Christopher Knowles has spent much of his adult life abroad. He has taught English in France and Italy, and led groups of tourists in many countries of the world, from Albania to Zimbabwe.

He has spent many challenging months in the USSR over the years and has had the opportunity to visit a great part of this vast country, which he likes for its variety and the exotic nature of its people. In 1985 has was one of the first Westerners for 39 years to cross the frontier from Soviet Kazakstan into Chinese Turkestan.

This is his second book, following *Shanghai Rediscovered*. He is now working on a book on Florence and Tuscany.

To Ming and Daniel

Acknowledgements

I am indebted to many people for the production of this book. My thanks to Lezcek of Voyages Jules Verne for never failing to find an answer; to Ann Frost for her time and resourcefulness; to Alla Musaelyan and family for their help in trying times and for introducing me to Alexander Popov, Yuri Brickman, Slava Shaginyan, Yuri Posokhov, Ann Titova, Oksana Omelchenko, Sergei Stepanov and Alexander Fofanov; to Marina Slavin, Olga and Andrei Slavin and family, Sergie Mineyev, and Nina and Irada for all their help in Leningrad; to Alexei Azarov for his suggestions; to the staff of BBC Moscow for their time; to Eleanora Ermoshina and her assistant Natasha for their assistance, sense of humour and tolerance; to Dr. David Jones for thorough editing; to Jim Helme for permission to use some of his photographs — particularly St Basil's on the front cover; and to all friends in the USSR and elsewhere for taking an interest or not, as the case may be.

A Request

The USSR is undergoing many changes. Keeping up with them is only possible with your help and thus the author and publisher would be only too pleased to hear of any new developments, corrections, recollections or suggestions. Please write to: Christopher Knowles, c/o the publisher. A free copy of the new edition will be sent to anyone making a significant contribution.

Lascelles City Guides

MOSCOW and ST PETERSBURG

Christopher Knowles

Roger Lascelles, Cartographic and Travel Publisher
47 York Road, Brentford, Middlesex TW8 OQP. Tel: 081-847 0935

Publication Data

Title	Moscow and St Petersburg
Typeface	Phototypeset in Compugraphic Times
Photographs	The author and James Helme (as indicated)
Printing	Kelso Graphics, Kelso, Scotland.
ISBN	0 903909 90 1
Edition	First Aug 1991
Publisher	Roger Lascelles
	47 York Road, Brentford, Middlesex, TW8 0QP.
Copyright	Christopher Knowles.
	Dr. James Helme (Cover photographs and others where indicated)

Distribution

Africa:	South Africa —	Faradawn, Box 17161, Hillbrow 2038
Americas:	Canada —	International Travel Maps & Books, P.O. Box 2290, Vancouver BC V6B 3W5
Asia:	India —	English Book Store, 17-L Connaught Circus/P.O. Box 328, New Delhi 110 001
	Singapore —	Graham Brash Pte Ltd., 36-C Prinsep St
Australasia:	Australia —	Rex Publications, 413 Pacific Highway, Artarmon NSW 2064. 428 3566
Europe:	Belgium —	Brussels - Peuples et Continents
	Germany —	Available through major booksellers with good foreign travel sections
	GB/Ireland —	Available through all booksellers with good foreign travel sections
	Italy —	Libreria dell'Automobile, Milano
	Netherlands —	Nilsson & Lamm BV, Weesp
	Denmark —	Copenhagen - Arnold Busck, G.E.C. Gad, Boghallen, G.E.C. Gad
	Finland —	Helsinki — Akateeminen Kirjakauppa
	Norway —	Oslo - Arne Gimnes/J.G. Tanum
	Sweden —	Stockholm/Esselte, Akademi Bokhandel, Fritzes, Hedengrens Gothenburg/Gumperts, Esselte Lund/Gleerupska
	Switzerland —	Basel/Bider: Berne/Atlas; Geneve/Artou; Lausanne/Artou: Zurich/Travel Bookshop

Contents

Introduction

Part 1: Planning ahead

Before you go
In a group or by yourself? 13 — Advance
reservations and how to make a booking 14 — Tour
operators 15 — Passports and visas 17 — Addresses
19 — Health and vaccinations 19 — What to take 20
— Climate - when to go 21 — Temperature chart 22

Getting there
By air 23 — Moscow by train 23 — By sea 25 — By
car 26 — What to take 26 — Finance 28

When there
Security 31 — Photography 31 — Food and drink -
what to take 33 — Duty free allowances 34 — Gifts
34 — Useful items checklist 34 — Advance Reading
35 — Maps 35

Part 2: The Soviet Union: a background

Geographical perspective

Historical Background
Introduction 37 — A vast, volatile land 38 — The
Tartar-Mongol yoke 39 — The rise of Muscovy 40 —
Ivan III, the Great 42 — Ivan the Terrible 43 — The
Romanovs 46 — A false dawn 46 — Alexis the
Gentle 48 — The Polish question 49 — Peter I, the
Great 50 — A woman's prerogative 55 — Catherine

the Great 56 — Paul I 61 — Alexander I 61 — The
Great October Socialist Revolution 67 — The
Bolsheviks take power 69 — The road to Stalinism -
an old New Economic Policy 71 — The coming of
Stalin 71 — The Stalin years 72 — The Great
Patriotic War 75 — Stalin at home 77 — After Stalin
78 — Nikita the table thumper 79 — From
Khrushchev to the present day 80

The Russian persona
History and geography 82 — The Church 82 —
Stalin and the Second World War 83 —
Temperament 83 — The Great Slav Soul 84 —
Folklore 85 — The Matryoshka doll 86 — The
peasant view 86

Part 3: Practical information: general

Upon arrival
Customs and immigration in general 90 — Arriving
by car 90 — Intourist 91

Daily practicalities: Electricity 91 — Laundry 91 —
Soviet money 91 — Etiquette and custom 92 — Post
94 — Public holidays 94 — Time changes 94 —
Tipping 94 — Getting about: From city to city 94 —
Soviet railways 95 — By car 95 — Moving around
cities 96 — Berioska shops 98 — Commission shops
98 — Art and antiques 98 — Good buys 98 —
Newspapers 98

**Hotels, restaurants, food and the Russian
tradition**
Hotels 98 — Restaurants 98

Food and the Russian tradition: Meal times 102 —
Typical dishes 102 — Soups 103 — Meat dishes 104
— Fruits and vegetables 105 — Cereals, grains and
bread 106 — Cakes and chocolate 107 — Dairy
products 108 — Eggs 108 — Ice cream 108 — Drinks
108

The Russian Ballet 110

Part 4: Moscow

Arrival and departure

Airports 113 — Railway stations 114 — Facts and figures 116 — Getting around the city 117 — Accommodation 120 — Restaurants, bars and cafés 122

Exploring the city

History 127 — The Kremlin 129 — The walls 130 — Within the walls 132 — The Palace of Congresses 133 — The Government Building 133 — The Presidium 134 — Lenin's bust 135 — The King of Guns and the Queen of Bells 134 — Cathedral Square 136 — The Great Kremlin Palace and the Armoury 140 — The Diamond Collection 143 — Potieshny Palace 143 — Red Square and Kitai Gorod 143 — Opposite the Kremlin 146 — The State History Museum 147 — The Pit 147 — Lenin's Mausoleum 148 — Kitai Gorod 148 — A walk in the centre 154 — A walk along Kalinin Avenue and the Arbat 163 — A walk along Gorky Street 173 — Behind the KGB 179 — South of the River 183

Other places of interest within the city: Museums 189 — Botanical gardens and parks 192 — Donskoi Monastery 192 — The river 193 — The zoo 193 — Cemeteries 193 — Exhibition of Economic Achievements 193 — Kolomenskoye Estate 193 — Lenin Hills and University 194 — The metro 194 — Parks 194

Outside Moscow

Butildochny Domik (Bottle House) 195 — Abramtsevo Estate Museum 195 — Arkhangelskoye Estate Museum 195 — Yasnaya Polyana - The Leo Tolstoy Estate 196 — Zagorsk 197

Practical information

Shopping: Berioska and foreign currency shops 198 — Art and craft 198 — Beauty shops 199 — Books 199 — Clothes 199 — Department stores 199 — Foods 199 — Glass and porcelain 200 — Flowers 200 — Jewellery 200 — Markets 200 — Posters 200 — Records 200

Entertainment: Bars, cafés, clubs 201 — Baths 201 —
Boating 201 — Chess 201 — Horse riding 201 —
Performing arts T201 — Snooker 202 — Sporting
events 202 — Swimming 203 — Tennis 203 — Winter
sports 203 — Services: Airlines 203 — Banks 203 —
Car hire 204 — Car spare parts 204 — Chemists 204
— Church services 204 — Co-operatives 204 —
Cultural organisations 204 — Doctors 204 —
Embassies 205 — Emergencies 205 — Gayline 205 —
Intourist 205 — Libraries 205 — Lost property 205
— Post offices 205 — Shipping agent 205 — Taxis
205 — Visas office and registration for foreigners 205

Part 5: St Petersburg

Arrival and departure

By air 207 — By rail 207 — By sea 210 — By river
210 — Getting around the city 211 —
Accommodation 211 — Restaurants 212

Exploring the city

Introduction 215 — Facts and figures 216 — Walking
the city 217 — Ploshad Vosstanya 219 — The
Anichkov Bridge 221 — Ploshad Ostrovskovo 223 —
Gostinny Dvor 224 — The Kazan Cathedral 226 —
The Admiralty 229 — Merchant's Lodging to St
Isaac's Square 231 — The Russian Museum 232 —
The Summer Garden 235 — The Winter Palace 238
— The Hermitage 240 — The rest of Palace Square
242 — St Isaac's Cathedral 244 — St Isaac's Square
245 — The Moika Canal and The University
Embankment 246 — The Peter and Paul Fortress and
Petrovsky Island 254 — Smolny 261 — Museums 267

Other places of interest within the city: Botanical
Gardens 269 — Canals 269 — Churches 269 —
Markets 270 — Parks and gardens 270 — The
Planetarium 270 — The zoo 270

Outside St Petersburg
Petrodvorets (Peterhof) 271 — Pavlovsk 272 —
Pushkin 272 — Gatchina 272 — The countryside 274

Practical information
Shopping: Berioska and foreign currency shops 274 —
Other shops 274 — Art and craft 274 — Beauty
shops 274 — Books 275 — Department stores 275 —
Foods 275 — Glass and porcelain 277 — Jewellery
277 — Posters 277 — Records 277 — Shoes 277

Entertainment: Bars, cafés, clubs 278 — Cinema 279
— Performing arts 279 — Sport 279

Services: Airlines 281 — Church services 281 —
Consulates 281 — Emergencies 282 — Lost property
282 — Pharmacy 282 — Photograph developing 282

Introduction

If there were a prize for the most exotic country on earth, Russia would probably not spring to mind. Yet, if exotic means strange, foreign and enigmatic, then Russia would win the *Victor Ludorum*. Russia, despite its popularity as a traveller's destination, remains something of a mystery. Recent events have certainly opened the country more than ever before, but tend to be interpreted according to our own prejudices. Empty shops and rebellious republics are not the only aspects of Soviet life. Nor, before the coming of Gorbachev, was the Soviet Union simply a communist monolith. To understand this you must visit the country, and when you do it is essential to visit Moscow or St Petersburg, or preferably both, for few countries have their history so concentrated in their capital cities. This book is devoted to both of them and this introduction makes some general points about the country itelf.

Russia is overpowering in a number of ways. It is easy to become confused by the size of everything, by the alphabet, by politics, and above all by the people and their attitude to their country and rulers. It is essential to arrive with as open a mind as possible both to past and present events, otherwise the country cannot be understood. Reading the history section and the sections on etiquette and the Russian persona will help. It is essential to realise too that Russians, despite some indications to the contrary, want to be helpful, but events get in the way — patience and a sense of humour are indispensable for the foreign visitor, who after all is unlikely to experience the frustrations of living an ordinary Russian life. Don't get angry when you are getting nothing but *nyet* (no) but nudge people with friendliness and humour. *Nyet* often means *nyet* but sometimes an obvious solution is overlooked and your suggestion, courteously made, may work. Russian logic is not always your logic. Learning the alphabet is a big help, for many Russian words are similar to English or French words once you can pronounce them.

Even if you are on a tour try to do some things for yourself - Intourist guides cannot do everything for everyone and have the same problems as everyone else. When you get to your hotel, read the signs, many of which are written in English, and use the Service Bureau for obtaining tickets and information. If you have a problem in the restaurant, ask for the *administrator* (maitre d'hotel). Bargain hard in markets and with street sellers. Take a supply of Western cigarettes and glossy magazines — bribery has become a way of life. Learn to see the funny side of Soviet life — Russians have had to do so in order to stay sane. Finally, look hard around to see why Russians, despite all, adore their country. At the end of your stay you may not wish to live in Russia but you will have enjoyed a unique experience.

This book is based around walks which include the major places of interest. But if you wish to visit the Winter Palace, for example, without the walk leading up to it, refer to the contents and index. As it happens many of the things to see must be visited on foot.

Abbreviations in the text: Pl. = *Ploshad* (Square), Ul. = *Ulitsa* (Street), Per. = *Pereulok* (Lane), Pr. = *Proezd* (Passage)

N.B. Some streets and metro stations are assuming their original names and may not correspond to names given here. Changes, where known, are indicated.

The Russian Holy of Holies: Cathedral Square in the Moscow Kremlin, viewed from across the Moskva River (Photo: Jim Helme).

Before you go

In a group or by yourself?

It is commonly thought that individual travel to the Soviet Union is out of the question. This is not so, although you cannot simply show up at the frontier (see Passports and visas). However, to go in a group remains both the easiest and the cheapest way of seeing this enigmatic country. Some will baulk at the very idea of sharing a holiday with a bunch of strangers but despite a more open political climate tourism is still organised around group travel and remains under the aegis of the state tourist company, 'Intourist'. Hotel administrations prefer to deal with groups. So, pity though it is, travelling alone in the USSR is only for those whose patience is exceeded by the amount of money at their disposal.

Individual travel
The determined independent traveller will heed none of this and set off alone anyway. Of course any traveller worth his salt will prefer that. Nevertheless, independent travel in the USSR, although technically possible, remains an illusion. Arrangements must still be made through Intourist, who will decide your hotel and arrange all internal travel — all at greater cost than if you were part of a group. Once in the country it is often difficult to change a prearranged itinerary; obtaining tickets for trains and planes at short notice is a nightmare. Your visa specifies not only entry and exit dates, but also the places to which you are entitled to visit. Changes can be made to the visa, but not easily.

In the end it is better to choose the places you want to visit, select a company that offers the nearest to that, and once you have arrived in each city, set off, if you so wish, to discover things by yourself. Nobody minds that — nobody is going to trail you — but some of the hassles (hotel accommodation, travel tickets) will be taken out of your hands.

Advance reservations and how to make a booking

In a group

There are a number of tour operators offering tours and a selection is given at the end of this section. Their brochures are obtainable from most travel agents or directly from the operator concerned. Obviously price will depend on the itinerary and on the international flights, but also on the 'expense category' into which the tour falls. All Western tour operators have to go through Intourist, whose charges are based on the standard of service requested (i.e. hotels, food and drink, sharing arrangements on trains, etc.) — there are several categories. If such matters are of concern to you, it might be as well to get some idea from the tour operator of what to expect. Do not be surprised if they are only able to give you rough information about things such as hotels because Intourist will not usually guarantee any single hotel, only the category, which may include a broad and disparate selection. Once in the country the standard of service (see Service and what to expect) is highly variable and usually depends on local organisation rather than on the tour operator.

Each operator will have its own itineraries and specialities but most first-time visitors are likely to want to visit either St Petersburg or Moscow or both, and many itineraries include them. At least two clear days in each should be allowed.

For a fee most tour operators will obtain the visa on your behalf. (See Passports and visas).

Intourist have offices in London, Manchester and Glasgow (as well as in major cities throughout the world), and operate their own tours at competetive rates. However, their tours are not 'fully escorted': in other words, although there will be a Soviet guide to accompany the group once it has arrived in the USSR, there will be no company representative to and from the country.

Finally, make sure that you see exactly for what you are paying when choosing a holiday with a tour operator, that it is clear why one company is cheaper than another for seemingly the same thing: how many excursions are included? Will you be sharing with one or three people on an overnight train? Is there a night in an aeroplane rather than in a hotel, and so on.

The independent traveller

It is possible to visit the Soviet Union without going in a group. The only advantage is that you can devise your own itinerary, but remember that all basic arrangements must be made in advance, and that the cost will be more.

Your best bet (unless visiting friends or going on business), is to make all the arrangements through your nearest Intourist office. The visa cannot be obtained without a letter from Intourist, so you may as well let them take care of that for you too.

At the very least you will have to book hotels through Intourist. As for plane and train tickets, the unhelpful attitude of Intourist offices is legendary, but there are two factors in your favour — foreigners frequently mistake Russian bluntness for rudeness, and the newly introduced innovation of cost accountability may induce staff to at least make suggestions in the event that there really are no tickets available.

You will have to fill in a form and provide the following information:

- Exact dates of travel with arrival/departure details
- Cities to be visited, with dates
- Type and class of accommodation/transportation
- Deposit of £40 (non-refundable)

Since so much of the available space is allocated to groups, it may be the case that there really are no tickets. In this case it may be worth your while trying tour operators who will have a direct line to Moscow. Naturally this will be more expensive.

Tour operators

UK
London

- Intourist, 219 Marsh Wall, London E14 9FJ. Tel: 071-538 8600.
- Knowles & Gray, 32B Atwood Road, London W6. Tel: 071-723 0912.
- Thomson Holidays, Parway House, 202/204 Finchley Road, London NW3 6XB. Tel: 071-435 8431, 071-493 9191.
- Voyages Jules Verne, 10 Glentworth Street, London NW1 5PG. Tel: 071-486 8080, 071-486 8084.
- Serenissima, 21 Dorset Square, London NW1. Tel: 071-730 9841.
- Progressive Tours, 12 Porchester Place, London W2. Tel: 071-262 1676.

- Cosmos, 17 Homesdale Road, Bromley, Kent. Tel: 081-464 3444.
- Swan Hellenic, 77 New Oxford Street, London WC1 Tel: 071-831 1616.
- Contiki Travel, Royal National Hotel, Bedford Way, London WC1. Tel: 071-637 2121.
- Top Deck, 131 Earls Court Road, London SW5. Tel: 071-370 4555.
- Cedok, 17 Old Bond Street, London W1. Tel: 071-629 6058.
- Trafalgar, 15 Grosvenor Place, London SW1. Tel: 071-235 7090.
- Express Boyd, 15 Bonhill Street, London EC2. Tel: 071-628 6060.
- Tracks Travel, 12 Abingdon Road, London W8. Tel: 071-937 3028.
- Yugotours, 150 Regent Street, London W1. Tel: 071-439 7233.
- Tedmans, 76 Westow Street, London SE19. Tel: 081-653 8260.

Outside London
- Page & Moy, 136/140 London Road, Leicester LE2 1 EN. Tel: (0533) 524463.
- Virgin Holidays Ltd, Sussex House, High Street, Crawley, W. Sussex RH10 1 BZ. Tel: (0293) 775511.
- Wallace Arnold, Gelderd Road, Leeds, W. Yorkshire LS12 6DH. Tel: (0532) 634234.
- Redwing, Groundstar House, London Road, Crawley, W. Sussex. Tel: (0293) 561444.
- Regent, 13 Small Street, Bristol BS1 3DE. Tel: (0272) 211711.
- Yorkshire Tours, 319 Cathedral Street, Manchester M4 3BT. Tel: (061) 832 1766.
- Goodwill, Manor Chambers, School Lane, Welwyn, Herts. AL6 9EB. Tel: (043) 871 6421.
- First Trade Union Country Club, Play Hatch Hall, Sharpthorne, E. Grinstead, Sussex. Tel: (0342) 810373.

From North America
Intourist have offices at 630 Fifth Avenue, Suite 868, New York NY 10011, Tel: 212-757 3884, and will be able to tell you about the many companies that operate tours to the USSR. However, it is often cheaper to buy a tour through the UK.

From Australasia
Contact Intourist at Underwood House 37/49 Pitt Street, Sydney, NSW 2000. Tel: (02) 277 652. Tx: INTAUS AA 176604.

The Cost

Package holidays to the Soviet Union have been traditionally rather cheap (this may begin to change with new government policies). The basic package is normally very good value, often including return flight, full board and lodging, all internal transportation, services of Intourist guide, and at least some sightseeing. Even soft drinks (and sometimes beer) are provided with the meals. Thus, it is possible to spend almost nothing more than the cost of the package.

However, in some ways the country is surprisingly expensive, and this largely depends whether you use roubles or foreign currency. When roubles can be used, costs are less for a foreigner, but when payment is expected in foreign currency, it is more expensive because the less favourable exchange rate is used (see Money).

Passports and visas

Without a visa you cannot enter the Soviet Union. Although there are different types of visa, they all have certain requirements in common:

- Three identical, signed passport-size photographs, trimmed to size and affixed to passport copy/application form as instructed.
- A full five- or ten-year passport (a British Visitor's passport is not acceptable), *which will still be valid a month after your date of return home.* Clear photocopies of the first five pages of your passport, trimmed to size, are also acceptable.
- Visa application filled in and signed.

Your visa is a separate document and no stamps or entries are made in your passport. Addresses of the embassy and other relevant organisations are given at the end of the section.

Tourist visa — group travel

If you are travelling in a group it is worth paying a few pounds to have the company concerned process the visa on your behalf. Precise instructions will be given you on making the booking, but do not be surprised if your visa and other documents do not arrive until a few days before departure. However, it might be sensible to contact the company if nothing has been heard a week before departure.

Tourist visa — independent travellers

If you are travelling alone you will need a letter from Intourist in order to obtain the visa from the Soviet Consulate, so you may just as well let Intourist take care of the application for you. Try and allow ten weeks for all arrangements connected with the application. If your projected journey involves visits to other countries, you will probably need to show a visa for the first country to be visited after leaving the USSR. (Making onward arrangements, therefore, involves working backwards; that is to say organising dates and itinerary in the Soviet Union after having confirmed your onward arrangements). At the same time you will obviously want to be reasonably sure that there will be no difficulty in realising your intended itinerary in the Soviet Union. In the same way, if you are going overland to the USSR, via Poland for example, your Polish visa can be obtained only on production of a Soviet visa. Complicated though it sounds, it is by no means impossible, but time, patience and flexibility are vital.

Business visa

For a business visa you need not go through Intourist. Apart from the standard prerequisites, you will need a letter from your company outlining your business and a written invitation (letter, telex or cable) from the relevant organisation in the Soviet Union. For information about doing business in the Soviet Union you may contact one of the many Western organisations with appropriate experience. Some addresses are given below.

Visiting friends or relatives

This is easier than in the past, but still not a simple matter. You will have to show a written invitation with an undertaking to provide accommodation and to cover expenses in the Soviet Union during your stay. Easier by far, however, is to take a package tour which includes a stop at the nearest point to where your friend lives.

Transit visas

You may need a transit visa if you are passing through — check. It is possible to obtain a three day visa on arrival at Moscow airport.

Do remember to obtain photocopies of your visa and the first five pages of your passport before departure.

Addresses

- USSR Embassy, 5 Kensington Palace Gardens, London W8 4QS. Tel: 071-229 3215. (Open 10.00-12.30, not Wed. or Sat.).
- Polish Embassy, 73, New Cavendish Street, London W1N 7RB. Tel: 071-636 4533. (Open 10.00-14.00, not Wed. or Sat.).
- Embassy of the Mongolian People's Republic, 7 Kensington Court, London W8 5DL. Tel: 071-937 0150. (Open 10.00-12.00, 13.00-17.00).
- Embassy of the People's Republic of China, 31 Portland Place, London W1. Tel: 071-636 1835/5726. (Open 09.00-12.00 Mon. to Fri.).
- Society of Cultural Relations with the USSR, 320 Brixton Road, London SW9.
- British-Soviet Friendship Society, 36 St John's Square, London EC1V. Tel: 071-253 4161.
- Great Britain-USSR Association, 14 Grosvenor Place, London SW1X. Tel: 071-235 2116.
- East European Trade Council, 10 Westminster Palace Gardens, Artillery Row, London SW1P. Tel: 071-222 7622.
- British-Soviet Chamber of Commerce, 2 Lowndes Street, London SW1X. Tel: 071-235 2423.

Health and vaccinations

Although there are currently no requirements for people travelling from the British Isles, North America or Australasia, you should always check with a doctor or with one of the innoculation units that specialise in travel abroad (addresses given below) about the latest situation in any given area. On the whole there is very little to fear in a visit to this part of the world but certain safeguards are advisable. It is always as well to be innoculated against tetanus, and to consider the limited protection that vaccinations against hepatitis can offer. If you are arriving from an area where certain diseases are endemic, a certificate may be required, but this changes from time to time, so check.

Inoculation centres in the UK
- British Airways Passenger Immunisation, 75 Regent Street, London W1. Tel: 071-439 9584.
- Thomas Cook Medical Unit, 45 Berkeley Street, London W1. Tel: 071-499 4000.
- Trailfinders, 194 Kensington High Street, London. Tel: 071-938 3999.
- Heathrow Airport Clinic. Tel: 081-562 5453.
- Gatwick Airport Clinic. Tel: 081-668 4211.

Drinking water
On the whole the standard of the tap water is not bad — it is considered safe to drink in Moscow, but in St Petersburg try to avoid drinking tap water as it can give rise to a particularly unpleasant form of diarrhoea. But if you are unsure, don't drink it. In any case mineral water is nearly always available, and failing that, tea. If you do not care for the local mineral water, which is too metallic for some tastes, imported water is often for sale in the Berioska shops.

Medical services
It is provided free of charge to foreigners visiting the USSR. The standards, while excellent in some specialist fields, leave a lot to be desired in general medicine. However, as a foreigner, you are sure to receive the best care available.

Some hotels have clinics and pharmacies for minor illnesses and new private services are surfacing, at least in Moscow (see Useful information at end of Moscow section).

What to take

As well as a supply of proprietary medicines (aspirins etc.), you must ensure that you have a pentiful supply of personally required medicines. Just because you were prescribed something at home does not mean that it will be readily available in the USSR. If possible try to have the name of any such medicine translated into Russian.

The following items may be useful:

- Tablets against diarrhoea
- Elastoplast
- Insect repellent
- Tampons
- Contraceptives
- Throat lozenges
- Talcum powder
- In the summer a sunhat, sunglasses and suncream are useful, as well as a water bottle and electrolite powders (to replenish minerals lost through sweating, one of the main causes of diarrhoea).
- In the winter sunglasses are useful against glare from the snow. In very low temperatures chapped lips can become more than just an irritation — take a good moisturiser.

Climate — when to go

The climate is somewhat variable, as you might expect in a country of such vastness. The whole of the Soviet Union spans almost the entire width of the Eastern Hemisphere. Even that part of the country which extends to the Ural mountains is about the same size as the whole of the rest of Europe. However, it is true to say that summers are hot almost everywhere (even in Siberia!) and winters are cold (in January the entire country has an average temperature of 32°F). The Moscow winter is colder than Leningrad's but shorter. Moscow has essentially a dry climate, while Leningrad is rather damp (and thus more uncomfortable in winter). Both cities have up to twenty-four inches of rain a year. The best times to visit Moscow or Leningrad are usually May and September, although both cities are at their most beautiful under a coverlet of snow. Leningrad is also uniquely attractive in June, especially during the White Nights Festival from 21 to 29 June, when the sun never fully sets.

Temperature chart

ST PETERSBURG

Month		JAN	FEB	MAR	APR	MAY	JUN	JUL	AUG	SEP	OCT	NOV	DEC
TEMPERATURE C°	Av. Monthly Min	-24.5	-24.8	-18.8	-7.3	-0.5	4.4	7.1	7.0	1.5	-3.5	-11.0	-18.9
	Av. Monthly Max	1.7	2.2	6.3	17.3	23.7	26.5	28.5	26.7	23.6	14.9	9.4	3.6
	Av. Daily Min	-13.4	-11.9	-7.9	0.4	5.8	10.5	12.7	12.5	8.5	3.7	-2.1	-7.9
	Av. Daily Max	-7.1	-5.4	-0.2	8.0	15.1	19.8	21.2	20.3	15.4	8.8	1.8	-3.1
Rain m.m. per mth.		35	30	31	36	45	50	72	78	64	76	46	40
Bright Sunshine Hours p. mth.		13	45	121	144	244	313	270	257	145	72	15	3

MOSCOW

Month		JAN	FEB	MAR	APR	MAY	JUN	JUL	AUG	SEP	OCT	NOV	DEC
TEMPERATURE C°	Av. Monthly Min	-29.4	-26.1	-19.1	-8.2	0.9	4.0	7.6	6.3	-0.2	-7.5	-14.3	-22.9
	Av. Monthly Max	-0.1	1.7	6.3	19.8	27.4	26.5	29.4	28.5	25.1	18.2	9.9	3.1
	Av. Daily Min	-16.2	-13.6	-7.8	1.3	7.9	10.6	12.9	11.9	7.3	2.9	-3.3	-9.5
	Av. Daily Max	-9.3	-5.7	-0.1	10.2	18.7	21.0	22.8	22.0	16.3	9.0	1.5	-4.5
Rain m.m. per mth.		39	38	36	37	53	58	88	71	58	45	47	54
Bright Sunshine Hours p. mth.		39	92	139	179	263	296	284	254	169	77	41	18

Getting there

By air

From UK

There are direct flights every day from London to Moscow (Aeroflot, British Airways, flying time approximately 4 hours), and others, regular or charter, from some of the other UK airports. There are also direct flights to St Petersburg, and occasional flights to other cities (e.g. Yalta). The cost is about £400 but sometimes cheaper flights are available on other airlines, by changing planes en route or on a charter, especially in winter.

From N.America

There are flights on Aeroflot and Pan Am but the situation is variable. It is often cheaper to go via London.

From Australasia

Aeroflot flies only as far as Singapore but there are some good deals available. Speak to Intourist.

Moscow — by train

This is the most interesting way to go — sleeper tickets can be booked from London through British Rail for a journey that takes about fifty hours. A major advantage is that you arrive in the centre of the city, and it is likely to be cheaper. There are two convenient routes, via Ostend (from Victoria) and Hook van Holland (from Liverpol Street), the latter being a little shorter. In both cases the services interlock so that the boats meet the trains from London, and the trains to Moscow await the boats. Once aboard you do not change trains again (unless you are going to St Petersburg, in which case you must change at Berlin Friedrichstrasse).

From Ostend and Hook van Holland, you travel in carriages

belonging to Soviet Railways, staffed by Russians. Although you will stay in the same carriage all the way to Moscow, the train that leaves the European coast is a composite one and is broken up and rearranged at least once.

The international carriages of Soviet Railways are quite comfortable but differ somewhat from the ones that you will meet in the USSR itself. On international routes the compartments can accommodate up to three people. This is very cramped, so it may be worth spending extra in order to travel first class, which reduces the number of occupants to two (effectively you buy two seats). Each compartment has a basin with running water (not drinkable). There are two lavatories per carriage, one at either end, and a drinking water tap set into the corridor wall near the stewards' quarters. There are no showers.

The stewards have a *samovar* (boiler) in their room, and it is part of their job to provide hot water for tea and coffee. A hard currency tip is to be reccommended to ensure good service from the stewards, but they are usually pretty jovial and a nip of whisky and a show of friendliness will usually do just as well.

The journey across Europe to Moscow is likely to be pretty eventful. Both routes take you across Germany, Poland and the Soviet republic of Belorussia. In other words there are a number of border crossings to deal with. When you board the train at Ostend or Hook van Holland, the stewards will ask you to hand over your passports. They are doing you a favour because the border guards of the West European countries are usually satisfied with seeing the passports and not the passport-holders. On approaching the first East European border your passports will be returned.

Some hours later you will be in Berlin. Not much more than a couple more hours will see you at the German/Polish frontier. You need a transit visa to cross Poland which must have been obtained before your departure — *you will not be able to get one at the border*. This may change so check with the embassy before departure.

Poland is a large country and most of the day will pass in going from one end to the other. The timetable varies from year to year of course, but generally a long stop is made just inside the Polish frontier in order to reshuffle the train — carriages are added and subtracted according to their final destination. This stop may last up to three and a half hours, during which time your carriage will disappear and reappear at different platforms. The opportunity to stretch your legs will be welcome, but keep an eye on your carriage.

In the evening you will arrive at the Soviet frontier (the formalities are explained under Arrival procedures), where the wheels (bogies) are changed to accommodate the wider Soviet gauge. You will also put your watches forward by two hours. The following afternoon you will be in Moscow.

Throughout the journey there is an assortment of restaurant cars, depending on the territory you are crossing. For example there may be a small snack bar across Holland, a full dining car across Germany and a buffet car across Poland. Any Western currency is acceptable on these services. You are advised, however, to bring your own food for the first night (packed meals are available on the boat), and snacks for the remainder of the journey in the event of there being no dining car of any sort, an unlikely occurrence, but not unknown. There is always a dining car attached at the Soviet border so breakfast and lunch are available on the last day. Meals must be paid for in roubles so you will have to change money at the border station bank.

It is not possible to register luggage through to Moscow from London, only as far as Hook van Holland or Ostend, where it must be retrieved and taken to the carriage. Space is at a premium in the compartments, so pack wisely.

You are advised to book some time in advance as these routes become quite crowded at certain times.

For timetables speak to British Rail on 071-834 2345.

There are similar services from other major European cities.

By sea

No doubt to go by sea would be the most relaxing way to arrive in the Soviet Union. The journey from London to St Petersburg takes five or six days but there are only a limited number of sailings per year. An alternative is to get on a container ship to Helsinki. There are cruise services to Odessa and Yalta on the Black Sea; and ships from Hong Kong and Japan dock at the Soviet port at Nakhodka, where you can board the Trans-Siberian Express.

Addresses
Baltic Steamship Company, c/o CTC lines, 1-3 Lower Regent Street, London SW1. Tel: 071-930 5833.

This formidable building is in fact a hotel, the Moskva.

By car

It is possible to take your car into the Soviet Union providing you are willing to follow routes prescribed by Intourist. Bear in mind, however, that facilities are poor — spare parts, for example, are almost unavailable.

What to take

Luggage
You should take as little as possible, which usually means less than you think you need. As for the bag itself, that depends to a certain extent on the type of holiday you are taking; but at any event durability and portability are the main criteria. Even on a package holiday there is always the possibility that for some reason you may have to carry your own bag, and any airline is capable of lacerating a suitcase.

If taking a suitcase, take either one that is already battered, or one of the Samsonite type. Whether it should be hard or soft is a moot point, but experience seems to favour the soft variety. A backpack is not to be sneered at, even if it is not your usual choice — they are perfect for train travel. Make sure that all bags are lockable and well labelled, preferably not with your home address. A second label inside is a sensible precaution.

A second foldable bag is useful for carrying overnight things in the event of a late arrival or delayed departure.

A spare nylon strap is a useful item in the event of your bag beginning to fall apart.

Hand luggage should be small and stowable. Airlines everywhere are becoming stricter on this matter.

Clothes

Comfort is everything. Provided that your attire remains within the realms of decency, informal clothing is acceptable almost everywhere.

Nevertheless Russians have their own idea of what is correct and what is not. Although far from prudish, Russians do not approve of shorts being worn in city streets, and certainly not on a visit to the Kremlin or to Lenin's tomb. In the winter you are obliged to hand over your coat to a cloakroom attendant upon entering theatres and restaurants — not to do so is considered rude. As for a hat, anyone without one in the winter is simply considered mad. People might think twice about wearing jeans at Covent Garden, but it is quite acceptable at the Bolshoi.

Obviously what you take depends when, where and how you go. If you are likely to be flying a lot, bear in mind the possibilities of long waits at badly appointed airports; if travelling by rail, remember that it is always difficult to remain clean on a train, especially on long journeys. Take as little as possible (there is a laundry service of sorts in most hotels), but at the same time take what you need — don't rely on being able to easily replace anything you forget.

Business

A suit and tie in keeping with the climate is quite acceptable. While Russians are on the whole rather informal in dress, business suggests America, and Americans wear suits.

What to take in summer

Summers are hot and rather sticky. Lightweight, natural fibre clothes are advisable, and a sun hat and sunglasses. A light pullover, cardigan or jacket will be useful for the evening in some areas or for during the day in some northern zones. Sandals are cool, but very poor for walking. It is far better to buy a carefully chosen pair of walking shoes. Towels are provided on the trains but are rather small — take another. A lightweight raincoat may be useful; shorts are fine on beaches and in the country (but bear the mosquitoes in mind), or on the train, but will not be popular in the cities. Bring your own supplies of toiletries as some things are hard to come by.

What to take in winter

Winter on the Black Sea or in the southern republics is rather mild, but in northern areas it is severe. Yet the sun, snow and crisp dry air can make it highly enjoyable if you are properly dressed — it is like swimming through iced vodka. Northern Russia is at its most magical in the snow, its palaces and cathedrals seemingly designed for it. At the same time coastal areas can be cold and damp, and intermittent thaws are a nuisance.

Interiors are often over heated. Thus you need to be warm when outside and not to suffocate inside. A long, thick, well lined and waterproof coat is best, combined with thermal underwear, a scarf, gloves and a fur hat with ear flaps. Temperatures inside are usually high enough to be comfortable in shirt sleeves. Fur hats are obtainable in the USSR: though expensive, they are cheaper than at home.

Your footwear needs to be able to withstand snow, cold and water. Boots of some kind are excellent for outdoors but not so good for inside. Stout winter shoes with galoshes are ideal.

Bring your own supply of toiletries.

Finance

How to spend your money is explained elsewhere, but before you go, you need to know what to take with you.

Despite what travel agents and tour operators might tell you, it is better to take cash with you to the USSR. That way you can control the number of roubles you buy — with cheques you may find yourself with more than you want.

Travel agents invariably recommend travellers cheques partly through ignorance and partly because they are a safe bet. In this last respect they are completely in the right — if travellers cheques are lost or stolen they can be replaced. Although theft from foreigners in the Soviet Union is a comparative rarity, it is not unknown and more liberal policies have the unfortunate side effect of loosening the traditional respect for authority. Nonetheless the particular circumstances of the country mean that travellers cheques are impractical.

The solution is to work in cash (preferably dollars, since the pound coin is a nuisance), and to have a reserve sum in travellers cheques available for emergencies.

Most of the major credit cards are acceptable in a limited way. They can be used without problem in the Berioska shops and in some restaurants and bars.

Drawing cash in the USSR is likely to be a problem and Eurocheques are not widely accepted.

You are able to change surplus roubles back into foreign currency at your point of departure from the country providing you have the bank exchange receipts and declaration form to prove that they were changed legally.

It should be noted that it is illegal to export roubles from the Soviet Union and that therefore you should not be in a position to reimport them. Theoretically and legally roubles can only be bought in the Soviet Union, although sometimes recently returned visitors from the USSR are to be found selling them on the streets of the cities of neighbouring countries.

The magic of the Russian winter: the entrance to the fantasy that is Zagorsk monastery.

When there

Security

Theft is becoming more common. Nevertheless people in the Soviet Union are comparatively honest. However, do make sure that your luggage is lockable, and keep it locked when out of your sight. Photocopy all your important documents before leaving (photocopies are not yet easily available in the USSR although this is changing), and keep two separate supplies of money. A money belt is sensible.

Photography

Regulations

Photography has always been considered a problem in the Soviet Union by Western tourists used to taking photographs willy-nilly. According to a guidebook published in the Soviet Union for the benefit of foreign tourists 'it is prohibited to photograph military objects and equipment, sea ports, bridges, tunnels, radio stations, etc. It is also forbidden to film from on board aircraft. At factories, farms, and state institutions, photographs may only be taken with the permission of the management.' At first glance this looks too specific to hinder the average tourist, but it becomes a matter of interpretation. Railway stations, for example, inoffensive enough one would have thought, can be difficult; or people queuing up to buy food may be regarded by a zealous policeman as the stuff of anti-Soviet propaganda. Nor is it only the police who may show an interest in what to you is a perfectly harmless picture of Russians going about their business — particularly on stations there are volunteer administrators wearing red armbands who may step in if they think you are stepping out of line. Unless you really are a spy there is nothing to be frightened of. You may well have inadvertently broken the law. Officials are normally very polite, and will simply ask you to desist. The worst that is likely to befall you is the confiscation of your film.

But it is unlikely that you will encounter any problems, particularly at a time when openess is the watchword. Secondly, try to understand the Russian attitude towards cameras. Westerners tend to regard the taking of photographs practically as a basic human right. It does not occur to us that people might find offensive the unrestricted wielding of cameras. Not all Russians own cameras and therefore do not regard them as indispensable, and there is a certain amount of diffidence towards foreigners. This stems not only from political events during the last 50 years, but from an insularity that dates back over hundreds of years. Nevertheless, Russians are warm-hearted and welcoming people by nature, and basic observance of the rules and politeness when photographing will bear fruit. Photographs at railway stations, for example, should not present a big problem. However, do not take photographs at frontiers and if you want to photograph people, it is better to ask unless you are able to be very discreet — the Russian for 'may I take a photograph' is 'fotografeerovat mozhna?'.

As for taking photographs inside, the rules vary from museum to museum and from theatre to theatre. In some places, for example, it is forbidden to use a camera at all, while in others photography is permitted provided that flash is not used. It is advisable to ask in advance. In those theatres where photography is allowed, please remember that too much enthusiasm can spoil the performance for others. These days it is possible to buy film with a very high ASA rating which permits photography inside without the use of flash.

Video cameras are as acceptable as standard cameras and subject to the same restrictions. If in doubt, ask.

X-rays

X-ray machines are in use at some Soviet airports but are considered film-safe. Film exposed to these machines will only suffer if it happens many times over or if the film has a particularly high ASA rating (1000 plus) and even then not much. If you are worried about your films, ask the guard to hand search them — but he is unlikely to oblige.

Polaroid

Polaroid cameras are often useful for breaking down barriers in countries where photography is regarded with suspicion. The negative aspect is that adoring mothers tend to live under the misapprehension that all cameras are capable of producing instant pictures. If someone expects you to send them a copy of a photograph, do try and remember to oblige on your return home — it is a small thing that may mean a great deal.

Film availability, developing, repairs
Bring everything you need with you and bring more than you think you need. While it is sometimes possible to find print film (usually Kodak) in the Berioska shops, there is absolutely no guarantee of this, although this is another area where things are improving. For the time being depend upon only your own supplies.

Locally-produced film is more readily available but unless you intend to have it developed in the USSR there is no point in buying it since the laboratory techniques differ from those at home.

There are few places where film may be developed; see the information section at end of each city section. Camera batteries are unlikely to be easily obtainable.

There are no appointed agents for carrying out repairs on foreign cameras. There are, however, plenty of repair shops. You may find someone able to carry out repairs but it is a question of luck.

Filters
Filters may be necessary against glare in winter.

Food and drink — what to take

Foreign visitors certainly will not suffer from a shortage of food in the hotels. The problem lies in the quality, not the quantity. Of course the standard varies from hotel to hotel, but on the whole meals are reminiscent of school, especially those served to tourist groups.

It is common knowledge that in many parts of the USSR the shops are not well stocked. Allowing for exaggerations in the Western press, this is more or less true. Cravings will have to be satisfied from whatever is available in the Berioska shop (although variety in local shops varies from region to region) where you may be able to buy chocolate or packeted snacks for hard currency. The alternative is to take your own but this is mostly impractical. Fruit, fresh vegetables and coffee are the items most usually missed. All are available but not easily. So take coffee or coffee bags, tea if you have your own favourite blend (although Russian tea is good) and vitamin supplements. Milk is easily found but supplies of anything, including sugar, are erratic.

Intourist meals will usually include something to drink, some sort of fruit drink or mineral water or Soviet beer when available. Wine and vodka are available from the waiter or in the Berioska shop (difficult to find in the local shops these days); foreign beers are sold in Berioska shops; drinks such as whisky are sold in the hotel bars but usually at high prices. If you have preferences, bring your own. The same applies to cigarettes — some foreign brands are sold but the variety is limited. It is better to buy in advance.

Duty free allowances

Standard, but nobody ever checks.

Gifts

Under certain circumstances you may feel inclined to show your gratitude with a gift. Tipping is discussed elsewhere so here are a few suggestions for those times when money is not acceptable: foreign cigarettes for porters, drivers etc.; ballpoint pens when requested; perfume or headscarf for female guide, floor lady; books and cassettes for guides in general. Remember that the new laws have made vodka, or at least good vodka, hard to find, but that it can be purchased in the Berioska shops for hard currency. Do resist the temptation to give things like chewing gum to begging children — they can live without it. If you want to take 'useful' items such as stockings, it is as well to ask the recipient in advance in order to avoid embarrassment. Make it clear what your intentions are, but do not be offended by a refusal.

Useful items check list

These are items that are not easily obtainable in the Soviet Union or are not conveniently bought: sellotape, film, batteries of all descriptions, proprietry and prescribed medicines, ready cash, spare spectacles or contact lenses, detergent, cosmetics, toiletries, instant coffee, tissues, lavatory paper, tampons, contraceptives, wide rubber bath plug, maps, preferred reading material, dictionary.

Advance reading

The possibilities are endless but a little history, a little analysis and
a novel or two will help to prepare you:
● Any novel by Tolstoy or Dostoyevsky.
● The best analysis of the Russian mentality is *Journey into Russia*
  by Laurens Van der Post (Penguin 1965).
● A book that combines Russian history with Russian culture is the
  superb *'Land of the Firebird'* by Suzanne Massie (Hamish
  Hamilton 1980).
● Otherwise: *Holy Russia* by Fitzroy Maclean (Weidenfeld and
  Nicolson 1978) *The Soviet Achievement* by J.P. Nettl (Thames
  and Hudson 1967).

Maps

It is possible to find reasonable maps in Russia now but supply is
erratic. 'Falk' do city plans of Moscow and St Petersburg. Other
maps are available from Collet's bookshop on the Charing Cross
Road in London.

The mightiest bell in the world: it never rang but remains both a work of art
and of engineering.

Trezzini's masterpiece: the Peter and Paul church.

Geographical perspective

The Soviet Union is the largest country in the world with an area of 22,402,000 square km (8,647,172 square miles). It is comprised of 15 republics of which the largest is the Russian Federation, or Russia. It is roughly 11,265 km (7000 miles) from west to east (covering 11 time zones) and 4,023 km (2,500 miles) from north to south. It lies both in Asia and in Europe, the Ural Mountains providing a rough boundary between the two. It is essentially a massive plain surrounded by great mountain ranges (Pamirs and Caucasus) and drained by vast rivers, some of which are among the longest in the world (Ob, Yenisei, Lena). It is punctuated by immense lakes (Aral Sea, Lake Baikal, Lake Ladoga near St Petersburg the largest in Europe). There are climatic areas of every sort except tropical. Moscow and Leningrad both lie in the northern, European part of the country.

Historical Background

It is commonly said that the Soviet Union is actually Russia in disguise. Certainly Russia, or the Russian Federation as it is now called, is the largest of the 15 republics of the Soviet Union and its capital, Moscow, is the capital and political centre of the entire country. Foreigners mistakenly refer to the Soviet Union as Russia and Russians themselves indignantly correct them. Yet the fact remains that power and influence in the Soviet Union are essentially Russian in character; if the country has a persona, then it is Russian. In one sense, therefore, the Russian sense, the Soviet Union can be said to be part of Europe — after all, the Russian language and the Russian people are European. Yet the history of the country is at the same time curiously separate. Many aspects of life in the Soviet Union that Westerners find so eccentric have their origins in traditions that have grown out of Russian history. The Revolution of 1917 did not, nor could not, alter a mentality overnight; and the changes currently taking place, slowly and painfully so it seems to outsiders, are doing so in uniquely Russian fashion.

Setting foot in the Soviet Union is a mystifying, almost exotic experience. Much is familiar but little is immediately comprehensible. To visit, for example, China, whose exoticness is more obvious, is for the Westerner somehow less startling. The differences are great but coherent. To appreciate Russia, you must appreciate the quixotic nature of the Russians; and to do that, you must know a little of their history.

Modern Russian history may be broadly divided into four periods — the creation of Rus, the rise of Muscovy, the expansion of the Russian Empire, and the establishment of the Soviet Union.

A vast, volatile land

Until the rise of Kiev in the ninth century AD, the vast area that is now the European Soviet Union was the hunting ground of nomadic and semi-nomadic tribes vying with each other for power over the steppeland. Some established relations with Greek settlements on the shore of the Black Sea; others were accomplished in many fields. On the whole however, there was little stability and the land belonged only to those who could defend it from the next wave of invaders from the east.

In the sixth century AD came a significant change. The Slavs, a nomadic people united only by a common language, split into three — the West Slavs (the predecessors of the Czechs and the Poles), the South Slavs (later to become the Serbo-Croations) and the East Slavs (who were to become the Belorussians, the Ukrainians and the Russians). Simultaneously they began to change from nomadism to farming, founding settlements such as Smolensk, Novgorod and Kiev. But Slavs lived in thrall to the Khazars, the dominant tribe of the time, until the ninth century, when they rose against them. The citizens of Novgorod turned to their near neighbours, the Norsemen, for help. The Khazars were vanquished and the first Russian dynasty, a mixture of Slav and Norseman, was established in Novgorod. The next generation absorbed Smolensk and then Kiev, which was to become the capital of the new state and known as the 'mother of Russian cities'. The state came to be known as Rus, a name given, so it is said, by the Norsemen.

Until the eleventh century Kiev grew and prospered. Its rulers were a mixture of pagan and Christian until Vladimir of Kiev married the sister of the Emperor of Byzantium in 988, after which Christianity became a permanent factor in the government of Russians until the Revolution in 1917. Russia was thus brought onto the margins of the European fold. Vladimir could equally have married into Islam but he preferred, it is thought, to be on the eastern flank of Christendom than to be the European bulwark of the non-Christian world. Another factor may more plausibly have been that Islam was teetotal and 'drink is the joy of the Russians'. Through trade and marriage alliances with European royal houses, Russia became closer to Graeco-Roman Europe than she would be for 500 years. During this time the Russian alphabet (the Cyrillic, named after its supposed inventer, St Cyril) came into being, and there were the bare bones of democracy and of an organised judiciary. Above all a sense of Russian statehood emerged.

Kiev's power was not to last however. Part of the problem lay in the system of inheritance. Instead of primogeniture, appanage was used, whereby each son, according to seniority, was given a portion of the state to govern. Thus the centre of power moved away from Kiev as principality after principality was created and carved up. Consequently many East Slavs migrated west to form the states of Galicia and Volhynia (later Belorussia and the Ukraine) which, unlike Russia, were much influenced by Catholic Poland and Lithuania; other principalities, such as Novgorod and Vladimir-Suzdal, jostled each other for overall power. Until the much later rise of Moscow none succeeded, and in the mean time the powerful force of the Tartar-Mongols came from the east.

The Tartar-Mongol yoke

Traditionally Russians attribute their historical backwardness to the 'Tartar-Mongol yoke'.

The first Mongol raids into Russia were in 1223, when Ghengis Khan still lived, but these were essentially for reconnaissance. But from 1237 they overran the country, and entered the West. They were quickly forced to retreat from Europe but only to the Russian steppes, where they remained for 250 years.

That they retarded potential advances in Russian society is undeniably true. Yet, once they had established their suzerainty, the Tartar-Mongols did not appear to take a great deal of interest in their new subjects, beyond the exaction and collection of enormous amounts of tribute from the various Russian princes. Certainly they were intolerant of rebellion, but they ignored religion and the Russian way of life, although there was a certain amount of intermarriage between the Russian and Mongol aristocracy. Their invasion ended contact with Byzantium and effectively cut Russia off from Europe, forcing the centre of power away from Kiev.

Once the Mongols were well established, they appointed Russian princes to collect tribute on their behalf. Once this and a few other obligations had been fulfilled, Russians were allowed to arrange their own lives.

The Tartar-Mongols began to lose their predominance in 1380, and finally abandoned Russia in 1480. Thus they were present for almost 250 years and the ruling force for about 150.

Judgements regarding their influence on Russian life and the Russian psyche are hard to make but would seem to be almost exclusively negative. If language is a yardstick, then their influence was negligible — only six words can be traced to the Mongolian language with any certainty, including the colloquial word *dengi,* meaning 'money'. The Mongols were accomplished in money management, and had developed a highly sophisticated communications system, something of which rubbed off on the Russians. Although the Mongol policy, having established their suzerainty, was to allow the conquered race to carry on as normal, political power remained in their hands and obviously cramped Russian style, perhaps fostering a cowed mentality. The Russians saw the might and effectiveness of a centralised, autocratic state, and imitated this style later, which lingered into the twentieth century. It has been said that the impact of the Mongols on Russia is similar to that of the Arabs on the West, without Aristotle or Algebra; 'They continued something to the general harshness of the age and to the burdensome and exacting nature of the centralising Muscovite state which emerged out of this painful background'.

The rise of Muscovy

Moscow began as a minor appanage and is first mentioned in historical chronicles in 1147. Its founder, Yuri Dolguruki (Yuri 'long in the arm'), was prince of the independent principality of Rostov-Suzdal, of which the Moscow area was a part. By the late thirteenth century it had become an independent principality under Daniel, the younger son of Alexander Nevski, whose descendents were to rule it for the next 300 years. In 1328 Ivan Kalita (Ivan the Moneybag) was the first prince of Moscow to be dubbed Grand

Prince by the Mongol overlords, who sold the title to the highest bidder. He thus appropriated the privilege — collection of Mongol tribute — that did more than anything else to render Moscow the most powerful city in the land. The only condition was Muscovite co-operation in the suppression of insurrection. Kalita was only too happy to oblige. It made the Mongols less tempted to leave their homelands, and so called 'Golden Horde', situated at Sarai on the Volga. But it also meant that other states saw their power and influence wane as Moscow's waxed. Moscow also became the religious capital and seat of the Orthodox Metropolitan. Close co-operation between the spiritual and secular leaders of Moscow became a strong feature of Muscovite, and Russian, government.

Kalita's grandson Dmitri proved an able and strong ruler. The Russians had never, in their hearts, given up the vow to expel the Tartar-Mongols from Russian soil. When factional fighting broke out amongst the Mongols, and dissident bands began to plunder Russian settlements, war broke out between Russian and Mongol for the first time in more than a hundred years. Although the Mongols were soundly beaten at the battle of Kulikovo, they continued to rule Russia for another 100 years, even returning to sack Moscow; but they never fully recovered their lost confidence. Moscow's claim to the leadership of all Russia became almost incontestable.

Dmitri was succeeded by his son Basil I who continued to enlarge and strengthen his realm. If the Mongols were now less of a threat, the Lithuanians and Poles were constant irritations on the west; and from the east came a new threat, Tamburlane the Great, but he contented himself with conquests farther east, leaving Moscow well alone.

Changing the laws of succession to that of primogeniture did not prevent quarrels amongst feuding relatives. The 20 years following the death of Basil I were largely taken up by fighting between Basil II, his son, and a variety of cousins and uncles. Basil eventually won, and several events of considerable significance took place during his reign. First, the Mongols were defeated again, this time by Tamburlane, in 1398, and the Golden Horde fell into disarray, splintering into different khanates. Basil was even able to create a Mongol princedom under his tutelage. Second, the Russian Church finally severed theological links with the Eastern Church in Constantinople after the Council of Florence (1438-45). Thus Russians were further cut off from the West when contact with Renaissance Europe might have been crucial to their development.

These, then, were the formative years for Russian character. It was born and nourished in Kievan Rus but particular traits were established under the distant but constant tyranny of the Mongols; and given succour by a church indissolubly tied to government affairs.

The oldest square in Moscow: Cathedral Square in the Kremlin.

Ivan III, the Great

The son of Ivan II, Ivan the Great reigned over Muscovy for 43 years. Under his rule the practice of appanage was ended. Novgorod, the most powerful of the princedoms not under Muscovite rule, whose domains extended as far as the Urals, capitulated in 1478. Step by step Ivan III brought most of northern Russia under his control — only the areas to the south and west, modern Ukraine and Belorussia but at the time part of Poland and Lithuania, remained independent states. The Tartar-Mongols, technically still the overlords, were finally dislodged during his reign. And his marriage to Sophia Paleologue, the niece of the last Emperor of Byzantium, persuaded him to adopt the double-headed eagle as a symbol of a burgeoning empire, and to take the name of Tsar, a word that derives from the latin 'Caesar'. Muscovy was now the largest state in Europe.

Expulsion of the Mongols enabled Muscovite rulers to look

westwards with more enthusiasm. The walls of the Kremlin, built between 1485 and 1495 by the Italian Aristotle Fioravanti, is an enduring example of early East-West co-operation. It was Fioravanti, too, whose designs created the familiar skyline of the Uspenski Cathedral, the Arkhangelski Cathedral, and the Granovitaya Palace within the walls.

Ivan III was essentially an autocrat, but there was a nominal parliament in the *Boyarskaya Duma* (Council of Nobles). The Boyars comprising it, were vassal princes of the Great Prince, and formerly ruled in appanage states now part of Muscovy. Theoretically they were entitled to leave the service of the Great Prince but in practice this was not so — they were far too much of a threat to his power. Ivan III and his successors expended a good deal of energy ensuring that the Boyars remained feeble. Thus, for example, a class of landowner was created to colonise newly conquered states and to replace their deposed princes, who became Boyars; but even they were ultimately tied to the Great Prince, for their continued ownership of land was dependent on the fulfilment of certain obligations to the state. nor was any such landowner able to bequeath his domains to his children without approval from the Great Prince. They were, in fact, no more than tenants.

Upon his death in 1505, Ivan was succeeded by his son Vasili III, who was even more autocratic than his father, and accepted counsel from only a few trusted advisors. Nevertheless, contact with the outside world grew during his reign, and Muscovy was firmly and finally established as the Russian power. Any remaining recalcitrant princelings were absorbed; and some notable successes were scored against the threatening Lithuanians.

Vasili married twice and the fruit of his second marriage, to a Polish princess, was Ivan IV, the Terrible.

Ivan the Terrible

When Vasili died, Ivan was a mere three years old. His mother ruled in his stead until her death in 1538, and was followed by a ten-year interregnum when no regent was appointed and the Boyars, theoretically in charge, squabbled amongst themselves. At 14, already well versed in the ways of court intrigue, Ivan showed that he was no longer a political innocent by making an example of one of the most troublesome of the Boyers by executing him. By his eighteenth birthday he had been crowned 'Tsar of all Russia' — Muscovy was now an empire.

The reign of Ivan the Terrible was a time of expansion. A professional army was created and the Tartar-Mongols finally driven out. The Tartar city of Kazan was taken in 1552 (St Basil's Cathedral on Red Square was built in celebration), and in 1556 the city of Astrakhan, home of another branch of Tartars. Only the Tartars of Crimea remained, but they were under Turkish rule.

The dispersal of the Tartar-Mongols gave the Russians access to the Caspian Sea, to the Volga and east, into Siberia. Ivan also turned his attentions westwards, and in a campaign against the Livinians, Lithuanians and Swedes drained the country of morale and money to such an extent that in 1571 Moscow was razed by the Crimean Tartars. These Tartars were roundly beaten the following year, but the 25-year war in the northwest, to obtain an outlet to the Baltic, finally proved unsuccessful, and in 1582 Ivan was forced to give up his Lithuanian territory, and renounce his claim to Livonia. The year after, the Swedes took back territory that the Russians had captured on the Gulf of Finland and annexed Estonia. Although the Russians had failed, for the time being, to gain direct access to the Baltic Sea, contact with the West was greater than ever before. (Following the journey of Richard Chancellor to Archangelsk in 1553, Ivan had granted a charter for the founding of Muscovy Company, and henceforward English ships anchored regularly at the mouth of the Dvina.)

A view of the golden domes of the Kremlin cathedrals.

Ivan's reign was in other ways an ominous portent of Russian government for generations to come. With the death of his beloved wife Anastasia in 1560, under suspicious circumstances, all the loathing of the Boyars who had treated him so ignobly during his childhood expressed itself in a fit of paranoia. In order to pursue his campaign against the Boyars and to create a state where his rule was absolute, he created the *Oprichnina,* a police organisation that was a law unto itself, an instrument of suppression of those who constituted a threat to the Tsar, but whose members were also never immune to the moods and whims of Ivan himself. At the same time he strengthened the land-owning class created by his father, and reduced the privileges enjoyed by the Boyars. yet none of this assuaged his increasingly maniacal behaviour. Having convinced himself that treachery was hatching in Novgorod, he sacked the city with his *Oprichniki,* who massacred 60,000 people.

With all this it might be safely assumed that Ivan would be remembered as a hated tyrant and his reign as a black period of Russian history. In part this is so, but a remark by Henry Lane, a contemporary English resident of Moscow, hints at that strange Russian ambivalence towards tyranny: 'I think no prince in Christendom is more feared of his own than he is, nor yet better beloved.' That he was psychologically disturbed, possibly insane, is not really in doubt — in a burst of uncontrolled fury he even killed his own son. Nevertheless his reign was a period of growth. The Russians extended their domain far into Siberia, and extended their contacts with the West, as well as expelling the Tartars. Moscow became a great city, the country more prosperous, and the understanding and appreciation of foreign culture encouraged. As for his relationship with the English, he became such an anglophile that his subjects sometimes referred to him as the 'English Tsar'. He imported the first printing press into Russia. He loved music, wrote hymns, and encouraged the teaching of music. The Armoury Palace in the Kremlin became a workshop for the painters of icons and for jewellers.

In Stalin's time he was even accredited as something of a genius, which view recent events in the Soviet Union are likely to discountenance, but there is no doubt that Ivan made as great an impact on Russian history as any figure before or since. He has passed into folklore and into the national psyche. 'In the popular imagination he is seen as a heroic and tragic figure standing in the moonlight, wrapped in shadows' (Suzanne Massie, *Land of the Firebird*).

The Romanovs

Fyodor, the youngest of Ivan's sons by Anastasia, became the next Tsar. The position was merely titular, however, for Fyodor was a pathetic individual: he ruled for 14 years but power was really wielded by his regents. The first of these was Nikita Romanov. Upon his death he was succeeded by Boris Godunov, a minor Boyar of Tartar origin. A man considerably less fanatical than Ivan the 'Terrible', he was nevertheless a man of action. disaffected Boyars were given short shift and soon found themselves in unpleasant places of exile. By the judicious placement of friends he made an ally of the Church; and the development of the tied, landed gentry class, as a foil to the power of Boyars, remained a major priority. He continued to colonise Siberia, made good some of the territorial losses in the northwest, and widened contacts with the West. Although the brutal *Oprichnina* no longer functioned, Boris had seen the effectiveness of a secret police organisation and built up his own, tamer version.

The country prospered under Boris's regency and when Fyodor died in 1598, with no children living, the first great Russian dynasty also ended. Boris was an obvious candidate for succession but he was challenged by Fyodor Romanov, son of the first regent. Boris prevailed, but his reign was not a happy one. His relationship with the Boyars remained uneasy, and for three successive years Russia suffered crippling famines. Boris behaved with commendable passion, but peasants fled the countryside and he was compelled to introduce laws tying them to the land, laws that were to culminate in the institution of full serfdom in 1649.

Boris died in 1605, and a bizarre period of Russian history known as the *Smutnoe Vremya* (Time of Confusion), began.

A false dawn

The time of confusion following the death of Boris began with the reign of Tsar Fyodor. He had a half-brother and heir, Dmitri Ivanovich, the son of Ivan the Terrible and his seventh wife, Maria Nagaya. Upon Fyodor's accession, Dmitri had been sent to a remote town on the Volga, where at the age of nine he had died under faintly mysterious circumstances, murdered, it was alleged by some, on the orders of Boris Godunov. In fact Dmitri's death was almost certainly an accident but the controversy engendered by querulous Boyars was enough to render plausible the rather fantastic events that took place a little before the death of Boris; in 1603 a man claiming to be Dmitri Ivanovich appeared on Russia's southwestern border together with a Polish army ready to seize power from the supposed usurper Godunov. Although his first attempt failed, it was during the second offensive that Boris Godunov died. His son, another Fyodor, was immediately proclaimed Tsar, but the vengeful Boyars had him and his mother killed. Dmitri entered Moscow in triumph and was crowned Tsar. The success of his mission had depended, however, on what was fast becoming a fixture in Russian political life — backing the right horse at the right time. The Boyars, led by one Shuiski, had backed Dmitri against Boris, but now found themselves attacked by Dmitri's army of disaffected Russian citizens, who themselves had no reason to love the Boyars.

Dmitri's rule lasted only one year. He repulsed the Poles, who had supported him in his original enterprise, and offered an amnesty to many exiled families, including the Romanov's. Yet he was not liked, for it was felt that his ways were not sufficiently Russian. Certainly he did not look Russian, and his refusal to take afternoon naps or to pay regular visits to the baths were held to be deeply subversive. Shuiski turned on Dmitri, had him murdered and his ashes fired from a cannon in the direction of Poland, and himself crowned Tsar. But Shuiski failed to placate an already disenchanted population, who rebelled. The rebellion was quelled but was followed by the appearance of the Second False Dmitri, who claimed to be both the original Dmitri and the one whose ashes had been shot towards Poland.

Shuiski, whose position was becoming untenable, managed to obtain help from the Swedes by making various territorial concessions, and at the same time to irritate the Poles who promptly declared war. They captured Smolensk and then Moscow. The Second False Dmitri died and a Third False Dmitri materialised to keep the ball rolling. Russia was close to anarchy.

The national consciousness was, as always, resilient in a time of crisis. Efforts were made to dislodge the Poles but only under the leadership of two popular heroes, and a local Boyar, Prince Dmitri (no relation) Pozharski, were the Russians finally able to prise the Poles from out of the Kremlin. There remained the question of the Tsar. A *Zemski Sobor* (Council of the Realm) was convened, possibly the most representative in the history of the Russian people, which finally chose Michael Romanov, the 16-year old grandnephew of Ivan the Terrible and the scion of a minor Boyar family. Thus began the Romanov dynasty, destined to rule Russia for 300 years.

Michael ruled for 32 years, but he ascended the throne at a time of appalling chaos and misery. Years of war had reduced Russia to ruin. Order was restored, although bands of marauding cossacks continued to wander the country. The Swedes abandoned Novgorod and the Poles gave up their designs on the Russian crown. Michael's father a Metropolitan following his banishment by Boris Godunov to a monastery, returned home to share power with his son, and indeed to rule the country.

Alexis the Gentle

Michael's reign is chiefly notable as a period when Russian life settled back into comparative order. The exploitation of Siberia continued apace — in 1639 the Russians had established themselves on the Pacific coast and soon after had conquered the Buryat Mongols around Lake Baikal. During his reign the distinctive towers on the Kremlin walls were built and the Kremlin palaces were renovated. Delicate of constitution, Michael nevertheless revelled, like his predecessors, in the pomp that his estate required — during his public appearances, he was so weighted down by gold that he had to be supported by his courtiers. Although serious of demeanour, he was extraordinarily emotional. It is said that his own death in 1645 was caused by the tears he shed over the death of his two eldest sons.

Michael was succeeded by his remaining son, Alexis, who was also 16 at the beginning of his reign. Fond of hunting and falconry, he was also very pious, as attested by his English doctor, Samuel Collins: 'In fine, no man is more observant of canonical hours than he is of fasts. We may reckon he fasts eight months in twelve.' And yet nor was any man fonder of court pomp and ceremonial. He was a mild man, though his reign of 30 years was not an easy one.

One thorn in his side was the Orthodox church. In 1652 Nikon, a peasant monk, was consecrated Patriarch. This had come about because of his influence over Alexis' pious nature and he all but ruled the country. Having acquired the title of 'Grand Sovereign', he set about introducing changes he deemed necessary to the church liturgy. There was not a little opposition to these changes, and the

'Old Believers', as the resistance movement members came to be called, continue to maintain a contemptuous distance from the seventeenth century innovations; but at the time people died for the right to cross themselves with two fingers. The changes remained although Nikon was eventually discredited and banished to a remote monastery.

The Polish question

The southern part of Lithuania (including the territory of Kiev) became part of Poland with the Union of Lublin in 1569. The Russian population of these areas was under considerable pressure from the Catholic Church and from Polish landlords. Friction between the Poles and the Cossacks that roved the border regions led to confrontations and by 1648 a Cossack resistance leader, Bogdan Khelmnitski, was leading his men to victory after victory and became master of the Ukraine. He had implored the Russians to come to his aid during the war and after much hesitating, when the Cossacks were beginning to weaken, Alexis did so. The Ukraine retained the right of self-government but became part of Russia — Alexis was now Tsar of all Great, Little and White Russia. He promptly declared war on Poland, and then, together with Poland, having made peace with her, on Sweden. Meanwhile the Ukrainian Cossacks, not altogether happy with the new arrangements, rebelled. War between Russia and Poland was renewed, continuing another ten years, at the end of which they made peace and divided disputed areas between them — Poland took Lithuania and the Ukraine west of the Dnieper, Russia took Smolensk, Kiev and the Ukraine to the east.

Long years of war had sorely tried the patience of the rest of the population and peasant rebellions had become fairly commonplace. Certain Cossack bands became so powerful that they were able to challenge the seat of government in Moscow. Control of the country was maintained only with difficulty and the reign of Alexis ended with his sudden death in 1676. Uneasy though his rule had been, it was as nothing compared with the tumult that had preceded the reign of Michael Romanov. Furthermore, he had presided over a period of change and also of exposure to new ideas and fashions. The Kremlin palaces were embellished as never before. Alexis introduced a postal system. Expeditions were sent to China, as a result of which tea became the national drink. Church art in the form of icon painting, ornate frame work and book illustrations, reached its apogee. The Armoury Palace in the Kremlin expanded, employing the very best of the country's artisans and artists, who were encouraged to fuse ideas from Russia with the styles of the East and the West.

Contact with the West was greater than ever. Poles, even during wars against them, were employed as architects at the Russian court; there were English and then Dutch traders, and as the foreign quarter expended, Armenians, Bulgarians, Genoese, Greeks, Venetians and Scots were to be found on the streets. The Tsar's doctor was an Englishman and his children's tutor a Polish Ukrainian. However, most foreign influence was restricted to Moscow.

But the Russian attitude to foreigners was ambivalent. Foreign residents were restricted to a special area of Moscow, the 'German Quarter', in order to protect the Russian way of life and to prevent foreign ideas from upsetting the status quo. But this placement had the opposite effect, providing a ready-made model cosmopolitan town for Russians to observe at leisure. Alexis mellowed in later life and married again five years before his death. Their son, Peter, was to make quite a mark on Russian history.

Peter I, the Great

When Alexis died he left two sons, Fyodor and Ivan, by his first wife, as well as an elder daughter, Sophia. Fyodor came to the throne and died after six unremarkable years. Ivan, a half-wit, should have replaced him but it was Peter, a bright and precocious child, who was named Tsar. Sophia disagreed and had soldiers under her command murder anyone connected with Peter's family — Peter himself, only ten years old, witnessed some of the barbaric scenes that followed. This resulted in Peter and Ivan being proclaimed joint rulers, with Sophia as Regent. Peter and his mother lived not far from the foreign quarter, where Peter's questioning mind was free to have its fill of Western ideas. He became fast friends with General Patrick Gordon, a Scottish mercenary, and with François Lefort, a soldier of fortune from Geneva — from them he learned not only the latest Western developments but also to drink and carouse.

Sophia was eventually banished to the Novodevichy convent at the edge of Moscow, and although Ivan was an entirely inept ruler

The Novodievichy Convent, Moscow: where the Tsar sent his bride when he tired of her (photo: Jim Helme).

it was only after his death that Peter, at the age of 24, became Tsar.

He was immediately presented with an opportunity to test his newly-acquired military knowledge. The Turks and the Tartars still presented a threat in the Crimea — Peter made as if to attack them, but instead, with his newly-formed navy, captured Azov, which gave him control of the Don valley. Simultaneously, he was planning an extraordinary journey that would make him the first Russian Tsar in 600 years to leave the purlieus of his country.

Peter's Great Embassy to Western Europe was to take him to Germany, Austria, Holland, and Great Britain. Curiously, for a man of seven feet, he chose to travel incognito, as a corporal in one of his own regiments, but this did not prevent him from meeting many of the most eminent people of science and government. His retinue consisted of some 270 people, decked out in the most elaborate of Russian styles; obviously they made a considerable impact wherever they went, rendering, one might think, Peter's disguise somewhat pointless. It was not his aim, however, merely to impress — he was there to learn, and during his first sojourn in Konigsberg he took a course in gunnery. From Konnigsberg he continued to Hanover and thence to Holland, where he worked in the shipyards of Zaandam, a little town not far from Amsterdam.

Russian architecture tends to be proportionate to the size of the country. The arch in the middle of the longest building in Europe, the General Staff Building, on Palace Square, St Petersburg (photo: Jim Helme).

A visit to Britain

Then he went to England, where he gained his most lasting impressions. There he pursued his study of the science of shipbuilding in Deptford, and met the king, William of Orange. The Parliamentary process was a puzzle, or even an affront, to him; but there were other things English that he appeared to look upon more favourably. He took back English teachers to Russia to establish a school of navigation, and it is possible that Peter's programme of social reforms, as manifested in the Succession Law of 1714, was based on the English model. He recruited gunners, goldsmiths, astronomers and mathematicians too, all of which were dispatched home to Russia. In total he collected almost a thousand experts.

Westernisation

He was on his way to Venice when news of unrest took him home. This was quickly suppressed and Peter got on with the business of the application of what he had learned abroad. One of the first things he did was insist that the Boyars shave off their great Muscovite symbol, the beard. This was not one of his more popular innovations and eventually beards became permissable again at the cost of an annual tax of 100 roubles. People were encouraged too, to dispense with the traditional *kaftan* and adopt Western-style hats and jackets. Peter himself often supervised the cutting of beards, and barbers and tailors, to the general merriment of the onlookers, were posted at the city walls. Women were encouraged to lead less closeted existences and parents not to force unwanted marriages upon their children. The calendar, which had been based on the Russian version of the date of the creation of the world, was altered to fall into line with the rest of Europe (which was in the process of changing to the Gregorian calendar, leaving Russia out of step for a further two hundred years).

The army was modernised still further. The potato was introduced. Technical and grammar schools were founded. Students were sent to Europe to learn new skills, and artists were encouraged.

Peter ruled for another 26 years, of which 21 were spent waging war for the possession of that elusive outlet to the Baltic Sea. A peace concluded with Turkey enabled Peter to defeat the Swedes, who promptly allied themselves with the Ukrainian Cossacks and marched against the Russians in 1708. They were defeated by Peter at the Battle of Poltava, establishing Russia as a major military power. The Swedes then allied themselves with the Turks and persuaded them to attack Russia from the south. Peter was forced to negotiate but by 1714 was in a position to threaten the Swedes with his new Baltic fleet. The war with Sweden came to an end only in 1721 with the signing of a treaty that forced Russia to give up most of Finland, but which gave her the Baltic coast from Riga to Viborg. Peter was not easily satisfied, for no sooner had he concluded this peace than he declared war on Persia, eventually acquiring the western seaboard of the Caspian.

During these years of war Peter had been trying to implement some of the ideas that had developed as a result of his journey to the West. In some cases he merely attempted to reorganise powerful institutions, to make them more just, but also to weaken their influence. Thus a table of ranks based on merit was devised for the government services, replacing the old system based on birth and wealth. The Church, which had tried to stand in the way of many of Peter's reforms, was made to step into line too — the Patriarchate was abolished and replaced with a Holy Synod that was directly responsible to the Senate. Peter continued with his programme of construction of schools and factories and founded the first Russian newspaper.

Some of the reforms were entirely new to the Russians. Others, like the modernisation of the army, had been started before Peter's time. What was extraordinary was the scale and speed of reform — Peter's genius lay in the vision behind them. In some ways the vision was greater than the results, for many of the reforms, of local government for example, failed to take root. The peasant was more a serf than ever. The reforms touched the lives of only a tiny part of the population, so that the gap between the privileged class and the rest merely widened. And for all that Peter was impressed with things 'Western', Russia, although by now an acknowledged power, remained somehow separate from Europe.

Yet a seed was planted for the future and the dilemma of the Russian people was at least recognised. The epitome of Peter's sense of destiny was the construction of his 'window on Europe', St Petersburg. This beautiful city symbolised Russia's newly acquired influence on the Baltic, but also served to emphasise that the new Russia was no longer merely 'Muscovite'.

A woman's prerogative

There remained the problem of an heir. Peter's son by his first wife had never been much impressed by his father's reforming zeal and was ultimately imprisoned by Peter as a traitor and tortured to death. Peter had changed the law so that he and all future rulers of Russia could dominate their successors regardless of their ties, but died in 1725 without naming anyone. Russia immediately plunged into another bout of squabbling and opportunism.

In the event, women were to play a major role in the government of Russia for the rest of the century; and German influence was to become unexpectedly significant.

1725-1741

First came Peter's second wife, Catherine, who ruled for two years, achieving little; she was followed by Peter's 12-year old grandson, who became Peter II. He died in 1730, bringing the male line of the Romanovs to an end, but was followed by Anna, niece of Peter the Great and daughter of his former co-Tsar, Ivan. German influence began to be felt at court, for her husband had been the Duke of Courland, from where she recruited many of her closest advisors. She ruled the country for ten years, remarkable only for high taxation and unsuccessful military forays into Poland and Turkey. Her designated successor was her niece's son, Prince Ivan of Brunswick-Bevern, who became Ivan VI. Due to his extreme youth his mother was made Regent, which meant that the court became more German than ever. Machinations on the part of those who found this state of affairs unsatisfactory led to the enthronement of Elisabeth, Peter the Great's younger daughter, in 1741.

Elisabeth

Elisabeth was a pretty, frivolous woman, generous of mind and body, who was happy to leave affairs of state to the Senate. In fact her 20-year reign was rather a quiet one in the political and military senses, but rather grand in the social and artistic worlds. Her Ukrainian lover, Razumovsky, had first attracted Elisabeth's attention when singing in the choir of the court chapel and their shared love of music led some observers to describe the reign of Elisabeth as the 'age of song'. Under Elisabeth the ballet became a Russian institution. It was the golden age of the jeweller's art, inspired by Elisabeth's love of balls and of spectacle, of colour and movement.

Science also made its mark. One of Russia's greatest scientists, Lomonosov, although largely ignored by Elisabeth's rather hedonistic court, made progress in the field of physical chemistry and was one of the founders of Moscow University.

Although Peter the Great had founded St Petersburg, it was during the reign of Elisabeth that it acquired much of its character. Her principal architect was the Italian, Rastrelli, who created a style, combining Russian and European elements, that became distinctly Russian.

Elisabeth died on Christmas Day 1761. Her reign had not been wildly productive, but it had been comparatively peaceful, it had glittered, and it had enabled the Russians to rediscover their identity.

Catherine the Great

Although Elisabeth had restored an essentially Russian atmosphere to the court of St Petersburg, foreign influence, notably Germanic, was still widespread. This dated back to Peter the Great who, in order to secure Russian influence in the Baltic region, had married his nieces and daughter into the appropriate royal families. Elisabeth, who was unlikely to marry officially and produce an heir, had named her successor within two years of her accession — Charles-Peter Ulrich, Duke of Holstein-Gottorp, the son of her sister Anna who had been married off to the Duke of Holstein-Gottorp by Peter.

Catherine was a member of the same family as Charles-Peter and was considered by Elisabeth to be an excellent match for him, if for no other reason that she came from a minor German family unlikely to make political waves. They married, although by the time Charles-Peter came to the throne (as Peter III), he had become a drunk and a pathetic physical specimen following a disfiguring bout of smallpox. Catherine had already overcome any reservations she may have had about marrying him, but now, after his illness, her reaction was quite plain — 'He had become, quite simply, ghastly', she wrote. She was, however, a woman of steely resolve, as characterised by the following extract from her memoirs: 'Here is the reasoning, or rather the conclusion that I reached, from which I have not deviated for even a single moment, as soon as I realised that I was to stay in Russia: 1) to make myself agreeable to the Grand Duke my husband, 2) to make myself agreeable to the Empress Elisabeth, 3) to make myself agreeable to the nation.'

Said to be the tallest monument of its kind in the world, the Alexander Column rises from the middle of Palace Square (photo: Jim Helme).

Peter was unable to consummate the marriage, and after eight years, Catherine took a lover, the first of many for which she was legendary even during her own lifetime (as Thomas Rowlandson's cartoon 'The Empress of Russia Receiving Her Brave Guards' testifies), a union from which it is supposed her first son, Paul, was the issue.

Empress of Russia

Peter was equally unpopular outside his marriage. He had no love for Russia, whereas Catherine had made considerable efforts to come to terms with the country. At the death of Elisabeth a plot was hatched to overthrow Peter who was considered far too pro-Prussian at a time when Russia was actually at war with Prussia. A conspiracy, carried out with the active connivance of Catherine, led to the fall of Peter the elevation of Catherine. She herself dressed in the uniform of a soldier in order to participate in the arrest of her husband. He stalled her by writing a note offering his abdication, but was killed in suspicious circumstances only a few days later. Catherine was now Empress of Russia.

Catherine was a remarkable woman. Not beautiful, she was nevertheless most attractive to men, and not only because of her exalted rank. She was highly sensual and had considerable intellect, as her reading material and her well-known correspondence with the French philosopher Voltaire imply. Above all, she was a survivor.

'The Great Instruction'

Peter III had, during his short reign, managed to make a few changes. One of them was the emancipation of the nobility, effectively freeing them from the tyranny of compulsory service to the throne. Nobles became able to travel abroad and the conditions of military service were relaxed. Catherine enforced this but failed to improve the lot of the peasant despite her publication of an extrordinary document, *The Great Instruction,* outlining the political and social circumstances of Russia and how they should be changed. Much of it was revolutionary by Russian standards. Despite her staunch defense of absolutism several startling recommendations were made: that it was the letter of the law that was important rather than the spirit (which leaves too much room for personal interpretation); that no citizen should be punished until proven guilty in a court of law; that torture was inhumane; and that all citizens be subject to the same laws. Nevertheless, she noted, too, that society requires a fixed order, that there are those for whom it is given to govern and those for whom it is given to obey. This was pretty bad news for the serfs, although in unpublished drafts Catherine suggested that serfs be allowed to accumulate sufficient property in order to buy their own freedom. The published draft, somewhat less liberal, was laid before a Legislative Commission but the Great Debate which followed produced no concrete results.

In 1769 Turkey had declared war on Russia, taking advantage of Russia's military involvement in Poland. Peace was made in 1774 after Russia had made many political and territorial gains. Poland, no longer the powerful kingdom of the previous century, had more or less capitulated to the Austrians, Prussians and Russians. Under this First Partition of Poland Russia gained control of what is now Belorussia.

Discontent

At home the deep discontent of the serfs and the Cossacks was bubbling angrily to the surface, a discontent compounded by an outbreak of cholera. The Cossack leader Pugachov tried the old trick of masquerading as the resurrection of a dead Tsar, in this case Peter III, and succeeded in gathering a large rebel force. As his victories took him ever closer to Moscow, Catherine became worried enough to send her best generals against him. Pugachov's defeat was followed by the exaction of terrible reprisals on his followers, leaving the serfs worse off than ever and with a resentment that would simmer for generations. The Cossacks were finally brought into line too — no longer were they able to range at will but were now part of the government frontier forces. The result of this uprising was the reorganisation of local government into smaller units under the jurisdiction of the noble class, a system that was to last until the Revolution of 1917. The nobles were not only in a position of some power, but now were under no obligation to serve the state.

Foreign affairs, however, were Catherine's main interest, and in 1783 she annexed the Crimea and allied herself with Austria. She had in mind the creation of a revived Byzantine Empire under the tutelage of Russia and with a Russian Constantinople as its capital. With her new Austrian (Emperor Joseph) and Polish (King Augustus IV of Poland was a former lover) allies, she made a state visit in 1787 to the newly acquired territories (of which another former lover, Prince Potemkin, was Viceroy). This was too much for the Sultan, who declared war on Russia and Austria.

Catherine had been convinced that victory would come quickly, but the Turks gave stubborn resistance. By 1792, when a treaty was signed, the Austrians had already concluded a separate peace and the Russians had gained almost nothing beyond a little land and Turkey's formal recognition of the Crimea as Russian territory.

Meanwhile Catherine turned her attention to Poland, where the adoption of a new and liberal constitution provided the excuse for a Russian invasion. In 1792 Poland was partitioned again, and then for a third time in 1795, following an insurrection against the Russian occupying forces. Russia ended up with Courland and Polish Lithuania; and Poland had ceased to exist.

In 1796, at the age of 68, Catherine died. She had intended to nominate her grandson Alexander as heir but had died without doing so. Thus her son Paul, for whom she had little affection and from whom she had usurped the throne some 34 years before, succeeded her as Tsar.

Catherine's achievements

During Catherine's reign Russia was firmly established as a European imperial power of the first rank. Russian influence was considerable and contact with the rest of Europe had become normal. She introduced some social reform but had not confronted the problem of the serfs. It was a reign where the intentions had been greater than the achievements. She realised that new ideas had necessarily to take into account Russian conditions and that sudden change was out of the question. She attempted to tone down the harshness of Russian life but when she made changes she was not always sensitive to the varying conditions from one area of the vast empire to the next. She was also unwilling to give the serfs too much freedom since she believed that Russia was not in a position to cope with the problems that emancipation would bring. She made some alterations to the legal system but in fact the idea of legality was alien to the Russian tradition and so, although a legal system was brought closer to the people, it was almost meaningless. It was more like a moral code, an example which in some respects has survived to the present day.

In foreign affairs, although the Empire was extended greatly, the manner was brutal and hasty in contrast to Catherine's handling of domestic affairs, which was by Russian standards subtle and humane. Indeed she was diverted by war from completing many of her domestic plans. On the whole, however, her reign was important for its possibilities and for the adoption of a new, more gentle tone. 'Those who remembered Catherine's rule looked back on it then as a time when autocracy had been 'cleansed from the stains of tyranny', when a despotism had been turned into a monarchy, when men obeyed through honour, not through fear.'

Paul I

Paul, having been mostly ignored by his mother, was mentally unstable. Nonetheless, he knew clearly what he wanted — essentially to rescind all the laws and changes brought about by his mother, and to bring back some of the old unpopular ways. Still, he was careful not to go too far since he saw the danger of alienating the aristocracy, without whose support he could not rule. He had hoped to stay out of foreign wars but the growing strength of Napoleon, who was on the way to conquering Europe and spreading the ideas of the French Revolution in the process, forced him into war against the French in Italy and Switzerland. His general, Suvorov, led Russian troops to some fine victories but ultimately felt let down by his allies, Austria and Great Britain. Relations were patched up with Napoleon but at home the Tsar's obsessive fears of revolution and treachery were becoming absurd. A plot was hatched against him by, amongst others, his son Alexander and the British Ambassador. He took refuge in the seemingly impregnable Michailovsky Castle but he was murdered all the same in 1801. His son became Alexander I.

Alexander I

Charming, handsome and intelligent, Alexander I was nonetheless the product of a mad father and an overwhelming grandmother. The result was a mystical aspect to his nature which had some bearing on the way he conducted affairs throughout the 24 years of his reign. It is during his reign that one of the greatest works of world literature, Tolstoy's *War and Peace,* is set.

He was a liberal by temperament, but his efforts to liberalise the constitution nonetheless fell at the usual hurdle — the threat to the autocracy. Some cosmetic changes were made — Ministries replaced the Colleges and a State Council, responsible to the Tsar, was introduced — but they had no real power.

Napoleon remained a threat and thus relations were re-established.

with Austria and Great Britain (Britain was also Russia's main trading partner). This upset Napoleon and war broke out again, the Russians suffering a severe defeat at Austerlitz. Under an alliance with the Prussians they fared no better and eventually Alexander decided to come to an understanding with Napoleon. They met on a boat in the middle of a river and agreed that Russia would control most of eastern Europe and be given a free hand in Sweden and Turkey (immediately after this meeting the Russians took Finland and Bessarabia) while Napoleon would control western Europe and Prussia. They agreed too to declare war on Great Britain but the British came to hear about it and the plan came to nought.

The alliance did not hold, however, and in 1812 Napoleon invaded Russia. The Russians had no coherent strategy and were forced to make an orderly retreat, much to the disgust of the Tsar who dismissed his general and recalled Kutuzov from exile. At the Battle of Borodino both sides lost vast numbers of men but the Russians continued their retreat to Moscow, which was abandoned to the French. This represented a great moral victory to the French, but was the beginning of their undoing. A fire destroyed much of the city and, backed by popular feeling, Alexander refused to parley with Napoleon. Napoleon suddenly found himself in an unenviable position, isolated thousands of miles from home, with winter coming on. He decided to fall back until the following spring when the campaign could be continued. On their journey west the French army was constantly harried by squadrons of Cossacks, the stoic indifference of the natives and a harsh, early winter. Alexander, the bit between his teeth, pursued the French across Europe, and although Napoleon was able to reform his army it was beaten again in Prussia by the Russians and their allies at the Battle of the Nations. Alexander, pursuing Napoleon right into Paris, began to see himself as the saviour of Europe. His latent mysticism began to assert itself and he began to call for a Holy Alliance. The other vanquishers of Napoleon were less keen on this idea but an alliance continued to hold for the time being as a useful tool for the suppression of revolutionary ideas.

At home Alexander's policy were far from enlightened. Power became concentrated in the hands of a minister called Arakcheyev who introduced the idea of Military Colonies where hundreds of thousands of peasants and their families were forced to perform a mixture of military and agricultural duties. Alexander (like Stalin) was popular because of his defeat of a foreign invader, but his solutions for the increasingly pressing problems at home were in the

Russian style, brutal and summary. He died in 1825, his only legacy a sense of Russian nationalism as a result of wars. (There are good grounds for believing the rumour that he in fact retired as a hermit to Siberia.) In any case he left no children and failed to nominate an heir. In theory power should have passed to his brother Constantine but he had renounced all claim to the throne some time before owing to his morganatic marriage. The remaining brother, Nicholas, thus became heir but he was unaware of the situation — along with many others he assumed that Constantine was to become emperor.

This confusion enabled the liberal element in Russia, given new strength following exposure to western ideas during the Napoleonic Wars, to rally its forces. New ideas found expression in the writing of Alexander Pushkin and others and took root during the interregnum. At the same time support for each of the brothers polarised, Nicholas seen as a reactionary and Constantine as a liberal. When to bring the confusion to an end Nicholas declared himself Emperor there had been enough time for a conspiracy among liberal members of the aristocracy and the army to come to maturation. Thus on 14 December, following the taking of the vow of allegiance by Nicholas, some 3,000 soldiers assembled in Senate Square to protest. Nicholas wanted to reason with the leaders of the conspiracy but they were nowhere to be found; in the evening he took drastic action and loyal troops opened fire on the demonstrators. The ringleaders were found but in the end only five of them were executed, the others being exiled to Siberia. The Decembrists, as they came to be known, have become an integral part of socialist mythology.

These events made Nicholas vow that revolution would never happen in Russia. He realised that changes needed to be made but was unable to see how. His vision extended only as far as the institution of a pervasive bureacracy and the widening of the powers of the police. Despite this, the strength of the liberal intelligentsia managed to grow, although they were themselves somewhat out of touch with real life. There were two main groups, one of whom looked to the West for inspiration, the other to pure Slav orthodoxy and the peasant commune.

Nicholas's foreign policy was also little different from his predecessor's. The Poles, similarly affected by liberal ideas, rose up and provided the Russians with a new excuse for annexation. At the same time, when relations between Turkey and Egypt deteriorated Nicholas used this to try to force Turkey under his protection and thus further his ambitions in the Balkans and Constantinople. Britain was most alarmed and for a while war looked possible until an uneasy peace was agreed. Peace did not last, and when the Russians marched into Turkish domains in 1854 the already concerned Western powers joined forces with Turkey with the aim of destroying Russian naval power in the Black Sea. Thus began the Crimean War.

However, Nicholas died in 1855. His successor, his son Alexander II, also had a reputation as a disciplinarian but was perceptive enough to realise that change was essential if Russia was to escape turmoil. First he ended the Crimean War in 1856, withdrawing from Moldavia and Wallachia (later to become Romania) and guaranteeing Turkish integrity. The Black Sea became neutral. Then he turned his attention to the serfs. By 1861 they were freed and theoretically able to purchase the land of their own. Enthusiasm for the reform was muted in all quarters and constitutional government was still a long way off, although a start was made with the election of local councils. The legal system was modified, educational facilities improved and the army reformed. Poland was allowed a certain amount of self-government but when this provoked cries for total independence it was followed by repression. In the east the Russian borders were widened considerably with expansion to the Pacific and the creation of the port of Vladivostok. Russia also took large areas of what is now Soviet Central Asia, the homelands of the Kazakhs and Tadjiks, much to the consternation of the British who felt that the Russians were getting uncomfortably close to India and Afghanistan. In fact Russia still had designs on Constantinople, for they still saw themselves as protectors of the Byzantine ideal. The Pan-Slav movement was in full swing at the same time and thus when the Turks savagely put down insurrections in Bulgaria and what is now Yugoslavia the Russians had another opportunity to intervene. They declared war in 1877 and by 1878 were in Constantinople. But so were the British, worried about the neutrality of the Straits between the Mediterranean and the Black Seas. Another peace was made, Russia making some small territorial gains and the Turks maintaining control of the Balkans. Again the peace was an uneasy one. And now Germany was becoming a force to reckon with.

At home revolutionary groups were flourishing as a result of the reforms. There were the Populists, the Socialists and the People's Will, which was openly dedicated to the assassination of the Tsar. Terrorism was rife, and the term Nihilism was coined. It was the age of classical Russian literature and yet there was a strong sense of foreboding.

Alexander was killed in 1881 by a terrorist bomb and hopes of gradual reform went with him. His successor, Alexander III, ignored his father's constitutional plans and brought back repression. Persecution of minorities became commonplace, the power of the nobility increased and the secret police sharpened their claws. When he died in 1894, handing power to Nicholas II, he had merely kept the lid on a boiling pot.

Nicholas was an ineffectual believer in autocracy and out of touch with the real nature of the country's problems. Freeing the serfs had not been a wholly successful operation (there was a lot of jealousy between those who had made good and those who had not) and yet, despite an uneasy political situation, the economy was growing fast. The peasant population was diminishing at the same time as industry grew in importance and with it the means to finance it, banking and commerce. In its wake came Marxism and the first Marxist party, known as the Russian social Democratic Party, was founded in 1898. In 1900 this split into the Mensheviks and the Bolsheviks, the latter being the more radical. Terrorism continued and Jews were blamed for it, resulting in a series of pogroms.

The Russo-Japanese War of 1904 might have been a useful way of defusing tension behind patriotism if it had not been such a fiasco. The Japanese were concerned at Russian encroachment in their sphere of influence in Manchuria. They completely outmanoeuvred the Russians, who were forced to give up all claims in China and whose status as a military power was rather lessened. Thus public discontent deepened further. On 22 January 1905 crowds of workers carrying icons gathered in the square in front of the Winter Palace to petition the Tsar. The Imperial troops panicked and several hundred deomonstrators were killed in cold blood. This day came to be known as Bloody Sunday. The rest of the year was dominated by strikes and riots, culminating in a general strike in October and the formation of a Workers's Soviet in St Petersburg. There were uprisings in the country and mutinies abroad naval ships. Even Nicholas began to realise that something needed to be done and in 1906 a *Duma* (National Assembly) was introduced, housed first in the Winter Palace and then in the Taurida Palace. Other reforms were made in other spheres of life. By now three quarters of the land belonged to the peasants and there was a beginning of Trade Unionism. There was a glimmer of democracy but it came too late.

Events outside Russia were to render these small changes insignificant. A realignment of the European powers sparked off the First World War. The Russian army was large but badly equipped and badly led. In three years Poland was lost as well as the Baltic Provinces, vast areas of Belorussia and the Ukraine, and two million men. Nicholas was an incompetent military leader and his unpopular German wife, seemingly hypnotised by the self proclaimed holy man Rasputin, interfered too much in government affairs. Rasputin was murdered in exasperation by Prince Yusoupov but the Royal Family carried on regardless. Revolution was inevitable.

The Great October Socialist Revolution

By the winter of 1916 it was obvious to foreign observers that the Russian people were at the limit of their endurance. 'The conditions of life have become so intolerable, the Russian casualties have been so heavy, the ages and classes subject to military service have been so widely extended, the disorganisation of the administration and the untrustworthiness of the Government have become so notorious that it is not a matter of surprise if the majority of ordinary people reach at any peace straw. Personally, I am convinced that Russia will never fight through another winter.' So wrote Sir Samuel Hoare in a dispatch to London from Petrograd where he was stationed.

The time was ripe for revolution. In view of what was to happen in later years, it is perhaps hard to imagine that there was really a popular mandate for a communist revolution, but the hardship of war was only one factor. Russia was completely different from the other great powers, all of whom had, one way or the other, evolved from autocracy to the beginnings of parliamentary democracy. Not so Imperial Russia where the Emperor was in effect an autocrat. Following the uprising of 1905, an elected assembly, the *Duma,* had been constituted but was all but powerless. An observation by Sir Samuel Hoare is revealing: 'The meetings were uncertain and liable to arbitrary adjournment. The Ministers, appointed and dismissed by the Emperor, and in no way responsible to the assembly, generally kept away . . . worst of all, the deputies themselves, impotent and irresponsible, were obviously disillusioned and embittered by the hopelessness of their position. The Duma, out of touch with reality, cold shouldered by authority, was eking out a precarious and often purposeless existence.'

In Russia, in the absence of an open forum for intellectual debate, rebellion tended to be violent and its suppression equally so. Thus revolutionary and conservative were locked in endless battle, with no prospect, or indeed means, of agreeing to a truce. At the turn of the century opposition to the government could be, broadly speaking, divided into four groups: liberal middle-class intellectuals; the anarchists at the extreme left; the Populists who championed the cause of the Russian peasant; and finally the various Marxist groups, of whom the Mensheviks, whose philosophy was of a mass party open to all supporters, and the Bolsheviks, whose leader Lenin envisaged a mass movement led by a disciplined and intellectually exclusive party, were of the most importance. At the crucial moment, in 1917, when an opportunity for action presented itself,

Zagorsk: the heart of old Russia.

only Lenin seized it, and only he had positive ideas of where the movement should go.

That the Tsar would have to go was acknowledged by all in 1917. A peaceful demonstration before the Winter Palace in St Petersburg was savagely broken up and the strikes that followed it forced the Tsar into making concessions (that he later abrogated or diluted). Nicholas was an amiable man but terrified of change. Sir Samuel Hoare, who met him several times, concluded that 'he was one of those over-sensitive and self-conscious personalities that create around them an atmosphere of doubt and hesitation.' Thus when the Revolution came the only question was whether the entire system would have to go as well as the Tsar.

It seemed that it would. Many of the ministers close to the Tsar, even the more liberal among them, who were eager to see the departure of the Tsar, were unrelentingly stubborn in other areas and the 'Minister of the Interior . . . can scarcely even be considered a psychically normal person.' Since the Tsar had no time for liberal reformers a mass movement, probably violent, seemed to be the only solution and disenchantment with the war was the ideal touchstone for revolution. Lenin saw it as a golden opportunity. 'Turn the imperialistic war into civil war.'

Although much of the groundwork had been laid by revolutionary groups, the first uprising in March 1917 was a spontaneous reaction to the lack of bread. Regiments of guards went over to the rioters and thousands of workers went on strike. The Tsar was forced to abdicate and a provisional government headed by Prince Lvov was established. The Russian war effort, to the relief of the allies, was sustained.

The Bolsheviks take power

The new provisional government eventually included socialists too, some of whose revolutionary fervour promptly abated. Lenin arrived in Petrograd from exile on 16 April 1917, determined to push the Bolshevik political line. He refused to make compromises, alienating many of his colleagues in the process, but drawing Trotsky, who realised that only the Bolsheviks were following genuinely revolutionary tactics. But the Bolsheviks, although powerful in Petrograd, lacked support in breadth and were well behind the Mensheviks in popular appeal. However, as the war continued so the left grew stronger and 'Soviets' (organisations which helped to coordinate strike movements and became the administrative arm of government) were springing up all over the country — in the Petrograd Soviet the Bolsheviks were all powerful. On 7 November 1917 (25 October in the old Russian calendar), the day of the meeting of the All-Russian Congress of Soviets, the Bolsheviks, to the tune of cannon fire from the cruiser Aurora, seized and held the principal buildings of Petrograd. Thus began the Soviet Union.

When in the following November free elections for a Constituent Assembly still failed to produce a Bolshevik majority, Lenin remained undeterred. The Bolsheviks continued to infiltrate the most important organs of the state while the other members of the coalition bickered about the ethics of the truce that had been made with the Germans. Lenin, convinced of imminent revolution in Germany, was firmly in favour of peace negotiations, despite the manifestly unfavourable terms of the treaty, and by the middle of 1918 his was the ruling party. The Constituent Assembly faded and all power was deemed to lie with the Congress of Soviets, whose executives were mainly drawn from the Bolshevik party. 'The concept of exclusive power to one party thus sprang not primarily from doctrinal disposition, but from a revolutionary situation in which neutrality or indifference was meaningless. Those who were not with the Bolsheviks were against them. The notion that power might be shared outside the Party was buried for ever.' (J.P. Nettl, *The Soviet Achievement*).

When Bolshevik rule appeared to be threatened, the *Cheka,* the special police led by Dzerzhinski, would step in. By the autumn of 1918 the so-called Red Terror was in full swing in an attempt both to rally people to the cause and to stifle opposition. It was at this point that the Tsar and his family were executed, but bloodshed, given the circumstances was kept to a minimum. Recrimination for past crimes was not, on the whole, Bolshevik policy at this stage. That was to come later. At this stage the Communist movement was rather more flexible in the mistaken belief that revolution on an international scale was sure to follow the Russian lead.

However, opposition to the Bolsheviks was not about to wither away and the Civil War of the following two years was savagely fought. A 'White' counter-revolutionary government (broadly in favour of reform but along liberal or even monarchical lines) had been established in Western Siberia and at one time all looked lost for the Bolsheviks; but the Whites were divided amongst themselves while the Reds enjoyed widespread support among the peasants.

The Mensheviks and their like fought alongside the Reds, if only because Red rule was preferable to White restoration. At any event, by the end of 1920 the Civil War had all but ceased and the Bolsheviks were not only in power by default, but had proved their strength.

The road to Stalinism — an old New Economic Policy

The country was on the brink of economic collapse. Clearly socialist ownership was out of the question for the time being, if for no other reason than that the expected world-wide Revolution was rather slow in coming. The implementation of the NEP (New Economic Policy) was an attempt to render the country economicaly strong by reverting to a measure of private production at the cost of ideological correctness. By 1924 the currency was stable and industrial production increasing. Economic stability was very fine but the Party continued to function as if the NEP was not really there. Discipline and correctness were all important, the NEP merely a temporary measure. To be so divorced from reality was later to lead to tragic circumstances.

The anti-Kulak movement was an example. The *kulaks* were rich peasants who had been encouraged to buy land in order to produce more and who then became a focal point for class hatred from those Party members who were against the NEP. By 1928 the anti-Kulak movement was in full intellectual swing, but nobody quite knew how to act on it. (The problem was solved by forced collectivisation in the not too distant future).

The coming of Stalin

At the end of 1922 Lenin suffered a stroke. Once recovered, he revised his opinions of Stalin's actions in Georgia — Stalin, a Georgian and who had been in charge of the Nationality question, had forced Georgia to follow the Bolshevik line — realising that they amounted to precisely what he had wanted to avoid: bullying of smaller nations. Lenin came to treat Stalin with more circumspection but his illness was to prove a telling factor in Stalin's career. Since early 1922 Stalin had been moved from the Commissariat for Nationalities to the Central Committee of the

Party (for which the Politburo was a sort of inner cabinet) of which he was General Secretary. He obtained the job by default — no one else wanted it, for the work was detailed and routine. It was not considered a post for an ambitious man. Having seen Stalin emboldened by a hint of power, Lenin attempted to have him stopped in his tracks, but his illness intervened. Documents written by Lenin which, if they had been revealed to the rest of the Party, would most certainly have led to Stalin's downfall, or would at least have provided a brake on his progress, only came to light after Lenin's death, when to have used them as evidence would have seemed churlish. Stalin was aware of Lenin's feelings, and also that many of his colleagues were aware of them too. He mollified the Party at the Twelfth Congress in April 1924 by appearing to give way on all the major issues, and by stressing the importance of unity at a crucial time. In so doing he opened the door to power, for Lenin died without naming a successor.

The Stalin years

When Lenin died, Trotsky seemed to be the natural choice as leader. But he did not enjoy high esteem amongst his colleagues, some of whom were no doubt jealous of his natural abilities, a state of affairs that Stalin used to his own advantage. From his position as General Secretary he initiated a campaign against Trotsky which would consign him to the second rank for ever. By 1926, Trotsky had been removed from the Politburo and in the following year he was expelled from the Party itself.

It might be said of Stalin's rise that it was almost inevitable in a party where the party line was sacrosanct. An ambitious, ruthless individual like Stalin understood that the sense of ideological correctness that had been drummed into the faithful could be easily manipulated. It was really he who made Leninism into a cult, not because of its intrinsic value but because it was easy to dispose of heretics. If Stalin was the supreme interpreter of Leninism then it was but a short step to the easy toppling of potential enemies.

Policies
Most of Stalin's policies became wholly inward looking when it was realised that world revolution was not to be. This 'Socialism in one country' smacked also of the old Russian preoccupation with the outside world disguised as Soviet 'revolutionary correctness'.

Economically the aim of Stalinism was the transformation of a backward rural economy to fully-fledged industrialisation. In 1928, with the formal abandonment of the NEP, he began his programme of Five Year Plans and mass-collectivisation of the peasant farms. By 1934, 75 per cent of farms had been collectivised but the cost in human suffering was appalling. This wrong-headed policy led to the neglect of crops and the slaughter of livestock causing widespread famine in the early 1930s, when hundreds of thousands of farmers starved.

Although economics and politics had by now become inseparably fused, some aspects of Soviet life were surprisingly open at first. The family came to be considered a bourgeois concept and therefore expendable. Divorce was made very easy and sexual promiscuity was encouraged. The church was not subject to repression until after 1929, although ways were sought to wean worshippers away from total dependence. The arts enjoyed a period of creative excellence where they were able to celebrate the new freedom that the Revolution had brought without feeling the need to conform to the Party line. This was the era of Pasternak and Eisenstein, of Gorki and Mayakovski. Teachers were encouraged to have a more comradely relationship with their pupils and attempts were made to relate subjects to each other rather than to teach them as distinct.

Purges

All came to an end in the 1930s — the decade of the purges.

Crisis became institutionalised — production levels were never sufficiently high. Equality, one of the basic tenets of the Revolution, was cast aside as an obstruction to better production. This was the age of Stakhanovism — Stakhanov was a miner who enjoyed over fulfilling his work quotas and telling everybody else how to do the same. Writers, who had enjoyed a free rein throughout the 1920s were expected by the 1930s to concentrate solely on the merits of socialism. Canvases were covered with healthy, happy farmers and proud workers. Architecture was grandiose and awesome. History was rewritten according to the new criteria: 'the class struggle became the main component of history since the Neolithic Age'. Hundreds of churches and monasteries were closed, yet divorce became difficult once again and abortion illegal. Experimental education was consigned to the scrap heap.

The average citizen's life was at best a drudge. Housing was in short supply: 'housing conditions for workers in Moscow are at present infinitely worse than the slums I have seen in the East End of London, in New York, or in any other capital of Europe' (*From Baltic to Black Sea* by Archibald Forman, 1931). Shops sold nothing more than the basic necessities; and there was no consolation in religion or the arts. Evenings were taken up with meetings where government ethos was discussed. Yet by the end of the 1930s there were relatively more doctors in the Soviet Union than in any other industrialised nation. Paid holidays and sick leave were introduced. Recreational sport became a popular aspect of Soviet life. But the Party was everywhere and in its shadow the secret police. Russians learned the art of beating the system to obtain their daily needs, but above all they learned the virtue of silence to stay alive.

The system forced Russians to find ways of beating it, and the system had to find new ways of stopping them. It was the most vicious of circles.

Ancient and Stalin: in the foreground the pretty fifteenth-century church of St Anne; in the background a block of flats circa 1950.

Stalin was not a great thinker. Practical steps would be taken to deal with a problem, only to become part of the official ideology. This makeshift approach to uniting the country behind the Party and its ideology was insufficient. Stalin chose to use terror in order to make people comprehend the rightness of Communism.

Stalin's purges turned the Party into a still more elitist organisation and lifted it ever further from the reach of ordinary people. Party members were careerists for whom membership was an end in itself, rather than a means of fulfilling an ideological dream. This came about because all the old guard were literally wiped out. It was clear to Bukharin, who was removed from his post in 1929, that Stalin was interested only in power: 'Whenever necessary he will from one moment to another change his theories in order to get rid of someone. He will strangle us all.' Prophetic words.

Thus as opposition to Stalin's collectivisation campaign grew, he simply removed the opposition from power. He went on in this way through the 1930s. At first only people in the public eye, particularly politicians, were purged. When in 1934 the secret police, the GPU, became part of the Department of the Interior, the campaign for ideological purity became a witch hunt. When Kirov, the rising star of the Politburo and a possible rival to Stalin, was assassinated, allegedly through a conspiracy on the part of the opposition, but quite possibly on the orders of Stalin himself, the purges on a mass scale got under way. By 1936, while distinguished Bolsheviks were being openly tried in mass 'show trials', millions of ordinary people disappeared into prison camps. Many of these prisoners were simply cheap labour. In 1939 the purges came to an end although prisoners who had been wrongfully arrested were still in the camps at least until the mid 1950s. There was talk of 'excesses', but Stalin remained in power proclaiming that the Soviet Union had never been stronger.

In the mean time there was Hitler to deal with.

The Great Patriotic War

Stalin had noted the threat of Fascism and had tried several times, unsuccessfully, to seal a pact of non-aggression with Hitler. Finally they came to an arrangement in 1939. The pact not only ensured the Soviet Union's security, but also decided Soviet spheres of interest in eastern Europe. Thus, in the interests of security Stalin was able to annexe the Baltic republics, eastern Poland and what is now Moldavia, and invade Finland. A confident Germany, however, ignored the pact and by invading the Soviet Union forced her into the war.

The Soviets were badly prepared for war and the Germans advanced as far as the outskirts of Moscow and of Leningrad. Part of the problem was the loss of so many experienced generals in the purges; but although the Russians incurred enormous losses, Stalin succeeded in maintaining industrial output by moving factories eastwards. The Germans just failed to take Moscow and were forced to retreat. Sheer stubborness and the spirit of self-sacrifice kept the Germans at bay while the Soviet army remained in some disarray throughout 1942. New officers were trained and the army permitted to get on with the job, unencumbered by interfering political commissars who had until then had equal ranking. By the end of November 1942 the Russian army was on the offensive and the Germans were retreating. Towards the end of 1943 victory seemed assured and Stalin began to think politics again. He particularly began to think about his near neighbours in eastern Europe. Here were the beginnings of a plan to extend the Russian sphere of influence.

In justifying his determination to split Europe, Stalin was fond of pointing to the German threat. This at least was a view possibly shared by all the allies. To simply carve up Europe into spheres of influence was not everybody's choice but it suited Stalin, who wished for the Soviet Union to be shielded from 'imperialist' encroachment. It was acknowledged that the Russians had played a key role in the allied victory but now Stalin wished to retreat into isolation again, despite the fact that Communism in western Europe was no longer treated with the same suspicion as before the war. The countries of eastern Europe were to become client Communist states and a convenient source of cheap goods for the Russians, as well as providing a convenient buffer against potential attack. It seems certain that Stalin was not really interested in world revolution. He was more concerned with the Soviet Union, all the more so when it was clear that there were those, like Tito, who were not afraid to stand up to him.

Thus the Soviet Union emerged from the war as a 'superpower', at least in the sense that it wielded direct influence in several countries of eastern Europe and would for the next 40 years be regarded at least as an advisor to any country which aspired to Communism, and as the alternative to the U.S.A.

Stalin at home

The war had brought great suffering to the Russians but had temporarily relegated politics to second place. After 1945 it returned to the forefront of Soviet life. Stalin was eulogised as the great marshall who had led the USSR to victory. An era of austerity and ideological rigidity began to permeate all areas of life. Nationalities (e.g. Kalmyks), deemed to have been disloyal, began to be deported. Stalin was deeply suspicious of the Jewish population, particularly after the creation of Israel, when thousands of Soviet Jews wished to go there. Purges began again, not on the scale of the 1930s, but of many influential people. The purge became institutionalised, a peculiarly Soviet method of keeping people up to the mark. The economy was in a mess — the war had destroyed a fifth of Soviet potential output — and pre-war methods were reinstated. Heavy industry remained of primary importance and totally under state control. By the mid 1950s the country was back on course in output but the whole system was becoming increasingly unwieldy. Stalin refused to countenance any changes or adjustments — if something was not working it was not because the method was incorrect, but because it was incorrectly applied. More control was required, not less.

Stalin died in March 1953 of a brain haemorrhage, to genuine mourning. His legacy was remarkable. He had led the largest country in the world for 25 years and had moulded it into a global power. For outsiders the Soviet Union was as mysterious as ever, but a good deal more terrifying. Stalin also left positive achievements: illiteracy had been all but eradicated; some measure of culture was available to all; sports facilities, catering for ideologically acceptable recreation, were well provided for; workers were entitled to holidays, even if they were to be taken 'collectively' at a resort affiliated to their place of work. The country had survived the war and had made considerable progress on the industrial front.

But the achievements were overshadowed by the failures. Economic planning failed and left the country top-heavy — the emphasis on industrial development had been at the expense of the countryside and agricultural output. Relationships between Russians and other nationalities within the Soviet Union were worse than ever; Lenin's intention had been to free the other republics of Russian domination but now they were more 'Russified' than before the Revolution. The Party was ever more distant from the people and was run by careerists and bureaucrats — idealists and revolutionaries were eliminated in purges. Fanatical secrecy surrounded every aspect of daily life. Indeed life had become impossibly dreary. The country was stagnating and needed a shakeup.

After Stalin

The death of Stalin began a period of change. The first change was in the style of leadership. For four years there was a sort of interregnum: the country was run collectively while a slow power struggle developed. Several names were bandied about, but Khrushchev did not get the backing needed until 1957. Until then Malenkov, Chairman of the Council of Ministers, was considered the nearest to an outright leader. He was somewhat in the Stalinist mould but economic policies were changing from the Stalinist tradition. The main difference was an emphasis on consumer goods, implying a change of political direction.

The leadership may have been jolted into change by riots in the newly-created state of East Germany in July 1953. A shakeup in the Kremlin resulted in the death of the much hated Beria, responsible for Internal Security and the Secret Police. Thereafter the Secret Police were kept separated from the Ministry of Internal Affairs.

In 1955 Malenkov was elbowed out, but still no single person was obviously in charge. Khrushchev was preparing himself for power — at the Twentieth Congress of the Party in 1956 he made a fairly full-blooded denunciation of Stalin. By 1957 despite evident restlessness in Poland and in Hungary — for which some in the party blamed him — he managed to establish himself as the leading figure of the party and of the government. The process of de-Stalinisation had begun, although it was Stalin himself who was under fire, not the system that bred him.

Nikita the table thumper

Nikita Khrushchev, a Ukranian, was in a completely different mould to Stalin. Stalin had been deemed suitable for the job precisely because of his apparently rather dull character. Yet he had become a sort of cult figure. Khrushchev, who aimed to ensure that this did not happen again, was a showman nonetheless, but lacked the ruthlessness of Stalin. He loved to travel and made frequent journeys abroad and throughout the Soviet Union. He was a pragmatist rather than a theorist and although the 'cold war' intensified during this time, the Soviet Union was more open than it had been for a long time.

On one hand, regular contacts with the USA were established — the party line now being that Communism would triumph on its own merits rather than through revolution; but on the other the Berlin Wall was built and in 1962 for the first time the world was perched on the brink of nuclear war when in the Bay of Pigs episode the USSR placed missiles in Cuba in the heart of the USA's most sensitive sphere of influence. The USSR's East European allies were allowed to de-Stalinise but the Chinese broke off relations because of Russian 'revisionism'. All this was caused by the Soviet Union's larger role in world affairs, in turn causing more scope for tensions to arise.

Internally attempts were made to decentralise the economy in order to improve efficiency and to rationalise the distribution system. Khrushchev realised the importance of agriculture, but lacked expertise. When he devised a plan for cultivating the wilds of Siberia and Kazakhstan, he was advised that it would be better to improve the efficiency of existing agricultural land. He ignored the experts and his plan failed dismally. Later, he listened and tried to make the countryside as politically important as the cities had been under Stalin.

Although more attention was paid to producing consumer items and although the quality of life improved, the annual rate of growth fell from an average of 10 per cent to 7½ per cent. Yet as Soviet political influence grew, particularly in 'Third World' countries, so did her exports.

A more liberal attitude was shown towards the arts and culture, but only comparatively speaking. By Western standards the constraints remained considerable although, in the absence of an extremist like Stalin, it was never clear what was subversive and what was not.

In 1964 Khrushchev was voted out of office. His rather haphazard ways had alienated quite a few people and he was forced into early retirement. Although not disgraced, he was not given the honour of having his ashes placed in the Kremlin wall, but was buried in the quiet obscurity of the Novodyevichy convent. Recently, however, his achievements have been reappraised and he has regained an honourable place in Soviet history.

From Khrushchev to the present day

Khrushchev was succeeded by Leonid Brezhnev, who remained in power for 20 years during what is now referred to as the 'Time of Stagnation'. The Soviet Union ceased to grow in any meaningful sense although her reputation as a 'superpower' was strengthened by interventions in Prague in 1968 and in Afghanistan in 1979. The economy grew very slowly, political repression was vigorous, while corruption became a way of life, and self expression and contact with the outside world were denied to most people.

Brezhnev died in 1984 and was succeeded by Yuri Andropov, a former head of the KGB, who maintained the status quo in the short time before he died. His successor, Chernyenko, died after only a few months. Then came a big change — the appointment of Mikhail Gorbachev. Here was a man who seemed sophisticated and practical, who, like his predecessor Alexander II in the nineteenth century, realised that change had to come, no matter how daunting the task. He quickly established a reputation in the West as someone 'we can do business with' and made the words *glasnost* (openess) and *perestroika* (reconstruction) known the world over. Yet the habits of decades or hundreds of years are hard to shift quickly. The problems are immense — although there is now freedom of expression and travel has been made much easier, the economy is in a perilous state, several republics are demanding independence and the crime rate has soared. Gorbachev, if he survives, has to juggle the forces of reaction against the forces of progress — anything may happen.

Opposite: The spire of the Peter and Paul Cathedral, Trezzini's masterpiece, a happy amalgam of Russian and Danish architecture.

Following page: Old traditions are coming back to the streets.

The Russian persona

'Loe thus I make an ende: no other news to thee, but that the country is too cold, and the people beastly be.' So wrote Ambassador George Turbeville of Russia and the Russians to Elizabeth I of England in the sixteenth century, an impression that one way or another has lingered in the mind of the westerner ever since. Others gave a contrasting view: 'What I admire in the Russian people is nothing barbaric, picturesque or exotic, but something eternal, universal and great — namely, their love of man and their faith in God.' — Maurice Baring earlier this century, but it is a minority view.

One factor has been sheer ignorance; another has been, until recently, the difficulties of leavening that ignorance through informal contact with Russian people. In fact visitors from the West have been travelling to the Soviet Union in considerable numbers since the 1960s but the combination of Russian intransigence and western propaganda somehow negated the value of contact. Thus the vision of the Soviet Union as 'Russia' (partly correct), as a huge land of darkness broken only by millions of square miles of snowy steppe, as a quaint yet menacing mixture of fairy tales and oppression, as a training ground for ballet dancers, bulky athletes and writers, most of whom defect when given the chance, has persisted until our own time. In this very broad picture there is some truth, but it is a simplistic view of a people who are complicated and often contradictory. Only by recognising that the Russians have a singular attitude to life, and are only too human, can one expect to enjoy a visit to the Soviet Union.

History and geography

There is no possibility of understanding the mentality of a people without knowing something of their history. The history section above outlines the salient points that have made Russia and the Russian character what they are. Russians tend to claim that the greatest restraint on Russia's development as a nation was the Tartar-Mongol yoke which prevented contact with the rest of Europe and encouraged people to be deeply introspective. Muscovy, the predecessor to Imperial Russia, grew powerful in the shadow of Mongol occupation, and her success was based on the exploitation of the other city states. Ruthlessness, suspicion and savage recrimination became a way of life. Secret police, or their medieval equivalents, were an early development. Total dependence on the state, and complete awe of autocratic rulers were bred into the ordinary Russian over centuries of absolutism. All this nurtured a fatalistic attitude to life mixed with fierce patriotism.

The vastness of the land made the peasant depend upon himself and his family. The extremes of the climate touched the Russian with extreme melancholy and extreme joy. Inconstancy of harvests sent peasants scurrying elsewhere and brought forth hard laws tying them to the land and their masters.

The Church

Russia was not called Holy Russia for nothing. In 1914 there were at least a thousand functioning monasteries throughout the country. They ran schools but almost never became great centres of learning. There was a great tradition of mysticism and ascetism; and hermits were revered. The institution of father-confessor played a large role in religious life. The icon was ever present in church and home as a tangible expression of holy love (replaced, it is sometimes said, by a portrait of Lenin after the Revolution). The main concern of the Russian Church was for the community rooted in spiritual love. The Church played an important role in the daily lives of the average person and this devotional attitude has not been blunted by official atheism.

Stalin and the Second World War

The Soviet Union lost twenty million citizens during the Second World War. Stalin has finally been unequivocally pilloried as one of the most appalling dictators of all time. He was responsible for the deaths of as many as thirty million mostly innocent people, in labour camps or by firing squads, by playing upon people's ignorance and fears. His recent death makes his crimes hard to forget.

Thus, although the average Soviet citizen's talk of peace may seem political propaganda, there is hardly a Russian alive today whose family was not affected by either the war or by Stalin.

Temperament

Visitors to the Soviet Union often say that Russians do not smile, and are exultant when 'they managed to make a Russian smile'. It would be fair to say that Russians are not a frivolous people and do not trade in casual mannerisms. Certainly the average citizen has not, in the material sense, much to smile about — life is still not easy. Yet this does not mean that Russians do not know how to enjoy life. On the contrary, they delight in life, but in its simple pleasures, of friendship, conversation, music and dance. In short, conviviality. Naturally people object to having to queue endlessly for even the basic necessities, and of course people complain about the problems that beset their daily lives, but all that is quickly forgotten when there is a chance of a party.

Nevertheless, frustration with some of the shortcomings of life in the Soviet Union means that people working in tourism do not always themselves give the best service. Instead of politely explaining that an item is unavailable, or why something does not work, an employee is likely to give what appears to be a sullen *nyet* and turn away to chat to the nearest colleague. This is highly irritating. But on the other hand, it can be explained, usually, by lack of training, years of resigned acceptance to poor organisation or to corruption, and powerlessness to change anything. A pleasant manner and a sense of humour, it might be thought, could at least render inconvenience less unpalatable — but Russians are proud and patriotic. To have to constantly admit to the failings of their country is not only tedious but also embarrassing. Taking refuge in a blunt answer, as if the questioner were contemptible and the question beneath contempt, is a way out.

Russians, traditionally, have mixed feelings towards foreigners — a sort of mixture of shyness, admiration, inferiority and arrogance. Extremely hospitable by nature, centuries of at best limited contact with foreigners have made for a slight feeling of uneasiness in their company, which runs quite counter to a natural tendency to welcome and to share. At the moment contact between westerners and Russians is comparatively easy, but a feeling that foreigners are a little dangerous may yet linger.

The Great Slav Soul

One of the hardest things to understand has been the docility with which Russians have accepted a way of life that would be intolerable to the average westerner. Odder still is the impression Russians sometimes give of not minding about the lack of material comfort or the indignity of living under a totalitarian government. Again the answer lies partly in the history of the country. Another part, however lies in something that is almost irrational, a bond Russians have with their country, almost physical, yet with mystical qualities. Russians who leave are frequently homesick, and not a few emigrants, happy though they were to have escaped totalitarianism, return. This is no doubt partly due to an inability to cope with democracy, where so much depends on the effort of the individual. But this is not all. The comfortable West proves a disappointment to a people for whom companionship is everything.

Russians like to extract the essence of life. For them this means people, forests and flowers ('mother Russia'). And if it is necessary to forego the comforts offered by the twentieth century, so be it. Unless it can be had in the grandest, most magnificent style, for Russians tend towards the immoderate. They would like to have the best, but if that is impossible then the average, the mediocre, is not worth having. The same person who adores caviare will be just as happy with pickles and a cabbage soup. If it is not possible to live in a palace, then a poky flat is just as good. Russians love poetry. There is poetry in life in the raw and there is the poetry of riches. There is no poetry in mediocrity.

Folklore

Russia has a colourful folklore. The vastness of the land, long, silent winters and a history whose heroes and tyrants are larger, grander and more terrible than most, have given rise to a love for the magical and the fantastic. What the stories often reveal, too, is the Russian love for their homeland and its simple beauties. The Firebird is a mythical creature that crops up regularly in Russian tales — they grew out of the following legend.

Once upon a time there was an orphan girl by the name of Marushka, whose embroidery was of unsurpassed beauty, but who would never accept more in payment for her work than the purchaser could easily afford. Her fame spread far and wide and when merchants came from beyond the mountains and beyond the seas, they marvelled at her skill and offered to transport her away to riches and glory. Modestly, she would always decline, preferring to stay in her humble village birthplace. Her fame came to the notice of Koshchei the Immortal who, enraged at the knowledge of something so beautiful that he had not seen, assumed the form of a handsome boy and flew across the world to Marushka's cottage. The beauty of her work and the girl's unaffected modesty angered Kaschei still further, for he considered that his own skills were matchless. He tried to seduce Marushka by promising to make her his queen. Yet she refused the offer, saying 'there is nothing sweeter to me than the woods and the fields of one's native place. Never shall I leave this village where live those to whom my needlework brings joy.' At that, Kaschei turned Marushka into a Firebird and himself into a black falcon. He grabbed the Firebird with his talons and hurtled high into the sky.

Marushka could do nothing but she was determined to leave behind the traces of the beauty she had created, and so, as she was swept further and further away from her own dear home, she shed her brilliant feathers one by one to let them float down amidst the forest trees and the meadow flowers. They became covered with grass and leaves and snow, but their power survives. Marushka died of a broken heart in the talons of the black falcon, but her feathers can still be seen by those who love beauty and who try to make things beautiful for others.

The Matryoshka doll

One of the souvenirs that you will encounter regularly during your stay in the Soviet Union is the ubiquitous Matryoshka nest of dolls. The word Matryoshka is simply a diminutive of the Russian name Matryona, and there are several explanations of the doll's origins. One tells of the existence of a goddess in the Ural foothills by the name of Jumala. She was made of pure gold, but was hollow and contained three other similar figures and she stood in a forest clearing where no one was permitted to set eyes on her. Passing travellers would leave a gold offering on a tree and would return to find that it had gone to help make another shell for the goddess.

Whatever the significance of Jumala, the Matryoshka dolls you see now contain only wooden images of a peasant mother, but originally the first would have been a girl in peasant dress, then a boy, then another girl and finally a babe in arms. They seem to be an endearing talisman of the great Russian mother.

The peasant view

God-fearing though the Russian peasant was, his world was also one where superstition and fable, stretching back to their Slav past, played a large role. All houses had their ancestral spirit or *domovoy* who was supposed to inhabit the ashes of the stove, which were transported with the family should they move to another house. That the bear is an enduring symbol of Russia is a testimony to the strength of old belief; for the bear was one of the most potent of ancient Slav godhead symbols. The bear has persisted as an important feature in the Russian circus; and superstitions where the animal plays a crucial role abound. After 12 December it is said that winter wears a 'bear's coat', which means that the weather will be turning colder. To appease the mischievous *domovoy*, you should hang a bear's head in the stable.

Fairy tales are a vital and copious ingredient in Russian life. It is manifest in some of the greatest works of Russian art — what could be more Russian than the Nutcracker? There is Stravinsky's celebrated *Firebird*, and one of the pictures at Mussorgsky's exhibition is of Baba Yaga, a traditional figure of Russian folklore.

Baba Yaga is a witch who flies through the air in a mortar using the pestle as an oar, and who lives in the forest in a house that is built on rooster's feet in order to catch her victims. Hag though she is, she is sometimes of crucial help to the heroes of the tales. In one story, where the Tsarevich (son of the Tsar) has had the misfortune to marry a frog, it is Baba Yaga who reveals to him the whereabouts of the beautiful princess who is trapped within. She is held prisoner by the wicked Koshchei (of the legend of the Firebird). The Tsarevich must kill Koshchei in order to have his bride but this is not easy for Koshchei is immortal. His death lies at the point of a needle which is in an egg which is in a duck which is in a hare which is in a stone chest at the top of a mighty oak-tree which is guarded unerringly by Koshchei himself. Needless to say, the young Tsarevich succeeds. Koshchei is always evil, and, mostly, so is Baba Yaga. But they are always defeated by a potent mix of perseverence, faith and a good heart. These characters, like Baba and Koshchei are the product of the peasant imagination in a huge world of steppe and forest, an attempt to explain the unpalatable and to make it not only tolerable but beautiful.

Sunbathing against the walls of the Peter and Paul fortress, with St Isaacs in the distance.

A picture in the Russian Museum, St Petersburg. Early Russian art has a singular style not always to Western taste — this example has universal appeal (photo: Jim Helme).

Upon arrival

The arrival procedures, while essentially similar at all frontier posts, will vary according to where you are entering the country. Entering the USSR used to be difficult, and still can be, but customs and immigration formalities are easier now. There is only one form to fill in:

Customs declaration form

There is no health declaration form or landing card. Only the Customs Declaration Form, a most important document. It is a record of what you bring into the country and what, therefore, should be taken out. Without it, money cannot be changed legally.

It asks you to provide the following information:

- your full name
- your citizenship
- your place of departure
- your destination (the answer is the USSR)
- the purpose of your visit (business, tourism, private etc.)
- whether you have any legal weapons, drugs, antiques or works of art or Russian roubles with you (the answer to all should be negative, so write 'NO' for each.

It will then ask you to list the foreign currency that you are carrying (it is unnecessary to list coins, but notes should be listed carefully) — do so both in figures and in writing, e.g. '£200', 'Two hundred pounds', under the appropriate headings. Travellers cheques should be listed as a separate item. You are then asked if you are carrying any roubles on behalf of others (answer 'NO').

There are a couple of questions about the amount of luggage you are carrying.

Then sign and date the form.

The reverse of the form is for official use only.

There is mention of precious stones and jewellery, and it is as well to inform the custom's officer if you are in possession of anything valuable so that it will be recorded on the reverse of the form.

The form must be presented to the customs officer, who will stamp it and hand it back. DO NOT LOSE THIS FORM — eachtime you change money at the Bank of the Soviet Union, a record of the transaction will be made on it and the form must be given up upon leaving the country.

Customs and immigration in general

You are officially allowed the standard amounts of cigarettes, perfume and alcohol, but this is pretty flexible. The main problem used to be books, but since the likes of Solzhenitsyn and Nabokov are now being restored to favour, things are easier; but avoid pornography, anything overtly anti-Soviet or more than one Bible. From time to time, exception will be taken to something, in which case it may well be confiscated. Then you will be asked to sign a document saying that you understand why it is being confiscated and that you will be able to reclaim it on leaving the country (providing you leave through the same frontier post). Gifts for Soviets citizens may be regarded with suspicion — ensure that everything appears to be for your own use.

Passport inspection is sometimes drawn out, with the officer staring at your features and your photograph seemingly for ever. This is normal. In the case of border crossings by train your passport is never stamped. Luggage delivery is sometimes particularly slow at airports and trolleys are few.

Should there seem to be a problem with something, whether it involves customs or immigration, do not panic and do not get angry. Patience is the only answer.

Arriving by car

Remember that this must be prearranged. Arrive at a reasonable hour. Once you arrive at your frontier crossing the basic procedures are the same — passport and visa inspection, customs and currency control, and the filling in of the Declaration Form. Motorists, however, will be expected to sign a declaration undertaking to take the car out of the country after their visit. Another form will ask for details of the itinerary, the car registration number, and so on. It will speed matters up if you have all the vehicle documents to hand, and if you know the precise location of the engine number, the chassis number etc. Insurance may be purchased at the frontier. Your driving licence may be validated for the USSR at the border. You may be required to pay a road tax of a few roubles.

Intourist
Intourist is the state tourist agency of the Soviet Union. It is responsible for the arrangements for nearly every tourist that enters the country. Tour operators abroad who sell tours to the USSR do so only with the consent of Intourist — once an itinerary and date is established, Intourist makes arrangements for internal transportation and accommodation. A number is allocated to the group and visas are issued. They undertake to follow the itinerary that the foreign tour operator has advertised in its brochure but reserve the right to make changes dictated by circumstances beyond their control.

Considering the size of the operation, Intourist does a remarkable job. The problems are immense — hotels are too few and too variable in quality, and the national airline, though safe, is badly organised, unhelpful and unpunctual. Despite this most visitors get what they pay for. There are times when Intourist may seem rather inflexible but there is usually a reason and they do their best. Most hotels have a 'service bureau', part of Intourist, which is supposed to help visitors book theatre tickets, reconfirm flights and so on. If there is a problem, the best thing is to start with the service bureau and take it from there.

Daily practicalities

Electricity
The mains supply is generally 220 volts, with some isolated areas of 127. Plugs are twin round pin, the pins being 2 cms. apart. Bulbs are the screw variety.

Laundry
Next to no public services. In the hotels there is usually a service of some sort, usually (with the exception of the best hotels where they have a normal service) a question of giving it to the chambermaid who will do it for direct payment. If there is a floor lady, go through her.

Soviet money

The basic unit of currency is the *rouble*. One rouble is made up of
100 *kopecks*. There are currently two exchange rates. The first
applies to the purchasing of roubles. When you exchange your
pounds, dollars etc. for roubles at a bank (all hotel banks are
branches of the Soviet Bank so the rate is standard) you will obtain
approximately ten times the value of the rouble's value on
international markets. Thus, if the international exchange rate is 1
Rouble to 1 Rouble, you will receive ten roubles for a pound in a Soviet
bank. Yet in the Berioska shops the rate will be 1 to 1 Rouble. Thus,
for foreigners who make all their purchases in roubles the USSR is
cheap. However, you will find that it is often difficult to buy what
you want with roubles and thus are compelled to spend foreign
currency directly. In order to buy roubles you must present your
Declaration Form. You will be given a receipt for each transaction,
which you must not lose. Change a few at a time until you see how
many you are spending, for although you will often be using your
own currency, there are times when roubles are essential (e.g. for
stamps).

Providing you have your Declaration Form and exchange
receipts, roubles can be changed back at your point of departure.
Remember that roubles bought on the black market cannot be
changed back because you will need a bank receipt. It is illegal to
export roubles.

Etiquette and custom

In some respects the Soviet Union is free of binding social
conventions. On the other hand, there are a few things that are
definitely not done, and care should be taken to avoid giving
offence.

In theatres, for example, or in restaurants, you are expected to
remove your coat and hand it in at the cloakroom. There is unlikely
to be a charge, but a tip of a few kopecks might be in order. This
is rather a good service but there will be a rush at the end of a
theatre performance.

Russians think that you are most definitely mad if you do not
wear a hat in the winter months — motherly women are likely to
reproach you for this unthinkable oversight. Do not be offended.
They mean well.

By Western standards, Russians dress informally most of the
time. A visit to the theatre in jeans would not arouse comment,
although Russian women tend to favour a skirt on those occasions.

Business and diplomacy require conventional smartness, however. In hot weather bare flesh is not approved of — shorts and bare torsos (for men) are acceptable only at resorts. Women should dress with discretion.

Russians can be extraordinarily brief and to the point on occasion. We tend to expect a question to be answered not only in the affirmitive or in the negative, but also to be accompanied by an explanation, or an apology, or at least by a bit of waffle. The telephone in the Soviet Union is likely to be answered with a simple 'Yes?' (*Da?*); and the negative *nyet,* sometimes accompanied by a little shake of the head, is frequently the only information available. The English, who like a bit of padding, sometimes find such bluntness rather disconcerting but at least you know where you stand.

As in England, queuing is a way of life. Western newspapers have always lampooned the empty shops and the endless queues of the Soviet Union. Certainly the laws of supply and demand take on a different form in the Soviet Union, necessitating store sieges by the eager public when longed for goods arrive. This is not the only reason, however, for the lines in the shops. Part of the problem stems from the longwinded method of making a purchase, which involves queuing to select your purchase, queuing elsewhere to pay for it, and queuing again to collect it. Because of this it is quite normal to obtain a place in a queue and to ask the person behind you, by pointing to your feet, to reserve it while you complete a purchase elsewhere. Queuing becomes a matter of honour.

The Russian system of names differs from ours. All Russians have three names — a given name, a patronymic (from the father's name), and a family name. The use of the patronymic dates back to time when families were larger and closer, its survival perhaps a subliminal yearning for the old days. It is formed by adding, in the case of a man, the suffix — *ovich* or — *evich* to the first name of the father; and in the case of a woman — *ovna* or — *evna.* Thus a woman may be known as Eleanora Ivanovna plus surname, a man as Dmitri Mikhaelovich plus surname. Not only is this a convenient method of distinguishing, for example, one Ivan from another, it is also respectful without being either patronising or obsequious.

The use of the word *tovarishch* is acceptable when you do not know the name of the person concerned. It is not quite as political as its nearest English equivalent, 'comrade'.

Post

Postcard airmail anywhere in the world — 35 kopeks. A letter costs 50. Internal charges are much less.

Public holidays (those with asteriks are likely to have fireworks) January 1, February 23* (Soviet Army Day), March 8 (Int. Women's Day, May 1—2* (Int. Labour Day), May 9* (VE Day), October 7 (Constitution Day), November 7-8* (Anniversary of the Revolution). Current political events may bring changes.

Time changes

Moscow Summer Time — one hour is added at the last weekend of March. At the last weekend of September one hour is subtracted.

Tipping

Tipping, strictly speaking, is illegal in the Soviet Union, and the handling of foreign currency is theoretically limited to those for whom it is part of their job although new laws are being introduced which will change this. However, the fact remains that a show of appreciation is sometimes expected. It is customary, for example, to give a cloakroom attendant a few kopecks. Taxi drivers are unlikely to refuse a sum additional to the fare. At the same time there are plenty of people who would not dream of accepting a penny from anyone, so always be discreet and don't press money on someone who refuses. There are those, too, who may not accept money, but for whom a gift might be welcome. Taxi drivers, for example, may negotiate your fare, once they know that you are foreign, in foreign cigarettes. Others may accept foreign currency at a rate rather better than you will get at the bank, which may be convenient. Remember, however, that such transactions are illegal and treat each circumstance on its merits. If in doubt (with Intourist guides for example) ask first, in private, and accept the answer. A gift from the Berioska may be more appropriate.

Getting about

From city to city

There is a comprehensive network of aeroplane and train services throughout the Soviet Union but remember that if you are, for example, in Moscow, and you decide to go to Irkutsk, it is not as simple as merely boarding a train or a plane. It is still difficult for foreigners to purchase tickets for roubles and your visa must be amended for an additional destination. This can be done through Intourist who will also purchase tickets for foreign currency. Tickets for roubles can be bought at certain outlets — see 'information' at end of city sections.

Aeroflot is generally a badly organised airline and notoriously unpunctual. For any flight, therefore, go armed with snacks, something to drink and patience. In the event of a delay do not expect to be given a reason — the flight will go in its own good time. Prices are reasonable.

Soviet railways

The railway system by contrast is good, punctual, tolerably comfortable and reasonably priced. If you have the time and the inclination, train travel is most enjoyable, even though certain routes are not open to foreigners. Because of the distances sleepers are widely used (e.g. travellers tend to take the seven-hour journey between Moscow and St Petersburg at night, since the scenery is unremarkable). Although there are several classes, you will travel either first or second (sometimes called soft or hard) class. In first-class compartments there are two berths, in second-class there are four. Four-berth compartments occupied by two passengers are also considered first-class. Facilities are similar to international trains (see Getting there) but there are no wash basins in the compartments. Bedding is provided but towels are flimsy. Take lavatory paper, soap and plug. Alcohol is not sold on board.

By car

The road system in the European part of the Soviet Union is variable in extent and quality (partly due to the extremes of climate which make road maintenance problematic). It is forbidden for foreigners to drive more than 40 kilometres beyond the city limits, so any journey must be planned in advance; therefore inter-city travel is practical only for recreation. Bringing your own car is discussed under 'Getting there'.

Car rental is still in its infancy but possible in many of the principal cities. You will have to keep to a prearranged itinerary beyond the 40-km limit, organised through Intourist, but it is possible to do it partly by train or plane and partly by car. In certain cities you are compelled to have a chauffeur. These constraints are becoming fewer all the time, however.

Russians drive rather fast, so take care. The police, however, are pretty strict, so drivers tend to follow the rules. Road surfaces are unpredictable, so fast driving requires attention. It is not unusual to see people driving at night only with side lights — you are advised to use headlights. International road signs are the norm but are scarce, which means that there is likely to be little warning of what is ahead.

In the cities it is often difficult to spot traffic lights because of the great width of the roads. U-turns may be made at designated places but these are not always clearly marked. Be aware of the trams — you are not allowed to drive in the tram lanes on the road sides, but may cross the ones in the middle of the road unless there is a white arrow on a blue background which is telling you to keep to your lane until the next junction. Remember that government officials in their limousines will often come bowling down the centre of the road.

You are expected to get out the way and the traffic police will tell you as much. The official speed limit in towns is 60 kph (37 mph) and 90 kph (55 mph) outside the city limits. Zebra crossings are ornamental although drivers should slow down as they approach them. Car theft is not widespread but theft of radios and windscreen wipers is, so take precautions. The traffic police telephone number is 02 (toll free). The wearing of seat belts is compulsory.

Moving around cities
Metro
The stations are recognisable by the letter 'M' above the station entrances. There is a fixed fare of 5 kopeks for a single journey regardless of distance, for which you need a 5-kopek coin. Before the barriers you will see an array of boxes on the wall — these are change machines. If you do not have a five-kopek coin, these will help. For example, if you have a 20-kopek coin, put it in the box marked 20, from which you will receive four 5-kopek coins. At the barrier you need only put your 5-kopek coin in the slot.

Make sure that you know your route before you go through. The escalators are rather fast. Once in the platform area consult the signs, which list all the stops in either direction on the lines available at that station. If you need to change lines, make sure you know the name of the station in advance, as there is rarely a map in the platform area (although there will be one in the carriage). At least know the colour of the line on to which you need to change — across the railway line from the platform is a strip listing the stations on the route and the other lines which it meets. Once on the train, know how many stops before you alight, because there is almost no visible indication. Instead, an announcement is made in the carriage as the train pulls in to each station, and another as the train pulls out, telling you what the next station is. Using the metro is not as complicated as it seems, providing you know where you are going in advance. As for maps, they are sometimes in short supply, but can be found at newspaper kiosks.

The service is fabulous. It is clean, fast, cheap, safe and, particularly in Moscow, a work of art. You will never have to wait more than about three minutes for a train. Smoking is not allowed anywhere on the system. Do not blind the drivers by taking photographs with flash as the train enters the station. It varies from city to city, but you may need to combine your journey with a bus or tram because of the distances between stops. If you lose your way, you will find that people are very helpful within the limitations imposed by language.

Buses, trolleybuses and trams
The fare is 5 kopeks. There are no conductors. Buy tickets from the driver or in advance from kiosks and punch them on the machine on the wall inside the vehicule. When crowded ask somebody to do it for you, as indeed you may be asked to do the same for another.

Suburban trains
Obtain tickets from a machine at the station. Check the fare zone of your destination and put in the right amount. Check the platform of your train and that it in fact stops where you want to get off (not all trains stop at all stations). The ticket may be requested occasionally by an inspector. Suburban stations can be rather rural, so have the address of your destination written down.

Taxis
An available taxi has a green light in the windscreen. They are temperamental — once you have got one to stop, he will decide whether to take you to your destination. As a foreigner, extra payment may be expected or you can offer more. Meters are often ignored. Find out the going rate beforehand and work accordingly. If desperate, flag down any vehicle — there are plenty of car owners (or sometimes drivers of empty buses) who make extra money by acting as taxis.

Berioska shops
These are the state-run shops aimed at the foreign visitor. Generally, although not exclusively, the best quality souvenirs are to be found in them. They are usually found, in varying sizes, in tourist hotels or in their own building in city centres. There are specialist versions too — for example, in Moscow there is one that specialises in books and records. The prices are always marked in roubles, but the merchandise is paid for in foreign, convertible currency i.e. pounds, dollars etc. Your change however, may come back in a mixture of currencies.

Berioska and other shop addresses are given at the end of each city section.

Commission shops
These *kmissionny* sell anything second hand (and sometimes new), from clothes to hi-fi equipment. They are to be found in most cities.

Art and antiques
Glasnost has at least meant that there are more artists selling their efforts openly and that antiques are more widespread. Export licences are often required — it is as well to check.

Good buys
Books, records, jewellery and lacquerware.

Newspapers
It is now easy to buy foreign mainstream newspapers but they tend to be two weeks out of date. *Moscow News* (in English and other foreign languages) has become an interesting campaigning paper but is short on hard news.

Hotels, restaurants, food and the Russian tradition

Hotels

Hotels cannot in general be pre-booked although you will be able to, at high cost, in the newly restored ones.

In general the standard is not high, although tolerable. Service is erratic and it is easier to enter into the spirit of things and accept their peculiarities, particularly as managers often appear not to exist.

When you check in you must hand over passport and visa. After registration you may have them back but you may just as well leave them safely with the hotel authorities (but remember to get it back before leaving the hotel).

The key will be kept at reception, at a neighbouring desk, or with the attendant on your floor. At any event the key is usually only obtainable on production of a hotel card, which will be given to you as you check in. The card is useful as identification for taxi drivers and will often be asked for as you enter the hotel.

The floor attendant will help you in other ways — if there is a problem with the room or if you want laundry done, she will organise it. Language may be a problem, but she may well speak one of the main west European languages; and if she does not, do not be put off by her gruff manner — it is merely shyness at her inability to communicate.

Restaurants

Much has been made of the new co-operative restaurants. From the point of view of service, quality and variety, they are most welcome. Some of them are rather expensive and some demand payment in foreign currency or with credit cards. Many are not licensed but permit customers to bring their own alcohol. Check in advance. Bookings can be made direct or through Intourist service bureaux (although you may then have to pay in advance). Otherwise you may have to queue. For listings see city sections.

The old state-run restaurants are, in some cases, much more genuinely Russian (though service is poor, and the variety of dishes small). The problem is to get into the better ones. Again booking through Intourist is possible, but this is expensive. Simply turning up is often problematic — even if there are plenty of free tables, you are likely to be told the restaurant is full. Bribery and corruption are the only answers, but the better ones are worth it. See city sections.

Food and the Russian tradition

The quality of the food in restaurants is improving. There is nevertheless a lack of vitality and variety in the dishes which belies the great pre-Revolutionary tradition of Russian cooking. The only dishes currently associated with Russia are Bortsh, Russian salad, Chicken Kiev and Beef Stroganov. Yet, at the turn of the century the wide range of natural ingredients and the infinite number of ethnic influences from east and west, combined with French savoir-faire and the peasant tradition, had produced a cuisine that was exotic, Russian and interesting.

The medieval diet was pretty similar for all classes of society — a great deal of pickled cabbage, turnip, swede and beetroot, and sour yeast breads made from rye. Any hope of creating something interesting out of this was dashed by the Church, who decreed that

The new face of Moscow: a co-operative restaurant.

certain foods could not be eaten on certain days thus keeping certain ingredients apart from each other. Efforts were made to improve flavour with the addition of seasonings and oils but Russian cooking remained rather plain until the coming of the Tartar-Mongols, who introduced, by way of China, new spices and pasta. Tea became the national drink.

These new luxuries were only for the wealthy and for the aristocracy — the peasant diet remained as before. Royal banquets were luxurious beyond belief. Foreign wines were much in evidence: French Burgundy, Muscat, Hungarian wines, Canary, Alicant and Malmsey. Trays were laden with storks with sweetmeats, black cock in saffron, spiced crane, goose with millet, cocks dressed with ginger and hazel grouse with plums. This might have been followed by hare with noodles or larks in onion and saffron. There were countless puddings, and then fruits and nuts.

By the eighteenth century there were additions to the Russian table as a result of Peter the Great's connections with northern Europe. Meat cutlets, sausages, omelettes, mousse and compote all became part of the language of Russian cooking. The Russian tradition of *zakuski* (a sort of cold buffet) was to spring directly from the fact that Peter employed Dutch, German and above all Swedish chefs. Traditional dairy products like smetana acquired a new lease of life among the aristocracy. By the nineteenth century French chefs were on hand to teach the subtle art of blending and combining. This led to the publication of the classic book of Russian cooking produced by Elena Molokhovets, whose recipes were essentialy Russian, even meeting the demands of Church ritual, but which had been refined by contact with French art.

Since 1917 Russian cooking has taken a beating. The reasons are not hard to ascertain. Inefficient farming has led to shortages of staple foods, never mind anything remotely exotic. Until recently all shops and nearly all restaurants were owned by the government, with the consequent loss of interest and quality. It was true, too, that good eating had been confined to the aristocracy and the middle class, whose influence, after the Revolution, was negligible to say the least. The peasant diet of pickles and bread was ideologically acceptable and within its limitations, good and wholesome, if unimaginative. Thus daily eating became basic and restaurant eating festive but limited.

Nevertheless, the Soviet Union is a big country and subject to a wide variety of influences. Oriental, Baltic and French influences have already been noted, but there are others too. The Jewish influence is strong (*blini* for example), and Azerbaijani (*plov,* or *pilaff*); above all Georgian cooking has made the strongest impression in recent years with its use of herbs and nut oil, but Armenian and Moldavian ideas have crept into the repertoire as well. The scope is almost limitless in a country whose area extends to all climates except the tropical. If the new economic and political policies are sustained, there should be a corresponding improvement in the standards of Russian cooking.

Meal times

Traditionally the Russian gastronomic day is dominated by the midday meal, *obeyed.* It remains the main meal of the day but is unlikely to be as huge, luxurious or as long as in days of old, when baked carp, roast turkey with marinated cherries, buckwheat kasha with sour cream and finest fruit with thick cream were the order of the day. Although the main meal, it could in fact have been eaten at any point of the afternoon especially if *zaftrak* (breakfast) was taken late. This meal mobility is still in evidence today — those who can afford to eat in restaurants at lunchtime tend to linger for long hours over their meal where they may eat *zakuski,* soup, a course of meat, poultry or fish, ice cream or a cake, and coffee; and breakfast can sometimes take on the appearance of a full meal, involving eggs, cheesecake, buttermilk and bread, and sometimes cold meat, porridge or chicken. Dinner *(oozhin)* may be similar to *obyed* but smaller and without coffee.

Typical dishes
Zakuski

This is the cold starter, or open buffet that precedes the main meals. It may come these days in the form of potato salad with chopped pickled gherkins, smoked, tinned or salted fish, fresh cucumber or tomato, or cold eggs with caviare on top. The most typical fish is cured sturgeon of which there are several types — *beluga,* the largest, *sevroga,* middle sized, and *osyotr,* the smallest and most delicate. Other *zakuski* might be small open sandwiches *(buterbrody),* and hot sweetmeats on toast *(tartinki)* cold chicken, turkey or game, sour cream, pate, plums and cherries.

Caviare *(ikra)*

This, the black egg of the sturgeon or the red egg of the Siberian salmon, is considered the king of *zakuski,* although it was not until the nineteenth century that it became very popular. It was considered highly nutritious, but not a delicacy, but is now something of an industry, although becoming increasingly scarce as pollution eats into the sturgeon population. At the best of times it is possible to buy it in restaurants or in Berioska shops; or on the black market from hotel waiters, who generally have only caviare of lesser quality. Even bought legally, it is still somewhat cheaper than at home.

You are likely to come across three types in restaurants. The best is the black granular variety — *ikra chornaya zernistaya;* the second is black pressed caviare — *ikra payusnaya;* and the third is red Salmon caviare — *ikra ketovaya.* It is served with *blini* (pancakes): spread butter on them and then the caviare. Drink chilled vodka with it.

The word *ikra* is also used to describe vegetable pastes.

Soups

Russian soups are often excellent and probably remain the one area of cooking that is wholeheartedly native. The classic ones are mentioned here but you may also come across *Chikirtma* from Georgia and Armenia; *Spas* or *Tanabour* from many of the southern republics; and Bozbash from Armenia, which is closer to a light stew.

Shchi: Often considered the national dish, the principal ingredient is sauerkraut, along with beef, carrot, turnip and potato, mushrooms, dill and sour cream — but there are many variations. A summer version uses fresh cabbage and young nettles, sorrel and spinach.

Borshch: In fact more Ukranian than Russian it has somehow become identified as the quintessential Soviet food. It is another soup which is infinitely variable apart from two invariables — beetroot and sour cream. The stock may be made of beef, ham, chicken or duck. Vegetables include cabbage, tomato, peppers, sweet corn and onion. Herbs may include garlic, pepper, parsley, dill and caraway.

Rassolnik: This is a soup flavoured with Rassol, which is the brine in which dill cucumbers are preserved. It is lighter than most Russian soups and may include celery and leeks as well as poultry giblets, or more luxuriantly, kidneys.

Solyanka: Something like Rassolnik but with the addition of olives, capers, lemon, tomato puree and boiled beef or fish.

Okroshka: This is a cold summer soup made with *kvas* (see Drinks), chopped meat and vegetables, herbs and sour cream.

Botvinya: Another cold soup, this time of beetroot leaves and nettle leaves, cucumbers, onions, dill, mustard, *kvas,* lemon juice, and poached fish and shellfish. A luxurious dish that you will be lucky to find, but you never know your luck.

Soups are sometimes accompanied by special titbits. *Pelmeni* are a sort of ravioli from Mongolia (where they are still eaten) introduced to Siberia in the Middle Ages. They are traditionally made with a mix of beef, pork and elk and are eaten in a clear broth.

Pirozhki are served with the soup as opposed to in it. They are like little pasties filled with minced beef, veal or chicken and again are eaten with a clear meat, chicken or mushroom broth. Other fillings might be brains, mushroom, fish, or curd cheese.

Meat dishes

Meat is still a scarcity for shoppers in the Soviet Union and in fact traditional peasant cooking has often been a search to find a substitute. Most meat that is obtainable is of moderate quality and has usually been frozen. Traditional Russian cooking makes considerable use of meat nonetheless, but generally speaking what is available in the Soviet Union is rather uninteresting. You will regularly come across the universal *bifshtek,* roast chicken, *bef-stroganoff* (made in honour of the head of one of the great Russian families at the end of the nineteenth century), and *bitki* and *kotlety,* which are sort a of meatball and hamburger respectively. Other possibilities which are more interesting are *vereshchaka* (pork and beetroot casserole), *bigos* (another sort of pork casserole from western Russia), *kostitsa* (Moldavian pork with garlic sauce), *zrazy* (Baltic states beef dish), and Armenian *kokony* or *kololak* (meatballs with herbs).

The main sausage of the salami type is *kolbasa.*

Shashlyk is lamb or beef on a skewer served with *plov* (pilaff rice) and came originally from Georgia. There are, however, varieties from Armenia and Uzbekistan too.

Chicken Kiev (chicken wrapped around hot butter) is apparently a modern Soviet dish and is sometimes done with beef. *Amich* is from Armenia and is chicken or turkey with almonds and apricots. Turkey with apricots is a Moldavian dish. Chicken *tabaka* is from Georgia and is boned chicken cooked flat under a heavy iron lid. Another Georgian dish is *chakhokhbili,* braised chicken with tomatoes, potatoes and herbs; yet another is *satsivi,* which is cold chicken with walnut sauce.

Game used to be widely eaten. No doubt it still is in the heart of the forest, but you will be lucky to find anything much in city restaurants. The traditional Russian game bird is the *ryabchik* (hazel-hen) which may appear from time to time in *Lesnaya bil* shops, which specialise in game. Some of the new restaurants should come up with something eventually because the possibilities are endless in a country so huge and most of which is comparatively unpopulated. It is a question of organisation.

Apart from sturgeon, there are many other salted and cured fish. *Selyedka* (herring) is popular, as is *vobla* (Caspian roach) — to be accompanied by chilled vodka. The commonest fish for frying or grilling are *treska* (cod) *hek* (hake), *makerel* (mackerel), *ledyannaya* and *mintai*. In the Lake Baikal region try *omul*.

Fruits and vegetables

One of the main complaints made by foreigners about the food of the Soviet Union is the lack of fresh vegetables. When they do appear they are generally overcooked; and a tossed salad seems not to be part of the cooking repertoire at all. Again, the situation is improving with the growth of the cooperative restaurant, but because of the short summers, the long winters and the problems of storage, Russians eat a great many pickles.

The potato *(kartofel)*, which arrived in Russia only in the late-eighteenth century, is popular in chip form, and sometimes as a cold salad. *Gulbishnik* is a Belorussian potato puree baked with curd cheese and herbs.

Beetroot is the vegetable most associated with Russian cooking, although it is really the national vegetable of the Ukraine. Of course it is part of the famous *borsch* soup, but it is also served hot or cold and dressed with cream or oil. Sometimes it is sliced up with potatoes, gherkins, onions and carrots and is known as *vinegret*.

The most Russian vegetable of all is the *kapoosta* (cabbage). The large white variety is the most common — it matures in the autumn and may be stored easily for the winter. Russians prefer to salt their cabbage, since the vitamins are better retained, but it is also frequently pickled in vinegar. It appears in soups, salads and pies and, dressed in oil, is often taken as a starter.

Tikva (pumpkin) is widely eaten in Armenia. Sweet red peppers are eaten as a sort of goulash in the summer. Aubergines, have been made popular through the influence of Caucasian cooking and thus figure particularly in Armenian, Moldavian and Georgian recipes.

Fresh cucumber *(ogooryets)* and tomato *(pomidor)* crop up

frequently in the summer months and are eaten cold as starters.

Mushrooms *(grib)* are a passion amongst Russians, for good reason, since between April and October the forests abound in them. It is not only love of the mushroom itself which motivates hordes of city dwellers to crowd into the country, but a need to be close to nature, for the joy of being in the forest and the pleasure of good fellowship. Dawn is supposed to be the best time for picking, when there are fewer people and when the mushrooms are at their most plentiful and at their freshest. There are at least 40 varieties of edible mushroom to be found in central Russia and Siberia. The best are considered to be ceps *(byeliye),* chanterelles *(leseechky),* brown caps *(pudbeeryozoviky),* orange caps *(pudosinoviky)* and morel *(smorchok).* Cultivated mushrooms are known as *champignons.* Wild ones are sold in the markets for those who are unable to gather them themselves. Some dry them on string for winter use but they are delicious when eaten raw or cooked alone, or baked with cream *(zhulien).* Salted mushrooms are those that have been salted to preserve them in their own juice — to be accompanied by vodka.

Good fresh fruit is a rarity. Apples *(ablaka)* appear in autumn but are usually of poor quality, and occasionally some oranges *(apyelsin)* or grapefruit. Water melon appears in abundance in the summer months, especially in the markets. Wild forest fruit on the other hand is much loved and, although it is less likely to be in the shops, there is always the chance of finding a seller of cranberries *(klookva),* wild strawberries *(zemlyinka),* bilberries and the like by the roadside, at a railway station or at one of the free markets. The sellers will often be disposing of homemade jam — it is of the highest quality.

Cereals, grains and bread
The national diet depends upon its rye *(rozher)* and buckwheat, the first for bread and *kvas* (see Drinks) and the second for *kasha.* You are most unlikely to find the 'corn flake' type of processed cereal, but unrefined grain — in the form of wheat *(pshenitsa),* barley *(yachmyen),* millet *(prosso),* and the aforementioned rye and buckwheat — is often to be found in the markets, if not in the shops. Oats *(avoice)* are found too, and rice *(riss)* is cultivated around the Black Sea.

Kasha, which is a sort of porridge, is actually a term used for the cooking of any grain in water or milk or cream or stock.

Buckwheat, however, which being related to sorrel and rhubarb is not really a grain at all, is often the basic ingredient for the simplest of *kashas*. It is added to boiling water which is allowed to boil away leaving a soft porridge to which butter may be added to taste.

Kasha is sometimes made, apart with any of the other grains, with cornmeal — another introduction from the south, it is known as *mamalyga*. *Mchadi* are small baked cornmeal cakes, also from Georgia.

Russian bread *(hklyep),* or indeed Soviet bread in general, is excellent. There is always plenty of it and it is almost always fresh (most bakeries have special spoons to allow the public to test without touching). The basic black *(chorny)* bread, made of rye, is not so much black as dark brown. It is delicious with vodka. Another black bread is *borodinsky,* which is dark and sweet and covered in coriander seeds. Some of the dark breads are flavoured with caraway *(tmin)* and some, such as *ukrainsky,* meaning Ukrainian, and *stolovy,* meaning 'of the table', are a mix of rye and wheat flour. The wheat brings lightness to the texture and to the colour. Another type, *Riga,* is similar but rather maltier. White bread can be sweet or sour, in various shapes, and with or without poppy seeds. Towards the south and east flat bread, in the Middle Eastern style, becomes common. The word for bakery is *boolochnaya.*

Cakes and chocolate

There is not a great variety of cake in Russia itself, although the Baltic republics share the central European love of afternoon coffee and cake or gâteau and the Moslem areas maintain their tradition of pastry, honey and nuts. Traditional Russian cakes *(tort),* on the other hand, often dense with honey and spices, have been replaced by fluffy and sugary white confections, which are unfailingly purchased on public holidays. *Bulochki,* a sort of scone, are also made — they are usually rather solid and dry but with good flavour. There is also an Easter cake, *kooleech,* which is almost a sort of bread. *Bubliki* are rings of hard choux pastry, which make good snacks. *Rum Baba* is claimed to be a Russian dish, although the chances are that it originated from Poland. You may also find *khvorost,* a Ukrainian speciality, which is a sort of doughnut; and Russian cheesecake, which is sometimes eaten hot at breakfast.

Russian chocolate *(shokolade)* is reasonably good, although there is not much variety and it is rather sweet.

A shop that sells only cakes and sweets is usually known as a *kondeeterskaya.*

Dairy products

Milk and yoghurts are extremely popular and remarkably good. True yoghurt is known as *prostokvasha* (in Georgia it is *matsoni,* in Armenia *matsun,* in Azerbaijan *katyk,* in Turkmenistan *egurt).* A common and delicious fermented milk is *kefir. Kumys* is fermented mare's milk and is drunk in Kazakstan. *Tvorog* is a sort of cottage cheese, very good by itself or in dumplings or fritters. It is the main ingredient of *Paskha* (Russian for Easter), along with candies, raisins and eggs, which is eaten with *kooleech* cake over Easter. *Smetana,* a cream soured by the addition of a culture, is very good both in soups and in sweet things.

As for cheese, apart from the already mentioned *tvorog* there is *brynza,* which is a sort of cottage cheese that has been pressed in brine, and is eaten in the Caucasus with fresh basil and tomatoes, or in the Georgian dish *khachapuri,* a cross between a cheese pie and a cheese fritter. Otherwise the standard hard cheeses *(seerh)* are something like Dutch cheese.

Eggs *(yaeetsa)*

Fried eggs *(yaeechnitsa)* are often served in their own little frying pans and are very hot. If you want your eggs to be soft-boiled ask for *vsmyatku.*

Ice cream

Soviet ice cream *(morozhenoye)* is excellent and is sold in kiosks all over the country. Russians like to add it to their coffee. Good though it is, it tends to crop up rather relentlessly in restaurants in the absence of any interesting puddings.

Drinks

Tea *(chai)* is as important to Russians as it is to the Chinese — it came to Russia with the Mongols in the thirteenth century. It is warming and considered to be health-giving, but is also, with the samovar, a symbol of welcome and hospitality. It is customarily taken in a glass with a metal holder and is drunk with sugar but without milk. Sometimes it is taken with lemon or with jam *(varenye).* The tea leaves are grown in Georgia, and in the area of the Black Sea. Green tea is drunk mostly in Central Asia. The samovar, basically a metal urn in which water is kept boiling in order to make tea, is Persian or Middle Eastern in origin, although it may actually be an offshoot of the Mongolian hotpot. Traditionally wood is burned in a vertical pipe in the centre of the samovar. The teapot is placed at the top and contains the tea leaves in a little water to which the boiling water is constantly added. Tula was the centre of samovar production in the nineteenth century and there was much competition amongst the factories and workshops to produce the most beautiful designs. A Russian saying goes 'you do not take a samovar to Tula'. The samovar still functions but is most likely to be electric these days, like a huge kettle.

Good coffee *(koffiye)* is in short supply, but is available, expensively, in hotel bars and in some of the new bars that are springing up in the major cities. Otherwise instant coffee can be found but is grimmer than most. The Baltic republics have a longer coffee-drinking tradition and in the Caucasian republics you are likely to find coffee in the Turkish style.

Mineral water *(mineralny voda)* is widely available but can be very obviously mineral for some tastes. However it is certainly better than much of the tap water which in some areas, like St Petersburg and the Central Asian republics, is definitely suspect.

Kvas is the standard Russian soft restorative. Although likened to a beer it is at most only mildly alcoholic and is very yeasty. In the summer months it is sold from large barrels with the letters KBAC stamped on the side, stationed in city streets. It is made from a fermentation of wheat, rye, buckwheat and water and sugar.

Good beer *(pivo)* is usually only available in Berioska shops.

Wine *(vino)* is available but the problem is to obtain what you want when you want it. It is said that Russians have a sweet tooth which would seem to be borne out by the wine supply. You can always find a sweet white (white is *byeli*) wine but a dry white, or particularly a dry red (red is *krasni*), can be rather hard to locate. Most of the wines come from Georgia and Moldavia and some are very good. From Georgia one of the most popular reds is *kinzmarauli.* One of the best dry whites is *tsinandali.* Another more robust red is *mukuzani.* Moldavia produces mainly light white wines. A lot of good champagne *(shampanska)* is produced in the Crimea but again there is a problem in obtaining the dry version. Sweet champagne is easily found, however.

The national alcoholic drink is vodka (meaning 'little water'). It is distilled from grain, usually wheat, and purified several times over. It is a great deal better than anything made in Britain or the United States. In bars and in restaurants it is served by weight and should be drunk cold from a small glass at one gulp, having eaten a *zakuski* beforehand. Of the unflavoured vodkas, the best known are *pshenichnaya* and *stolichnaya*. There are many flavoured vodkas, for example *limonaya* (lemon), and *pertsovka* (pepper).

Of course Russians say that vodka, being so pure, produces no hangover. Quantity is the important element — drinking a lot of vodka has the usual effect. Obviously it is better not to drink on an empty stomach, and Russians advise you to eat a bite of black bread or a pickle between gulps. As for a hangover cure, there is none better than to have a little more vodka, although the local cure is to drink the brine from salted cucumbers. Fermented milk *(kefir)* or yoghurt is as effective as anything else.

Good brandy *(konyak)* is made in Armenia and in Azerbaijan.

The alcoholic content of drinks in the Soviet Union is marked according to the actual percentage of alcohol present, rather than the proof measure.

The Russian way of drinking to the health of another is 'na zdorovye'. Toasts are an important part of table etiquette.

The Russian Ballet

There is nothing more Russian than the ballet. Although in recent years critics have agreed that ballet in the Soviet Union has lost some of the inventiveness that established its unparalleled reputation, there is no doubt that the impetus which developed ballet as an artistic form was Russian. Had it not been for its development in St Petersburg, ballet may have remained nothing more than an adjunct to opera and drama.

Ballet in Russia has its origins in the reign of the Empress Anna in the early eighteenth century. The greater ties with Western Europe established under Peter the Great led her to invite a Frenchman, Jean-Baptiste Lande, to live in St Petersburg in order to teach dancing to the court. Noting that the Russians possessed a natural feel for dance, he set up, with the approval and help of the Empress Elisabeth, a permanent company, which was the foundation of the Imperial Ballet. Ballet was then not at all as it is today — it was far more mannered and conventional, not much more than glorified court dancing, a choreographed ballroom. Creativity was less important than the correct execution of established steps.

In 1801 Count Sheremetev, who was something of a patron of the arts, invited another Frenchman, Charles Didelot, to St Petersburgh so that he might not only dance, but also become ballet master.

Soon the ballet school became a fully-fledged Imperial institution, where academic subjects were taught alongside ballet and where the aim was to cultivate native talent. By the time of Didelot's death in 1837, the Russian ballet had become the best in Europe. Ballets were set to the poetry of Alexander Pushkin, giving dance a sense of drama and purpose that took it to new heights of artistic expression. The ballet became a fashionable spectacle whose glamour spread to theatres and audiences alike. Ballet performances became glittering occasions. Composers of music like Glinka began to write specifically for the ballet.

By the end of the nineteenth century, ballet in Russia was the art par excellence, just as elsewhere in Europe it was in decline. This was firstly because the Russians loved it and secondly because the Tsar provided huge subsidies. Ballet was so strongly identified with Russia that it became a tradition. And it acquired dynastic elements in its teaching, where teachers passed their knowledge on to their successors.

For the students who were the successful ten percent of applicants, dedication was all, and their lives became ones of almost religious devotion to their art. Within a year of enrolment they began performing. They were graded according to their skill and experience, from corps de ballet to prima ballerina assoluta in the case of a woman and soloist to the Tsar in the case of a man. All expenses were defrayed by the state and the students wore special clothes that displayed to the world their high standing. The school itself (still in the same street in St Petersburg) was designed by Carlo Rossi, himself the son of a ballerina.

Didelot's successor was Marius Petipa, another Frenchman. He had been contracted to dance but soon turned his hand to

Kolomenskoye — a former Tsar's Palace.

choreography. In all he created 46 ballets. He choreographed new scenes for Giselle and created the original choreography for among others, Sleeping Beauty, La Bayadere, The Nutcracker and Swan Lake. In the case of Tchaikovsky, Petipa provided him with a detailed plan of the movements and the composer did the rest. He therefore presided over the greatest period of Russian classical dance, perhaps of world classical dance. This was the era of great choreographers, great dancers (Pavlova and Nijinksky) and great composers. Petipa retired in 1903 bequeathing a supreme artistic achievement. Nonetheless, the Russian ballet was in danger of becoming complacent, something that Petipa's successor, Mikhail Fokine, was determined not to allow. He thought there was still too much formality in ballet and he encouraged dancers to become part of the music rather than slaves to it. For Pavlova he created *Les Sylphides* and *The Dying Swan* and he encouraged a whole range of endeavour from the Russian artistic community, led by the impresario Diaghilev.

Sergei Diaghilev had already established himself as a great discerner of talent as well as a gifted showman. Thanks to his skills artists such as the bass vocalist Feodor Chaliapin were recognised outside Russia. At first he was reluctant to promote Russian ballet, but was persuaded by fellow members of the 'World of Art' group (a sort of a club for people interested in new creative art, who aimed to combine dancing, painting and music in a lively spectacle), to arrange a season of performances in Paris during 1909. The French were aghast at the thought but Diaghilev managed to stage *Le Pavillon d'Armide, Les Sylphides* and *Cleopatra.* The audience were ecstatic and the 'Ballets Russes' became the toast of Europe. Nijinksky, at a time when male dancers were out of favour, hypnotised the audience. Pavlova was compared to the poetry of Racine.

The following year they repeated the event, to an enraptured Europe. *Giselle* and *Scheherazade* were presented, and *The Firebird,* a ballet to the music of an unknown composer and Diaghilev protégé, Stravinsky, seen for the first time. Following this further success, Diaghilev ceased merely to borrow artists from the Imperial Ballet and formed his own company, taking Nijinsky with him. Every year he returned to Europe. His troupe performed in England for the coronation of King George in 1911 and later in Austria, Germany, Hungary, South America and the USA. Although he was never able to produce his ballets in Russia itself, Russian artistry was recognised as something unique.

Arrival and departure

Airports

There are several airports in Moscow. The main international airport is Sheremetyvo II (Tel: 578 7518 for info: and 578 5614 for Intourist). It is modern, 24 km (15 miles) from the city centre, designed by West Germans. After customs you will find yourself in the waiting area, where your Russian host will be waiting. In the unlikely event that your contact is not there go to the Intourist office (same floor), or to the Information desk (also same floor).

When you depart you must fill in another Declaration Form (you may change your roubles back with the old form plus bank receipts at the airport bank) — both new and old forms must be shown to customs, which you pass before checking in.

To and from the airport
Those travelling in groups will be met by Intourist guides and buses. An individual traveller not being met has a few choices. If you are desperate, one of the guides might be willing to give you a lift into town. The more formal methods are:

Taxi: The rank is immediately opposite the exit just beyond the waiting area. It is the quickest way, but some drivers ask absurd prices, based on the black market. Bargain hard.

Metro and bus: There is no metro station at the airport but there is a bus to Gorky Street and another to the city airport terminal (nearest metro 'Aeroport').

Facilities
Money exchange, cafe and restaurant but no alcohol for sale. Intourist office. Information desk with English-speaking staff. Small offices of most of the airlines. Good duty free shop (in cooperation with the Irish).

Domestic airports
The other Moscow airports deal mainly with domestic traffic — all of them have a bus service to and from the city airport terminal.

Sheremetevo I (the old international airport) handles flights to St Petersburg, the Baltic Republics, Murmansk and Archangelsk. Tel: 578 5973 (Information) or 578 5974 (Intourist).
Vnukovo serves the Caucasus, the Ukraine and the Crimea. Tel: 436 6230 (Intourist).
Domodedovo serves Central Asia, Siberia and the Far East. Tel: 234 8655 (Intourist).
Arriving at one of Moscow's domestic airports, as far as procedure is concerned, is like arriving at any other airport. However, if you have any problem, go to the Intourist desk.

Railway stations

There are nine major terminals, each serving different areas of the country. All are within the city limits and usually are conveniently located for metro stations. Some of them deal with international services. Some have an Intourist office and all have taxi ranks. The general number for timetable enquiries in Moscow is 266 9000. The main stations with their nearest metro stations are:

Belorussia *(Belorussky vokzal)*. Tel: 253 4464. A beautiful station serving the west of the Soviet Union and where you arrive coming from Berlin, Warsaw, London, Stockholm, Paris, Oslo, Brussels and Amsterdam. Nearest metro: Belorusskaya

Kiev *(Kievsky vokzal)*. Tel: 240 7345. Serves the Ukraine plus major cities of eastern Europe except Warsaw and Berlin. Metro: Kievskaya.

Kursk *(Kurskii vokzal)*. Tel: 266 4820. Serves Armenia, Azerbaijan, the Crimea, the Caucasus, and Georgia. Situated in the northeast of the city. Metro: Kurskaya.

St Petersburg *(Leningradskii vokzal)*. Tel: 262 4281 Situated in northeast on same square as Kazan and Yaroslavl stations. Serves St Petersburg, Murmansk, Baltic-republics and Helsinki. Metro: Komsomolskaya.

Kazan *(Kazanskii vokzal)*. Tel: 266 2843. Situated in northeast on same square as St Petersburg and Yaroslavl stations. Serves Volga and Central Asia. Metro: Komsomolskaya.

Yaroslavski *(Yaroslavski vokzal)*. Tel: 266 0218. Serves Siberia and the Far East. Its distinctive entrance is shaped like a traditional Siberian hat. Here you board the Trans-Siberian Express. Situated in the northeast on the same square as Kazan and St Petersburg stations. Metro: Komsomolskaya.

Riga *(Rishskii vokzal)*. Tel: 266 1372. Serves Riga and other cities in Baltic area. Metro: Rishskaya.

Paveletsky *(Paveletskii vokzal)*. Tel: 233 0040. Volga area. Metro: Paveletskaya.

Savelovsky *(Savelovskii vokzal)*. Tel: 285 9000. Local trains. Metro: Novoslobodskaya, plus bus 87, 194, 206 or 672.

Bylorussia station — gateway to the west.

Facts and figures

Situation: Between 55° and 56° latitude and 37° and 38° longitude.
Dimensions: 42 km (26 miles) from north to south and 35 km (22 miles) from east to west. There are more than 3,500 streets with a combined length of 3,600 km (2,237 miles). There are 360 bridges and tunnels, and 150 underground crossings. One third of the city is parkland.
Topography: Said to be built on seven hills but really on a plain about 30 m (100 ft) above the Moskva river. The river is about 152 m (500 ft) above sea level. The city itself is laid out on a system of ring roads.
Population: Over 8 million.
The Moskva river flows into the Oka, a tributary of the Volga and

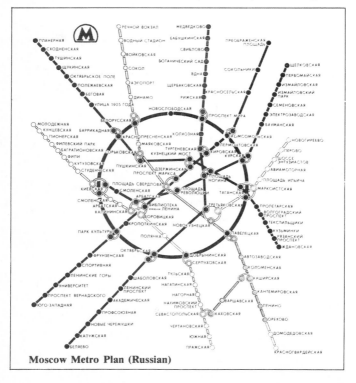

Moscow Metro Plan (Russian)

is navigable. Because of its meandering course it runs for 80 km (50 miles) within the city limits. There is direct water communication with five seas: the Caspian, Azov, Black, Baltic and White.

Getting around the city

Moscow is well served by public transport (metro, taxis, buses, trams, and trolleybuses) which is very easy to use once you get used to it. Try to buy a city plan which also shows the bus routes (they are theoretically available for a few kopecks from kiosks on the street or in hotels), for you will sometimes need to combine metro with bus or tram. How to use the various conveyances is explained on pp. 96-7. It is possible to hire cars — see Practical information.

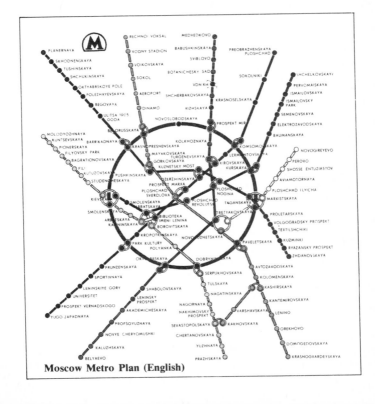

Moscow Metro Plan (English)

MOSCOW

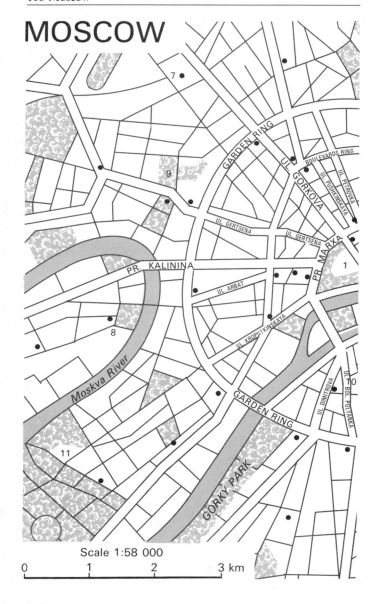

Scale 1:58 000

0   1   2   3 km

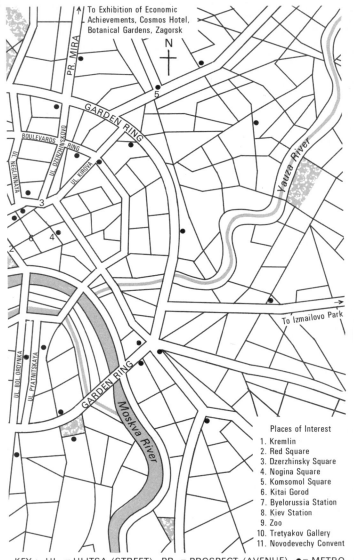

To Exhibition of Economic
Achievements, Cosmos Hotel,
Botanical Gardens, Zagorsk

N

PR. MIRA

GARDEN RING

BOULEVARDS RING

UL. DZERZHINSKOVO

UL. NEGLINNAYA

UL. KIROVA

Yauza River

To Izmailovo Park

UL. BOL. ORDYNKA

UL. PYATNITSKAYA

GARDEN RING

Moskva River

Places of Interest

1. Kremlin
2. Red Square
3. Dzerzhinsky Square
4. Nogina Square
5. Komsomol Square
6. Kitai Gorod
7. Byelorussia Station
8. Kiev Station
9. Zoo
10. Tretyakov Gallery
11. Novodevechy Convent

KEY : UL. = ULITSA (STREET)   PR. = PROSPECT (AVENUE)   ●= METRO

Accommodation

General information (checking-in etc.) — see p. 98.

Hotels in Moscow fall broadly into two categories. A few belong to the pre-Revolutionary era, are centrally located, have character and are comfortable in a shabby sort of way. The rest, dotted all over the city, are Soviet-built, usually too big, tolerably comfortable, but with erratic service. However, the old hotels are gradually being refurbished and there are plans afoot to build new hotels.

Most have a reasonable array of services. Most have a Berioska shop and a service bureau (for booking tickets to theatres, for flights and trains etc.), bars (hard currency and roubles), restaurants, newspaper kiosk, small pharmacy and so on.

The following list of Moscow hotels is arranged in sequence according to their closeness to the city centre.

Rossya: 1, Moskvoretskaya Nab. Tel: 298 1193.
A gigantic mid-1960s cube placed incongruously on the banks of the river, next to St Basils Cathedral and Red Square. With some 3,000 rooms it is the largest hotel in Europe, perhaps the world. The design is entirely unsuited to its size. Facilities: several restaurants and bars, discotheque, concert hall, cinema, large Berioska shop, ice cream parlour. Metro: Ploshad Nogina.

National: 1 Ul. Gorkovo. Tel: 203 6539.
One of the pre-Revolutionary shabby ones, it is smallish but with considerable charm; excellent location opposite Red Square. Fitzroy Maclean, in his book **Holy Russia,** says room 101 is the best, not least because of its looking glass, 'an Edwardian *chef d'oeuvre* that leaves one flabbergasted'. Not usually used for tourists; good restaurant for atmosphere; reasonable Berioska shop; art shop; beer cellar. Metro: Prospect Marx.

Intourist: 3 Ul. Gorkovo. Tel: 203 0131.
Up the road from the National. Good restaurants and bars; small Berioska but other shops not bad. Metro: as for National.

Metropol: 1—4 Prospect Marx.
The oldest, the most famous and perhaps the most attractive of Moscow hotels, built in 1903 in art nouveau style. It is situated close to the Bolshoi and has recently been refurbished. Good bars and restaurants, and a Russian Tea Room. Metro: Ploshad Sverdlova.

Berlin: see Savoy.

Savoy, previously the Berlin, now assuming its original name: 3 Ul. Zhdanova. Tel: 928 3780. Telex: 411620.
Another of the old hotels, small and used mostly by businessmen; it has period decor, which has been completely refurbished and is managed by Finnair. Reservations can be made direct or, better, through Finnair. One of the best restaurants in Moscow; business centre. Double room: US $200 approx. Metro: Kuznetski Most.

Belgrade: 5 Ul. Smolenskaya. Tel: 248 3520.
A modern tourist hotel composed of two buildings either side of a busy and almost uncrossable road; ordinary food; rooms adequately comfortable; good central location for the Arbat and Kalinin Prospect. Metro: Smolenskaya.

Ukraine: 10/9 Kutuzovsky Prospect. Tel: 243 3520.
Situated on the river in the western part of the city; not quite central but has good access to the centre. One of Stalin's Empire State Building lookalikes and therefore a sort of period charm. Rooms comfortable; classic Russian service (incomprehensible); reasonable Berioska; restaurants not bad; good views; convenient for river cruises and Kievskaya railway terminal. Nearest metro: Kievskaya.

Mezhdunarodnaya: 12 Krasnopresenskaya Nab. Tel: 253 2378.
Part of the World Trade Centre and one of the few hotels in Moscow of 'international' standard. A business hotel: swimming pool, business facilities, language centre, some good shops, a Japanese restaurant amongst others, a German bar, an English pub, car hire, and the Moscow offices of international companies (e.g. British Airways). Direct bookings accepted. Metro: Ulitsa 1905 Goda.

Sovietskaya: 32/2 Leningradskii Prospect. Tel: 250 2342.
A business hotel built on the site of the old Yar restaurant. Metro: Aeroport.

Cosmos: 150 Prospect Mira. Tel: 217 0785.
A Franco-Soviet production built for the 1980 Olympic Games. Too far out but only six metro stops to the centre. Huge (1,700 rooms) and unwieldy, it is the main and supposedly best of the 'deluxe' tourist hotels of Moscow: air-conditioned, spacious rooms; swimming pool; several restaurants (including one self-service;) discotheque; bowling alley; sizeable Berioska shop. Metro: VDNK.

Sebastopol, 1 Ul. Bolshaya Yushunskaya. Tel: 318 2263.

There are campsites — consult Intourist.

Restaurants, bars and cafés

General — see p. 100. The following lists aim to be as up to date as possible (there are new co-ops all the time), but you are advised to ring beforehand, if only to check whether alcohol is served or not.

State or Municipal run restaurants

Slavyansky Bazaar: 13 Ul. 25-Octyabre. Tel: 921 1872.
Situated between Red Square and Dzerdzinsky Square; an old restaurant which opened in 1870. It was here that Stanislavski and Nemirovich-Danchenko decided to found the Moscow Arts Theatre; and it was used by Chekhov as background in his *Lady with a little dog*. Then a large painting by Repin hung over the hors d'oeuvres table, and diners were able to select the sterlet of their choice from a large tank. 'The Old Russian Hall (of the restaurant), painted in glaring reds and greens on white with a vaulted ceiling in wood, was a special attraction and the scene of noisy concerts. To serve its highly praised *zakuski* the Slavyansky Bazar used wooden platters edged in silver, and offered what must have been a wonderful spread of salmon, beef, suckling-pig and crayfish, punctuated with bowls of sour cream. There was an excellent *solyanka* to follow, with *rastegai* (small salmon pies), and the house speciality, an orange salad.' (*The Food and Cooking of Russia* by Lesley Chamberlain). It is shabbier these days but there is good Russian food, and wines and vodka are usually available. Live music; very popular with locals; drunken, swirling atmosphere — very Russian.

Aragvi: 6 Ul. Gorkovo. Tel: 229 3762.
A popular Georgian restaurant with central location: good food and wine. The building that houses the restaurant was originally the Hotel Duseaux and then the Saxonia. According to Fitzroy Maclean, General Skobelyov, a nineteenth-century hero of the Balkan and Central Asian campaigns, collapsed and died here at the age of 38 whilst 'over-exerting himself with two young ladies of easy virtue'. Try telephoning for reservation or through Intourist.

Arbat: 26 Pr. Kalinin. Tel: 291 1445. Poor reputation.
Baku (Azerbaijani): 24 Ul. Gorkovo. Tel: 291 6692. Good.
Bombay (Indian): 91 Chausee Rublyovskoye. Tel: 141 5502.
Budapest (Hungarian/Russian): 2/18 Petrovskiye Linii. Tel: 921 4044.

Delhi (Indian): 23b Ul. Krasnaya Presnya. Tel: 252 1766; hard currency section: 255 0492.
Izba: out of town. Tel: 561 4244.
Minsk: 22 Ul. Gorkovo. Tel: 299 1248.
Moskva: 7 Pr. Marxa. Tel: 292 6267.
National: 1 Ul. Gorkovo. Tel: 203 5550.
Peking (Chinese): 1/7 Ul. B. Sadovaya. Tel: 209 1865. Much improved.
Praga (Czech/Russian): 2 Arbat. Tel: 290 6171. Reasonable.
Rus: out of town. Tel: 524 1307.
Russian Skazka: out of town. Tel: 184 3436.
Savoy: 3 Ul. Rozhdestvenka. Tel: 203 2065. Expensive but excellent. Hard currency only.
Sofia (Bulgarian/Russian): 32/1 Ul. Gorkovo. Tel: 251 4950.
Seventh Heaven: In the radio tower — good views.
Uzbekistan (Central Asian): 29 Ul. Neglinnaya. Tel: 924 6053.
Varshava (Polish/Russian): 2/1 Pl. Oktyabrskaya. Tel: 238 1055.

Co-operative restaurants
Russian and European
Aist (cafe): 1/8 Ul. Malaya Bronaya. Tel: 291 6692.
Atrium (cafe): 44 Leninsky Pr. Tel: 137 3008.
Belyi Lyebyed: 3/18 Sitsev Vrazhek. Tel: 203 1283.
Beryozka: 18 Karamyshevskaya Naberezhnaya. Tel: 191 1089.
Zaidi Poprobui: Kor.1, 124 Prospect Mira. Tel: 286 7503.
Kropotinkskaya-36: 36 Ul. Kropotkinskaya. Tel: 201 7500.
Lada disco video bar: 13 Altoofyevskoye Chaussee. Tel: 401 9501.
Likhobori: Korpus 3, 27 Dmitrovskoye Chaussee.
Razgooliay: 11 Ul. Spartakovskaya. Tel: 267 7613.
Rooslan: 32/36 Vorontsovkaya. Tel: 272 0632.
Smolenskyi Traktir; 1/9 Nickoloshchepovski Per. Tel: 249 3947.
Tigris: 81 Vaveelova. Tel: 132 0055.
Glazur: 12 Smolensky Blvd. Tel: 248 4438.
Traktir Zamoskvorechye: 52 Ul. Bolshaya Polyanka. Tel: 230 7333.

Abkhazian
Abkhazian Dvor: 35 Nakhimovski Pr. Tel: 124 1149.

Armenian
Arevik (cafe): Pavilion on Pl. Kievskovo Vokzala. Tel: 240 1528.
Armyanski Lavash: 9 Ul. Akademika Skryabina.
Moosh: 2/4 Oktyabrskaya. Tel: 284 3670.

Tsakhkadzor: 15 Lesnaya. Tel: 251 0257.

Azerbaijanian
Agdam: 22 Yurievski Per. Tel: 360 6840.
Araks: 5 Stroyenie, 52 Pr. Mira. Tel: 281 5223.
Garabakh: 52 Ul. Lipetskaya. Tel: 329 7100.
Nargiz: Korpus 4, 22 Lebedyanskaya. Tel: 329 7187.
Farkhad: 4 Bolshaya Marfinskaya. Tel: 218 4136.

Belorussian
Alesya: 37 Birulevskaya Ul. Tel: 326 4477.
Pokrovka: 4 Ul. Chernyshevskovo. Tel: 923 0282.

Caucasian
Bistro-Nedelya: 18 Ul. Oktyabrskaya. Tel: 288 9398. Open 24 hours
a day.
Ryleyeva 9: 9 Ryleyeva. Tel: 125 9149.

Chinese
Mei Hua: 2 Ul. Rusakovskaya. Tel: 264 9574.

The beauty of old Moscow and the functional present.

Italian
Arlecchino: 15 Ul. Druzhynnikovskaya. Tel: 205 7088.
Lasagne: 40 Ul. Pyatnitskaya. Tel: 231 1085.

Jewish
U Yuzefa':1 Ul. Dubininskaya. Tel: 238 4646.

Georgian
Gureeya: Korpus 1, 7/3 Komsomolski Pr. Tel: 246 0378.
Lahvash (bakery): Korpus 6, 3 Bolshaya Sadovaya. Tel: 251 7888.
Sayat-Nova: Korpus 1, 17 Ul. Yasnogorskaya. Tel: 426 8511.
Ooh Pirosmany: 4 Novodevichi Proyezd. Tel: 247 1926.

Korean
Zarya Vostoka: 4/2 Ul. 26-Bakinskikh Komissarov. Tel: 433 2201.

Scandinavian
Kooren: Posyolok Bootovo, 5 Bolshaya Bootovskaya. Tel: 548 7450.

Tatar
Saute-3: 12 Nagornaya. Tel: 127 2363.

Uzbek
Yakimanka: 2 Ul. Polyanka. Tel: 238 8888.

Cafés
Some of the above may also deserve to come under this heading (information welcome). Similarly some of the following may qualify as restaurants:

Beliye Nochi: 3 Pl. Komsomolskaya. Tel: 207 3036.
Vtorye Dykhaniye: 24a Profsoyuznaya. Tel: 338 1308.
Vytachi: 5 Novolesnaya. Tel: 258 0724.
Gourmand-2: 29 Ul. Chkalova. Tel: 266 5813.
Kondeeter: 1 Ul. Koneva. Tel: 194 8544.
Lakomka: 108 Yoonykh Lenitsoff.
Lastochka-1: 1 Ul. Ivana Franko. Tel: 417 4324.
Margarita: 28 Mahlaya Bronnaya. Tel: 299 6534.
Meridian: 16 Ul. Snezhnaya. Tel: 189 3768.
Mir: 22 Ul. Bobrooyskaya. Tel: 140 5474.
Raduga: 27 Bolshaya Polyanka. Tel: 238 8200.

Trinity Church in Nikitaiki, Moscow. Bang next to the Communist Party HQ, this is considered to be one of the most beautiful churches in the city (photo: Jim Helme).

Exploring the city

'From tiny little streams a mighty river flows,
From sources no less humble our Mother Moscow rose'.

The history of Russia and of the Soviet Union is also the history of Moscow. It was the capital of the principality of Muscovy and then of the Russian Empire. During the 200 years that St Petersberg was the capital, Moscow continued to play an important role in the affairs of Russia. Following the Revolution of 1917, Moscow again became capital of the Soviet Union.

Most importantly, it is the heart of the nation. St Petersburg is more splendid but it has always been peripheral to the Russian soul. For a Russian, Moscow never ceased to be the capital: St Petersburg is new but Moscow is the stuff of legends.

History

Moscow was founded, according to the chronicle, in 1147. There was in fact a settlement on the site long before that. A local Boyar by the name of Kucho dwelt in a stronghold at the confluence of the Moskva and Neglinnaya rivers, close to many of the important waterways of Kievan Rus. Yuri Dolguriki, ruling prince of the rapidly expanding Rostov and Suzdal, saw the strategic significance of Kushko's settlement, seized the stronghold, and is accredited with the founding of Moscow in 1147, the moment that he invited his peers to his latest conquest.

By the end of the twelfth century there was a wooden wall enclosing what would be a third of the area of today's Kremlin, later expanded and surrounded by stone walls.

The Moscow skyline was dominated by the brilliance of the golden cupolas of the cathedral walls within. Indeed, as Moscow grew in importance the Metropolitan of the Russian Church moved his seat there from Vladimir, making Moscow's influence countrywide. Moscow was becoming the Holy City, the Third

Rome. Over the next few hundred years much of the character of the city was to depend on the central role of religion in Russian life.

By the fifteenth century, Moscow was a city of about a hundred thousand souls. It grew outwards in circles, and was ringed by a great number of fortified monasteries, themselves almost little walled cities. By 1662 there were more than two thousand churches. The markets were filled with sellers of icons. Priests could be seen at every street corner offering their services to the owners of private chapels. The sound of the pealing of bells rang through the city air at all times.

But Moscow was far from being only a centre of religion. It was a colourful commercial centre too, with more than a hint of the orient about it. The city was divided into quarters: for nobility, merchants, armourers and craftsmen, and for foreigners and Tatars. Everybody lived in wooden houses. Red Square was a bustling market place (though dotted with small chapels and churches). In time of snow or mud gaily-coloured, ornately-carved sleds, sliced through the snowy streets. The kaftan was the standard form of male dress, in the case of nobles including a cap of silk and gold thread set with pearls. Below was a long garment of silk with the indispensible knife and fork thrust through a belt. Then would come a long kaftan; then another edged with fur; and finally, a cape.

It remained thus through the centuries. The city changed of course: fires destroyed all that was wood several times. Yet by the end of the nineteenth century it had the greatest area of any city in Europe except London, and by 1912 the population was more than one and a half million. Reflecting the Russian love of the countryside, one tenth of the city was given over to garden. There were still many churches (about five hundred) and a great many painted wooden houses, although there was now much more brick and stone. It had become a city of wide boulevards and had acquired, with its theatres and grand institutions, some of the trappings of Western Europe.

It had also become, by the end of the nineteenth century, the most important manufacturing centre in Russia, although exotic, for more than two hundred of the factories were devoted to the weaving of Moscow silk threaded with gold and silver.

The city had become more sophisticated but until the Revolution it still reeked of earthy Russia with its tea houses and gypsy restaurants. Bells still pealed throughout the city and religious processions remained a regular occurrence. Between the boulevards narrow winding cul de sacs led to charming little churches, the streets were filled with food and drink sellers and there was always a market or a festival in progress somewhere.

Much of old Moscow has survived. There have been twentieth-century additions to the skyline - some successful, others not — but the exotic street life has all but gone (although the new liberalism is allowing a sort of vitality to filter back).

The Kremlin

The visitor to Moscow is almost bound to be drawn first to its Kremlin. Metro: Biblioteka Lenina. Open 10.00—18.00; closed Thursdays.

Entrance to the territory of the Kremlin is free but if you want to visit the Armoury, or the Diamond Collection, or the interiors of any of the cathedrals you must purchase tickets in advance.

Tickets for the cathedrals and for the museum of seventeenth century Applied Art and Everyday Life in the Patriarch's Palace are available for roubles in a kiosk in the Alexandrov Gardens to the right of the entrance (Trinity Gate) as you look at it. They are not expensive.

To visit the Armoury or the Diamond Collection is rather harder. Foreigners are expected to pay for these in foreign currency through any Intourist Service Bureau. You must go on a guided visit at set times (the Armoury, for example, is open only at 10.00, 12 midday, 14.30 and 16.30). There is no prospect of getting into either by showing up at their entrances and looking hopeful or helpless. There is one other possibility — go to the 'KACCA' (Ticket Kiosk) at 1, Kalinin Prospect, between 10.00 and 11.00. (This is the part of Kalinin that is easily missed, for it has been cut off from the main part by Karl Marx Avenue, and lies behind the 'Manege', just in front of the Trinity Gate). Here you should be able to pay in roubles but as a foreigner you may be directed elsewhere. In any case it is worth your while making a reservation as soon as possible, since space is limited.

Soldiers stand at the gate of the Kremlin checking your bags. If you are carrying anything much larger than a handbag you may be asked to deposit it in the cloakroom below the bridge to the right. Lavatories are found on Cathedral Square. Try to keep to the paths — police tend to blow whistles and wave you back if you step on to the road in those parts of the Kremlin where cars pass.

The Kremlin cathedrals, the heart and soul of the Russian state (photo: Jim Helme).

The walls

The word Kremlin comes from the Mongol word *kreml* meaning fortified. There was a kremlin in every regional capital. In the case of Moscow it was the citadel both of the Church and of the Muscovite princes. The original walls, constructed by Yuri Dolgoruki in the mid-twelfth century, were of wooden beams three metres high. There was a set of double gates and some wooden towers. In 1365 they were replaced by whitestone walls. The present walls date from the end of the fifteenth century, when Moscow was establishing itself as the pre-eminent city of the region. The wife of Ivan III (the Great), Zoe (Sophia) Palaeologina, niece of the last emperor of Byzantium, urged her husband to build churches and a kremlin worthy of Moscow's position as defender of the faith. She had lived in Italy and brought the Bolognese architect Ridolfo Fioravanti to Russia. He is best remembered for his cathedral, but also acted as consultant for the walls. Building was supervised by architects and engineers from Milan.

The walls form a pentangle and look over Red Square on one side, the Alexander Gardens on another and the river on another. The most spectacular view of the Kremlin is from across the river, on the Maurice Thorez embankment, near the fine building housing the British Embassy. From there the cathedrals and the walls can be seen in all their glory.

The walls are 2,235 m long (7,333 ft), from 3.5 to 6.5 m (11.5 to 21 ft) thick and from 5 to 19 m (16 to 62 ft) high. They are riddled with passages and storage rooms. The walls are surmounted by merlons along their length, only interrupted by 19 towers, each of which was built to be self-contained. Four have gates. The oldest part of the wall, built in 1485 against possible Tatar attack, overlooks the river.

Looking at the wall from across the river, the tower on the far left at the corner is known as the **Vodovzvodnaya** *(Water Tower),* because it was from here, at the confluence of the Moskva and Neglinnaya rivers, that water was pumped through lead pipes to the palaces within. In 1812 this tower was destroyed by Napoleon's army, but rebuilt soon after.

Next is the **Blagiveshchenskaya** *(Annunciation Tower)* which has limestone slabs at its foot from the fourteenth-century whitestone wall. Next is the **Tainitskaya** *(Tower of Secrets),* which is the oldest of all the towers and so named because of the secret well inside. The others on this part of the wall are the first and second **Bezymyanniye** *(Nameless Towers),* **Petrovskaya** tower and **Beklemishev** tower.

Within the walls
Life in the Kremlin
'The walled city of the Kremlin with its complex of forts, armouries, palaces, cathedrals and cloisters was at the height of its grandeur during the sixteenth and seventeenth centuries, and the splendour of this miniature city within a city was extraordinary. Windows and pillars differed in design and colour. A multitude of cupolas in gold and bright colours crowded each other like bubbles. Gold, silver and later, in the seventeenth century, coloured tiles that gleamed like brilliant fish scales decorated the walls. When the sun shone upon its gilded roofs, its domes and tents of many colours, it was difficult to discern from afar whether these were indeed buildings or whether perhaps a flock of brilliant-plumed firebirds had landed and spread their fiery feathers under the sun' (Suzanne Massie, *Land of the Firebird*).

Despite this colour, the atmosphere was of regal silence: the social centre of the city had moved beyond the Kremlin walls to Red Square.

The Tsar was of course supreme. Subjects who failed to remove their hats when passing the Terem Palace were whipped. He sat in state surrounded by tall, axe-wielding guards. Every morning a box was lowered from the 'Petitioners Window' so that subjects with a grievance could petition him. When a Tsar was to be married, girls, often of humble origin, were brought from all over the country. Upon arrival they were housed in dormitories with a throne at one end from where the Tsar would survey his potential brides at his leisure. Once chosen she was handed over to the women of the palace, amongst whom she would live in utter luxury, surrounded by rugs, tapestries, enamels and shelves of religious books. Women spent much of their time painting their faces, attending religious services and doing embroidery. If they went out, they were screened from the public gaze and clouded in the aroma of cinnamon.

The entrance for the general public is the **Troitskaya** *(Trinity)* **Gate** on Manyeshnaya Street. At 76 metres (249 ft), it is the tallest of the gates and in front of it the first stone bridge of Moscow crosses what used to be the Neglinnaya River. The other towers on this part of the wall are, from the far left looking at the Kremlin, the **Uglovaya Arsenalnaya** *(Corner Arsenal)* and the **Snednaya Arsenalnaya** *(Intermediate Arsenal)*. Then to the right are the **Komendantskaya** *(Commandents)*, the **Oruzheinaya** *(Armoury)* and the **Borovitskaya**, which stands at the foot of the Borovitsky Hill, the core of the Kremlin.

Through the gate there are two buildings, left and right. The older, left, with a row of cannons (some made in Russia, others captured from the French) before it, is the old Arsenal. This was started by Peter the Great in 1702 for the manufacture and storage of weapons and as a museum for the display of weaponry captured in the battle. Construction was twice interrupted: by war with Sweden, and by fire damage. It was completed only in 1754, although it was damaged once again in 1812 by Napoleon. There are three plaques on the facade dedicated to those who fell in the Revolution, and to those who died in the defence of Moscow during WW II. It now houses offices and the detachment of the Kremlin Guard.

The Palace of Congresses

The modern building, right, just past older administrative buildings and the road (closed to the public) leading to the main palace, is the Palace of Congresses. It was built in 1961 on the site of buildings used by the grenadiers, court staff, the cooks and so on. With 6,000 seats it is regularly used for ceremonial occasions and international forums. The Bolshoi company frequently performs here — although it is comparatively difficult to obtain tickets for the Bolshoi theatre, there is usually no problem here. While it does not exactly harmonise with its surroundings (for Muscovites it is 'a spiv amongst the Boyars'), efforts were made to ensure that its height did not interfere with the beauty of the older buildings. Thus, a great part of it lies underground. It is linked by passages to the Great Palace and to the Patriarchs Palace.

The Government Building

Immediately after the Congress Palace there is a path leading right towards Cathedral Square. Ignore this and follow the main path ahead until it bears right and leads to a large square. On your left there are two buildings. The first, just at the point where the path bends, is the Government Building. This domed triangular building was built between 1776-88, by order of Catherine the Great, to house the *Duma* or Senate. Since the *Duma* never sat the building came to be used as the Law Courts. Catherine had ambitious plans for the Kremlin and thought to encase the whole in a palace surrounded with classical columns. Some of the wall on the river side was knocked down in preparation, but fortunately she lost interest. Catherine also had Annenhof torn down — this was a wooden palace built in the Kremlin grounds for Empress Anna and said to have been the most beautiful in the world.

However, the *Duma* is a legacy of enduring beauty. It is triangular in form, with three internal courtyards. The main room is a domed hall (previously known as the Catherine Hall, now the Sverdlov Hall in memory of the first chairman of the All-Russia Central Executive Committee) about 27 m (88.5 ft) high. When the Soviet government moved to Moscow the Council of People's Commissars and the All-Russia Central Executive Committee were housed here. Nowadays the building is used for Plenums of the Central Committee and the building contains the offices of the Council of Ministers of the USSR. On the third floor is Lenin's former flat and study.

'Leninism' may be on the way out in eastern Europe but Lenin will remain an important historical figure in Russian history. His study (a visit requires special permission) supposedly testifies to his simple, unassuming character. There is a desk with nothing more than telephones and pens; and the walls are lined with some two thousand books. During the Civil War this office was the headquarters of all military operations. An antique clock shows the time that Lenin left his study for the last time. Next to the study is a conference room. The flat where Lenin lived with his family from 1918 to 1923 occupies the second floor.

The Presidium

The building next to the Government Building houses the Presidium of the Supreme Soviet of the USSR. It stands beside the Spassky gate which is the gate for government officials and leads to Red Square. Built between 1932 and 1934 on the orders of Stalin, in neo-classical style, two ancient monasteries (the Chudov or Miracles and the Voznesenye or Ascension) were destroyed to make way for it. Originally it was built to house the All-Russia Central Executive Committee Military School. Later it became the Sverdlov Club and then the Kremlin Theatre. Following the construction of the Palace of Congresses, it became the office of the Presidium. During sessions of the Supreme Soviet its two chambers (the Soviet of the Union and the Soviet of the Nationalities) occupy the building in turn. It is to this office that foreign ambassadors come to show their credentials. Its main room is the Conference Hall which is finished in rare woods, polished stone and crystal.

Lenin's bust

At the far end of the square is a bust of Lenin in a pretty garden. This is supposed to commemorate the spot where Lenin rested during the first *subotnik* (a Saturday each year when citizens voluntarily work for nothing — their earnings go instead to help the state) in the spring of 1919.

The King of Guns and the Queen of Bells

Still on the square, opposite the Presidium, is a huge bronze cannon, the **Tsar's Cannon** *(Tsar Pushka)*. It was cast in 1586, is 5 m (17 ft) long and weighs 40.6 mt (40 tons). Had it ever been used, it would have fired cannon balls weighing two tons (although it is also said that it was in fact designed to fire grape-shot). The cannon balls beside the cannon are nineteenth century and purely ornamental.

Beyond the cannon rests the **Tsar's Bell** *(Tsar Kolokol)*. Weighing more than 203.2 mt (200 tons) it is the largest bell in the world. It was cast in the Kremlin in 1733-5 for the tower behind but as it was being hoisted into position it fell and smashed. It was recast but when a fire broke out in the workshop some water spilled on the red-hot bronze, and an 11.7 mt (11.5 ton) chunk fell off. It remained embedded in the pit where it was cast until 1836 when it was raised to its present position. It is easy to miss the exquisite engraving on its surface, depicting Tsar Alexei Mikhailovich and Empress Anna Ioannovna.

Following the road to the right, beyond the bell, is the entrance to Cathedral Square, right. Standing here one may identify the visible buildings, clockwise from the cathedral on your left: Cathedral of the Archangel Michael (with the shells near the top), Cathedral of the Annunciation, the Palace of Facets, Church of the Deposition of the Robe, Cathedral of the Assumption, the Patriarch's Palace and, to your immediate right, the Bell Tower of Ivan the Great (NOT the Terrible!).

Cathedral Square *(Sobornaya Ploshad)*

(Some of the cathedrals are open to the public — see Introduction.)
This is the most magnificent part of the Kremlin. The square dates
back to the fourteenth century although most of the buildings on it
date from the sixteenth century.

Cathedral of St Michael the Archangel *(Arkhangelski Sobor)*
This was built in 1505 by the Italian Alevisio Novi, replacing the
original one of 1333. Although the basic form is in the Russian
tradition, much of the decorative detail is characteristic of
Renaissance Venetian palace architecture (for example, the shells in
the gables). It served as a burial place for the rulers of Muscovy and
Russia until the eighteenth century. The interior is characteristic of
the Italian Renaissance.

Some of the original frescos, painted in the later part of the
sixteenth century, survive around the altar and on the west portal,
but the majority were painted by Russians, under supervision of
masters from the Armoury workshops in the mid seventeenth
century. They depict battles famous in early Russian history. There
are also full length portraits of Russian princes and heroes — one
of the columns has a portrait of Alexander Nevsky. Those on the
south wall depict the Moscow Grand Princes who are buried in this
cathedral.

The Russian Baroque iconostasis, with its gold fretwork, was
completed in 1681. The icon of St Michael (on the bottom tier) is
late fourteenth century. The earliest tomb (1340) is of Ivan Kalita,
the unifier of Russia. The tombs of Ivan the Terrible (southeast
chapel) and of the Great are also here.

Cathedral of the Annunciation *(Blagoveshchenski Sobor)*
This was built by architects from Pskov at the end of the fifteenth
century on the site of an existing church. It has white walls and nine
cupolas (originally there were only three) and became the marriage
and baptismal church of the Tsars. It also became a private royal
chapel and was the favourite of the Tsar's wives and sisters — the
choir gallery on the west wall was for their use.

The whitestone porch on the south side was added in 1570 for
Ivan the Terrible, so that he could be present at services from which
he was, strictly speaking, barred because of having a surfeit of
wives. The floor also dates back to his reign and is paved in mosaics
of agate and jasper. The walls are covered in frescos of 1508 by the
monk Theodosius. The iconostasis is said to be the oldest in Russia

and contains icons of masters Theophanes the Greek and Andrei Rublyev. Rublyev probably began his career in this church and is responsible for seven icons of the Festive Tier to the left of the north wall, and for one depicting Archangel Michael. The icons of the lower tier are older, dating back to the early fourteenth century. The iconostasis frame is nineteenth century. Portals leading from the inner court to the centre of the church preserve the ancient tradition of the wooden arch framed with columns of sheaves of corn; the oldest is the southern one. In the crypt is an exhibition of archeological finds from the Kremlin.

The Facets Palace *(Granovitaya Palata)* not open to public
This is the oldest secular building in the Kremlin, indeed the oldest in Moscow. It was begun by Marco Rufo and completed in 1491 by Antonio Solario. Its exterior is not dissimilar to the Pitti Palace in Florence and its faceted walls are in pure Florentine style. The ornate windows are a seventeenth century addition. The Facets Palace is only accessible from the Great Kremlin Palace.

Its lower floor was used for administrative purposes while the upper floor was a reception hall dominated by a massive gilded pillar decorated with ornamental painting in the Palekh style. It was here that ambassadors were received and where banquets took place — here Ivan I celebrated the capture of Kazan and Peter I the victory over the Swedes at the Battle of Poltava. Adjoining the Palace on the left was the Red Staircase (now incorporated into a modern building) upon which the Tsar would make his occasional public appearances. It was on these steps that the supporters of the young Peter the Great were murdered by the Imperial Guard.

Terem Palace *(Teremnoi Dvorets)* — not open to the public
This was the official residence of the Tsars until the capital was moved to St Petersburg and is part of the Great Kremlin Palace (behind the Faceted Palace and invisible from the square, despite its brightly checkered red and white roof). It was built in the typically exuberent style of the seventeenth century by adding three storeys to the existing sixteenth century palace. The older part had been designed by the Italian Alevisio but the new was of Russian design.

Although appartments for the entire royal family were here, the name Terem comes from the Greek word *teremnon* referring to the 'women's appartments'. The Tsarina's Golden Palace is on the ground floor. Others are on the upper floors, including the Tsar's bedroom and the room used by waiting Boyars. In another room the Boyars held their meetings. The stone attic held the appartments of the Tsar's son. Here too is the Throne Room with its Petition Window, from which a box was lowered to the square for people to place their requests (these were generally ignored — hence the Russian expression for putting things off, 'Do not put it in a long box'). The whole of this floor is surrounded by a terrace where women of the royal family could stroll. Some of the royal furniture remains, including silver chests one of which contains *The book of the election of Tsar Michael Fedorovich.*

Within the Terem Palace are four small churches: the Cathedral of the Redemption (or Upper Cathedral of the Saviour) which was the tsars' private chapel and whose 11 small gilt cupolas, on red brick bases covered in green ceramic, are just visible from the square (behind the Church of the Deposition of the Virgin's Robe); St Catherine's Church, which was the private chapel of the Tsarinas; the Church of the Resurrection of Lazarus, the oldest church in the Kremlin (1393); and the Church of the Crucifixion.

Church of the Deposition of the Virgin's Robe
(Rizpolozhensky Sobor)
This too was built by architects of Pskov between 1484 and 1486 in so-called early-Muscovite style. The walls and pillars were painted by Ivan Borisov who had also worked on the neighbouring Cathedral of the Assumption. The iconostasis is of 1627. The icons were painted by a group of Russian painters headed by Nazary Istomin. The two seventeenth-century candleholders recall Chinese enamel ware.

The church was at first the Patriarch's private chapel but from the middle of the seventeenth century came to be favoured by the royal family. There is a collection of ancient wooden sculpture and stone masonry on display.

The Cathedral of the Assumption or Cathedral of the Dormition *(Uspensky Sobor)*
This, for 400 years the main cathedral of Russia, stands on the site of a twelfth-century wooden church and a thirteenth- century stone one. At the time of its completion in 1479, under the supervision of its Italian architect Ridolfo Fioravanti, it was the largest building in Russia. It was modelled on the twelfth-century Cathedral of the Assumption in the ancient town of Vladimir in order to show the continuity of authority of the Muscovite Princes, and it was here

that tsars were crowned and acts of state proclaimed (for example the deed on the unification of the Ukraine with Russia in 1654). It was here too that appanage princes swore their allegiance to the Grand Princes of Moscow.

The walls of the spacious interior are lined with the tombs of the Patriarchs and Metropolitans. The seventeenth-century iconostasis, covered in nineteenth-century embossed gilt silver, is the frame for a display of twelfth- to seventeenth- century icons by Byzantine and Russian masters, some of which had been brought to Moscow by the princes of Constantinople, Kiev, Pskov and Novgorod. The oldest is the icon of St George, of the twelfth century. The icon in a case in the centre of the first tier, of the Virgin of Vladimir, was painted by an artist of the Andrei Rublyev school.

The interior walls are covered in frescos on gold in the Byzantine style. The pillars are painted with gigantic figures of martyrs, archangels in armour and New Testament figures. The entire west wall is a painting of the Last Judgement. The whitestone seat of the Pariarchs dates from the sixteenth century. The canopied wooden coronation chair was carved in 1551 for Ivan the Terrible. The bronze canopy dates to 1625. The 12 censers are of gilded bronze. The southern doors came from Suzdal in 1410. The huge central chandelier is made of silver that had been retrieved by pursuing Cossacks from the fleeing Napoleonic troops who during the occupation of 1812 had used the cathedral as a stable.

Patriarchs' Palace (Patriarshye Palat) and the Cathedral of the Twelve Apostles (Sobor Dvenadtsati Apostolov)

The patriarchs' palace and adjoining cathedral stand on the north of the square on the site of the former Church of the Solovetsky Miracle Workers. They are both seventeenth century. The interior of the palace, in marked contrast to the simple exterior, is luxurious and consists of a number of chambers and chapels. The most impressive is the 280 sq. m (3,014 sq. ft) Chrism-Making Hall ('chrism' is consecrated oil), which has no centrally supporting pillars. It was used for the sitting of church assemblies and for state banquets. The Cathedral was originally the Patriarch's private chapel. Following the banning of the Patriarchate both the church and the palace were turned into cells for monks. After the Revolution everything was restored to its original state.

The first floor of the palace is the museum of seventeenth-century Applied Art and Everyday Life. It shows the life of the ruling classes with examples of clothing, tableware, books, furniture, games and Russian and foreign watches.

Belfry of Ivan the Great *(Kolkovnya Ivana Velikovo)*
This was built in 1505-8 to celebrate the accession to the throne of
Boris Godunov. The upper tier was added in 1600, hence the
inscription around the base of the dome itself: 'By the command of
the Great Lord, Tsar and Grand Prince Boris Fiodorovich, autocrat
of All Russia, and of his son, the Orthodox Great Lord Fiodor
Borisovich, Tsarevich and Prince of All Russia, this church was
completed and gilded in the second year of their reign'. It is 81 m
(266 ft) high, surmounted by a gold dome of 10 m (33 feet)
diameter, and was for long the tallest structure in the country — in
fact no tower was allowed, by Imperial edict, to be taller. It was a
watchtower with a view of 25 or 30 km (15.5 to 18.5 miles) and in
the event of the approach of an enemy its bells were sounded. The
base used to house the church of St John Climacus, of 1329.

The belfry next to it was added in 1532-43 by the architect Maly,
in order to house the large bells. The part on the extreme left
(looking at it from the square), known as the Filaret (after Patriarch
Philaretes, father of Tsar Mikhil Fedorovich Romanov whose house
still stands on Razin Street), was added in 1624 by Ogurtsov. In all
there are 21 bells in the tower and campaniles, variously made
between the sixteenth and nineteenth centuries. The largest is the
Dormition or Assumption Bell, weighing 71 tonnes. They are rung
on Easter night as a signal for all the bells of Moscow to ring out.

When Napoleon left Moscow in 1812 he ordered the tower to be
blown up. The belfry and Filaret did not withstand the blast (they
were rebuilt by Domenico Gilardi in 1819) but the tower suffered
only a crack.

The Great Kremlin Palace and the Armoury

To reach these, leave Cathedral Square through the gap between the
Cathedral of the Archangel Michael and the Cathedral of the
Annunciation. Turn right, with the Kremlin wall and view across
Moscow to the left, and the Great Kremlin Palace is towards the
right. This is the building, with the letters CCCP written along the
upper part of the façade, that stands out when looking at the
Kremlin from across the river.

The Great Kremlin Palace stretches along the river opposite the
British Embassy and incorporates or is connected to the Facets
Palace and the Terem Palace (see Cathedral Square), as well as
some smaller churches — 'a composite architectural complex of

secular and ecclesiastical buildings erected at different times beginning from the fifteenth century'. The façade looking across the river was built by Nicholas I between 1839 and 1849. It replaces the last of several Tsar's stone palaces that had stood here since the time of Ivan III — this was a Rastrelli creation built for Emperor Elizabeth which had fallen into disrepair when the capital had moved to St Petersburg. It remained the official Moscow residence of the Tsars until 1917.

Although it seems to have three floors there are in fact only two, the upper floor having windows in two tiers. The palace is filled with vast saloons (there are some 700 rooms) with painted ceilings, massive bronze candelabra, and columns of marble and granite, or painted white or gold. Four of the rooms are dedicated to the great Russian orders of chivalry: St George, St Vladimir, St Alexander and St Andrew. Stalin combined the St Alexander and St Andrew rooms in order to form the meeting room of the Supreme Soviet. The Hall of St George is used for ceremonial purposes (Yuri Gagarin was honoured here) and the Hall of St Vladimir (the octagonal skylight of which is visible from Cathedral Square), built on the site of the old Boyars' Terrace, is used for the signing of important treaties. Parts of the older palaces have been incorporated into the building and there are passages leading to the Faceted Palace. Currently the Great Kremlin Palace is used for sessions of the highest legislative bodies of the USSR and the Russian Federation.

The Armoury (Open to the public — see Introduction)
Next to the Palace is the Armoury. The first Armoury was built in the sixteenth century for the manufacture of arms and armour, although there had been a treasure house on the site since the fourteenth century. The making of armour was of course an important craft for several war-torn centuries and art workshops had been established at several of the princely courts in the Kremlin since earliest times. Eventually, for practical reasons, these workshops were incorporated into the armoury workshops. Later it became the court workshop, scattered in buildings between its present site and the Trinity Gate, where the greatest craftsmen and artists worked side by side in producing embroidered gold, enamel ware and icons. The Armoury came to be known as the 'arts academy' and during the seventeenth century the Stable Administration was added to it, for the making of dress harness. When the capital moved to St Petersburg, the Armoury became the Romanov family museum, housed in a special building near the

Trinity Gate. When the Great Kremlin Palace was rebuilt in the middle of the nineteenth century, another two-storey building was built at its side, on the site of the Stable Administration, where the Imperial treasures have since been housed.

The treasures are arrayed in nine rooms and contain items of Russian and European applied art from the twelfth to the early twentieth century. In the weapons room the display includes the earliest examples of the Russian flintlock, royal dress armour of the seventeenth century, beautiful oriental weapons cases encrusted in precious gems and a thirteenth century Byzantine helmet.

Russian gold and silver work is well represented in the techniques of embossing, filigree and enamelling. Most of it dates back to the sixteenth and seventeenth centuries — note the gold cover for the 1571 Gospel, the three cameos in sardonix, and the collection of enamels. There is a large collection of seventeenth- and eighteenth century gold and silver scoops (shaped something like a duck and reminiscent of the wooden dishes in use among the peasantry) and of eighteenth- and nineteenth century tea services, samovars and snuff boxes.

The exhibition of silverwork from Western Europe (England, Austria, Holland, Poland, Sweden etc.) is one of the most important in the world. French decorative art is well represented — Paris silverwork from the eighteenth and nineteenth centuries and the Olympian service of Sevres porcelain presented by Napoleon.

There is a small collection of Turkish gifts (seventeenth century); and in another room a collection of fabrics. Some, like the vestments for the first Metropolitans, are Byzantine and date back to the fourteenth century. There are Persian fabrics with small floral and geometrical designs. And there are Turkish and Italian velvets, Moscow brocades, and late-eighteenth century garments of French glazed silk, like Catherine the Great's wedding dress.

The Regalia of State is displayed in the Armoury too, including the Monomachus Hat of State with its ring of fur, gold crown and pearl encrusted cross (thirteenth century), the gold crown of Ivan I, and the crowns of Peter I and his brother. The creative genius of Faberge is well represented and finally, there is a fine collection of carriages, of which the oldest is of English and Polish work from the late-sixteenth century.

The Diamond Collection (Open to the Public — see Introduction)

Although it is situated in the Armoury building, the Diamond Collection must be visited separately.

The collection was set aside from the main Imperial treasury in 1922 and opened as a permanent exhibition in 1967. The display consists of crowns, like that made for the coronation of Catherine II in 1762 with diamonds and pink pearls, and stones like the Orlov Diamond (189.62 carats) which is mounted on the gold imperial sceptre. The Shah Diamond was presented to Nicholas I by the Shah following the assassination of the writer and diplomat Griboyedov. The display includes the largest of most beautiful diamonds found in the USSR (e.g. the 232-carat Star of Yakutiya or the 51.66 -carat Valentina Tereshkova, named after the first woman (Cosmonaut) and other gems, as well as platinum and gold nuggets, one of which, the Large Triangle, is the largest in the world. Additions continue to be made to the exhibition.

Potieshny ('pleasure') Palace — not open to the public

This tall green building (again all but invisible) is situated between the Trinity Gate and the Commandants Tower, behind the Armoury and the Great Kremlin Palace. It was built in 1650-1 as a palace for the boyar Miloslavsky. In 1679, on the orders of Tsar Alexei, the ground-floor church was restored and the palace was transformed into a theatre. Although there were numerous changes made in the eighteenth and nineteenth centuries, and the seventeenth-century interior decoration has entirely disappeared, the palace has nonetheless retained much of its charm.

Red Square and Kitai Gorod

Red Square *(Krasnaya Ploshad)* lies beneath the eastern wall of the Kremlin and is the most famous and the most beautiful of Moscow squares. **Kitai Gorod** is the name of the area to the east of Red Square and is intimately connected to it. Metro: Ploshad Nogina or Ploshad Revolutsi.

The name is not a new one, nor does it have revolutionary connotations. The word *krasnaya* used to mean beautiful as well as red and the square acquired the name during the seventeenth century, when embellishments were added to the Kremlin towers.

As Moscow grew out of the original Kremlin, the area to the east came to be known as the Great Trading Quarter, or the merchant quarter. Immediately under the walls was the market place which became Red Square. In the fourteenth century the main entrance to the Kremlin was moved to this side and Ivan Kalita had all the merchant shops placed along the east wall. The square grew in importance and replaced the Cathedral Square within the Kremlin walls as the centre of social life. It became the principal market not only of the city but of the country.

It was the meeting point of the great commercial routes: from Novgorod, Tver, the Nikolskaya from the east, the Ordynka from the south and the Tartar Golden Horde. It was also the political and religious centre of the city.

Sleds loaded with produce came to the market from hundreds of miles away, carrying corn, fish, furs of all types, wax, honey, plums, red currants, asparagus and garlic. There were cranes and swans, sheep and cattle. Fabrics came from the east and metal objects from Russia and all over Europe. In oriental style objects for sale were grouped according to type in rows called *ryady*.

Modern Red Square is rather different although it remains an impressive sight. Apart from GUM there is no trace of the former market and crowds gather there for different reasons — it has a unique beauty and it is regarded by westerners as the symbol of communism.

(Lavatories are to be found just to the left of the Spassky Gate.)

Opposite: Red Square at night, visitors delight. The Spassky Gate, close to Lenin's tomb, complete with ruby star (photo Jim Helme).
Following page: The most familiar and beloved of all Russian churches: St Basil's on Red Square (photo Jim Helme).

Gates and towers

The east wall of the Kremlin looks over the square. Below it there used to be a deep moat. The principal entrance to the Kremlin is the **Spasskaya** *(Saviour's Tower),* highly distinctive with its gothic features and its clock. It was half its current height when built by Pietro Antonio Solario in 1491. The gothic-style tower and clock with its carillon was added in 1625 by the Englishman Christopher Galloway, although the clock you see now was installed in 1851-2. Until the Revolution there was an icon above the gate to which passers-by were expected to raise their hats. This entrance is not open to the general public.

There are a number of other towers on this part of the Kremlin wall. To the immediate left of the Spasskaya (looking at it from the square) is the most recent of them, built in 1680 — a turret from which the Tsar was reputed to watch events in Red Square. To the left of that is the **Nabatnaya** *(Tocsin Tower).* From it once hung a tocsin, rung when an enemy was sighted as a sign for citizens to take refuge within the walls. Next is the **Konstantino-Yeleninskaya** *(Constantine and Helen)* through which Dmitri Donskoy led his troops to victory over the Tartar Mongols in 1380 at Kulikovo. It was originally of whitestone and is named after a church that used to stand behind it.

To the right of the Spasskaya is the **Senatskaya** *(Senate Tower),* directly behind Lenin's Tomb, from which government members emerge for the May Day parade. Next is the **Nikolskaya** *(St Nicholas Tower),* the name being derived from the mosaic of St Nicholas which was above the entrance.

Around the square

The most striking and famous of all the monuments on the square is **St Basil's Cathedral** *(Khram Vassilia Blazhennovo)* with its distinctively bright-coloured cupolas. It was built in the reign of Ivan the Terrible between 1554 and 1560 by Russian architects to commemorate the victory at Kazan which was attributed to the intercession of Basil the Blessed, a mendicant miracle worker. It was originally red and white with green domes and recalls the native-style wooden churches of the countryside. The present colour scheme is seventeenth century. Legend has it that Ivan had the architects, Barma and Postnik, blinded so that they could never build another like it.

Despite the first impression of a chaotic congregation of colour and shape, St Basil's was built with harmony and symmetry in mind. It is the domes and belfries that attract, in the form of fruit, bulbs and pinecones. The central dome, which reaches a height of 57 m (187 ft), is encircled by four cupolas, and below them another four. The result is a fairy tale building whose charm is all the greater against the winter snow. The interior is in all senses the antithesis of the exterior — 11 plain chapels, now arranged as a museum of old Russian architecture.

The butcher and the prince
In front of the cathedral stands the memorial to Minin and Pozharsky. Minin was a butcher from Nizhny-Novgorod who organised the resistance to Polish invaders in the sixteenth century. Prince Pozharsky was the leader of the soldiers that drove the Poles from Moscow. The memorial is of bronze and was cast in 1818. The inscription on it reads: 'To citizen Minin and to Prince Pozharsky — Russia is thankful. 1818.' It originally stood opposite Lenin's mausoleum, but was moved in 1931 in order to clear the centre of Red Square for parades.

The Place of the Skull
A little way into the square before St Basil's there is a circular, stone-rimmed platform. This was known as **Lobnoye Mesto** (the *Place of the Skull* or the *Place of Execution).* It was not the scaffold or gibbet, which was nearby, but the place where death sentences were announced. In the reign of Ivan the Terrible many executions took place here. Here too, lay the body of the 'false Dmitri' in 1606. The Cossack leader Stenka Razin met his end here in 1671. And it was here that Peter the Great had all the *Streltsy* (the rebellious Imperial Guard) put to death. It was also a place for the delivery of Imperial proclamations and of theological debates. Its current form dates back to 1786. It was originally guarded by cannons, including the Tsar's Cannon now in the Kremlin.

Opposite the Kremlin

The whole length of this side of the square is taken up by nineteenth-century buildings built in the Russian equivalent of Victorian style, formerly known as **Torgoviye Ryadi** *(Trading Rows).* This part of the square has been associated with trading since the Middle Ages, and stone stalls were first placed here in the 1590s. The buildings that stand opposite St Basil's between Razin

Street and Kuibychev Street were built in 1901 and currently serve an administrative function. The others, between Kuibychev Street and 25th October Street, make up the most famous shop in the USSR, known as GUM **(Gossudarstvienny Universalny Magasin** or the **State Universal Store).** GUM has three floors and is cut by three passages which are linked by bridges and corridors. The roof is of metal and glass. It was built between 1888 and 1894. It has some 130 departments. You may not wish to buy anything but a visit is worthwhile for the bazaar atmosphere. Four hundred thousand customers are said to pass through its doors daily. (Lavatories inside on the ground floor.)

The State History Museum

At the north end of the square, opposite St Basil's, stands the State History Museum. To the right of the museum once stood the Iberian Gate (where Istorichiski Proezed now stands), part of the wall that used to surround the square and Kitai Gorod. The museum was built between 1878 and 1883 by V. Sherwood, an Englishman, in seventeenth-century style on the site of the first Russian university founded by Lomonosov. Inside there are something like four million exhibits and ten million documents. The museum is currently under restoration and likely to be so for quite some time, since several important architectural discoveries concerning Moscow in early times have been made under the foundations.

The Pit

To the right of the museum are two pink buildings, both part of what was the former Provincial Government Building, built in 1740. A notorious debtor's prison, the **Yama** *(the Pit),* formed part of this building. The plaque on the wall of the plain pink building testifies to the imprisonment of the thinker and author Alexander Radishchev. By going into the courtyard of the building next door (pink with white decoration), you will see ahead of you a lovely red brick building with pillars on the upper story, tilework on top and an ancient stone arch beneath. This was the mint, built in 1697.

Lenin's Mausoleum (Open to the public)

Under the Kremlin wall, about half way along it, is the red basalt tomb of Lenin. It was built by architect Shchussev in 1930, replacing an earlier wooden one erected immediately after Lenin died in 1924. Despite its angular form, it harmonises well with the wall and building behind it, particularly if viewed from the other side of the square. Inside, Lenin's embalmed body lies in a glass sarcophagus down some steps. During WW II his body was moved to Kuibyshev, on the Volga. Stalin lay next to him from 1953 until 1961, when he was interred at the foot of the wall behind. The doors are permanently guarded by a pair of soldiers - the guard is changed every hour with immaculate precision and is a memorable sight. Steps on either side lead up to a tribune from which Soviet leaders inspect the annual May Day parade. Behind Lenin's tomb, running along the wall, are the graves of many illustrious Communists e.g. John Reed, the American writer of *Ten Days that Shook the World* (the inspiration for the film *Reds),* Kirov, Dzerzhinsky, Stalin and Gorky.

Visitors may join the queue to enter the mausoleum on Tuesdays, Wednesdays and Thursdays, between 12 midday and 13.00. You should first obtain a permit (free) through an Intourist service bureau. If the one in your hotel cannot do this, go to the one in the Intourist Hotel on Gorky Street or to the independent ticket office next door. If all else fails show up at the end of the queue and show your passport — some policemen are quite content with that.

Although this is likely to be a contentious issue, there has been some talk about giving Lenin the normal burial that he would have preferred.

Kitai Gorod (A walk through the old merchant quarter)

In modern Russian *Kitai Gorod* would translate as 'Chinatown'. In fact it is no such thing, nor was it ever. The original meaning actually derived from the Mongol word meaning 'fortress'. The area called Kitai Gorod was originally the Great Trading Quarter, or merchant quarter, and grew in importance to the extent that a wall was built around it in 1538. The quarter extended eastwards from Red Square to the avenue that passes through the modern New Square, Old Square and Dzerzhinsky Square. Most of the buildings in that area are now ministries and offices. The wall has been all but demolished, but two bits remain, on Kitaisky Street, just off Ploshad Nogina, near the river and Rossya Hotel; and on Ploshad Sverdlova, behind the Metropole Hotel.

Three main streets run east-west across the old quarter between Red Square and Novaya and Staraya streets: Razin Street, Kuibshev Street and October 25th Street. In the old days all the streets off them were filled with trading stalls and were known as *ryady* (rows), each devoted to the sale of a single merchandise. Thus some of the history of these streets is preserved in their names i.e. Fish Street *(Rybny)*, or Crystal *(Khrustalny)*. Most of the architecture and layout of the area as it is today evolved during the nineteenth and early twentieth centuries, when the trading centre became predominantly a business centre with the modern connotations of banking and international commerce. Nonetheless, much of the bazaar atmosphere prevailed: in the fur section customers would have searched longingly for fine blue fox; or in the precious stones section for a perfect piece of turquoise.

A walk around this section should properly start on October 25th Street.

October 25th Street (Ulitsa dvyatsatpiatovo Oktyabra)

Its old name was Nikolskaya Street. The modern name commemorates the date of the Revolution and was one of the sites of battle between Red Guards and their opponents in 1917. During the seventeenth century it was the centre of Moscow intellectual and religious life, and was known as the 'street of enlightenment', although today's layout is more evocative of commercial Moscow. In the past there were numerous workshops, trading yards and taverns here.

On the corner of October 25th Street itself, now vacant, once stood the Kazan Cathedral. It was built in 1630 by Prince Pozharski, a Boyar who had led the Russians to victory over the Poles during the 'Time of Troubles'.

Number 5 is currently occupied by a legal committee. You then pass a Metro entrance and a post office. Continue along the street to number 9, on the left, where several old buildings used to form the *Zaikonospassky* (Saviour behind the Icons) Monastery, founded in 1600. During the reign of Peter the Great the Monastery was enlarged, new buildings being added to the design of the architect Zarudny. The monastery cathedral has an octagonal crown and what is left of it can be seen by entering the courtyard. It is now part of the Historical Archives Society. It was here that the first institution for higher education in Russia — the Slavonic, Greek and Latin Academy — was opened in 1687. Several eminent Russians, including Lomonosov, studied here. (Number 11 is also part of the Archives Institute.)

Just after number 9 is a little passage leading to Sverdlov Square.

Number 15 (enter by the porch inside the courtyard) once housed the first printing house in Russia, of which a couple of the original rooms survive in the courtyard. It has an eye-catching façade from the beginning of last century, unusual arch, one of the last remaining sundials in the city, and emblem of the Imperial Printing House. It was founded in 1562 by Ivan the Terrible, was rebuilt in 1644 and restored in the nineteenth and twentieth centuries. The first Russian book, published in 1564 by Ivan Fyodorov (whose statue stands in Tretyakov passage which connects the end of the street with Karl Marx Avenue), was the *Acts of the Apostles.* The first Russian newspaper, *Vedomosti (Gazette),* was published here in 1703. The press became part of the Synodal Printing House in 1814 and was also the site of the first public library in Moscow. It now houses another branch of the Archives Institute.

Opposite is a KACCA for the purchase of theatre tickets and a shop selling hand made souvenirs. Further up on the right is a little passage hiding a hamburger stand.

Also to the right is a major street, **Kuibyshev Passage** *(Kuibyshevsky Proyezd),* in which is the remaining church of the former Bogoyavlensky Monastery, a seventeenth-century baroque masterpiece. The splendid tombs are eighteenth century. Number 4 of this street is a fine example of Moscow Baroque.

Other churches that used to stand in October 25th Street (the Greek Monastery of St Nicholas, after which the street was originally named, and the Church of Our Lady of Vladimir built in 1691 near Dzerzhinsky Square) have disappeared.

Number 17, with its not very expressive façade and decorative arch with joined columns, houses the editorial offices of Lesnaya, the newspaper of the wood industry.

Number 19 is the **Slavyansky Bazaar** restaurant (formerly the hotel of the same name). In the past many eminent Russians and foreigners stayed here — Repin, Tchaikovsky, Rimsky Korsakov, Chekhov and the polar explorer Nansen. It was here that a dinner and concert were given in honour of a visit by the composer Dvorjak. For further historical information and details about today's restaurant, see Restaurant section.

Near the end of the street on the left is **Tretyakov Passage**

(Tretyakovsky Proyezd), named after the brothers upon whose land and with whose money the passage was built and whose collection of art work is the basis of the Tretyakov Gallery. This passage was built in 1870-73 — note the elegant archways at each end and the old fashioned Moscow street sign, small and high to the left, using the old Russian alphabet. (Public lavatories).

The grey building with the ornate canopy and the statues above it at 21 is one of the oldest pharmacies in Moscow. Behind the façade is the more usual red brick of Moscow.

To continue the walk, turn right at the end and continue past several lanes (and buildings, some of which are described in a later walk) until Kuibyshev Street on your right. On your way you will pass two cafes with distinctive blue signs: the first sells real coffee and a small variety of snacks; the other sells tea, bread and chicken, which you are expected to eat with your hands.

Kuibyshev Street *(Ulitsa Kuibisheva)*

In its heyday this was the main thoroughfare of Kitai Gorod, when it was called Ilinka Street or Prophet Elijah Street. In 1935 it took its present name in honour of an early Soviet statesman.

By the seventeenth century it was the centre of Moscow business life. There were a number of churches and monasteries as well which, during the eighteenth century, came to be used as banks. There were no shops but on the ground floor you would have found the warehouse and the accounting department; above, the church. During the nineteenth and early twentieth centuries, many of the properties, which had before belonged to the nobility, were purchased by the bourgeoisie. Mansions and gardens became financial houses built in art nouveau or pseudo-Russian style. Indeed most of what remains dates back to the beginning of the century, with heavy use of granite, bronze, concrete and thick mirror glass. If the prevailing atmosphere is one of austerity that is because many of the buildings along here are filled with functionaries of the Communist Party.

The part of the street farthest from Red Square used to culminate in the Ilinskye Gate in the old wall, which was razed to make way for Novaya Ploshad. Walking towards Red Square, number 21, with its tower and rotonda, and façade of natural stone, was formerly the Northern Insurance Society — it currently houses the Committee for People's Control, which is supposed to be responsible for 'quality of life'.

Number 15 is the site of the old Church of the Great Cross of St

Nicholas which until its destruction in 1933, had been considered one of the finest examples of early Moscow Baroque.

Number 14, with its balcony on the corner, is attractive, but of unknown function.

Number 9 was built in neo-classical style, very typical of last century.

Number 8 on the other hand is more typical of St Petersburg than of Moscow and stands opposite the grey building that is part of the Finance Ministry.

On the corner of the major street running off to the right (1 Kuibyshev Proezd) is a building in art nouveau style. This was a bank which belonged to the millionaire Ryabushinsky.

The former **Stock Exchange** *(Birzha)* is at number 6. This classically-colonnaded building (so like stock exchanges all over the world) was constructed in 1875 and has a small square behind it. It is now the seat of the Chamber of Commerce of the Soviet Union, an organisation that promotes internal trade and commercial ties with other countries.

Number 5, with the rotunda, was built in 1876 and for some years was the tallest building in Moscow.

At number 4, on the left, stands one of the largest buildings of old Moscow, a huge columned rectangle that extends to neighbouring Razin Street. This is the former **Old Merchants'** *Court (Stary Gostiny Dvor),* built between 1790 and 1805 under the aegis of Giacomo Quarenghi. This was the centre of wholesale trade. Now it contains an array of government offices, one of which is the supply base for the Moscow region.

Number 3 was the former Warm Trading Rows, while the last building on the left, not dissimilar to GUM and dating from the middle of last century, housed the Middle Trading Rows.

Razin Street *(Ulitsa Razina)*
Turn left at the end, walk along Red Square past St Basil's, and turn left into Razin Street.

This was formerly known as Varvarka Street or St Barbara Street. The current name was given in honour of the Cossack leader Stenka Razin, who was a great irritant to the Tsar during the seventeenth century. He was led along this same street to his execution in 1671.

Razin Street represented the limit of the trading rows and is testimony of the sheer number of churches there once was in Moscow. Beyond, as far as the river, lay the Zaryadye district, which acted as the port for Kitai Gorod. It was one of the insalubrious parts of the city, but doubtless one of the most colourful. Much of it is dominated by the vast Rossia Hotel, built in 1969.

At number 2, on the right, stands the pink and white **Church of St Barbara,** which dates back to 1796 and is an excellent example of late-eighteenth century classicism. At number 4 (white with the yellow bell tower), is the **Church of St Maximus the Blessed,** built in 1699 with a belfry of 1829, which houses the permanent exhibition of the All-Russia Society for the Protection of the Environment.

Between these two churches and below them is the so-called **Old English Tavern.** English merchants, according to a charter granted by Ivan the Terrible in 1556, were able to use this as their office — one floor was for living in, the other for storage. Envoys from England would have been accommodated here as well. It was built upon during the seventeenth century and thought to have been lost for ever, but restoration recovered much of the original walls and decoration.

The next buildings (below the overpass to the hotel) belonged to the former Znamensky Monastery. The first one, red, in baroque style and with no onion dome, belongs now to the Ministry of Cultural Propaganda, and was the belfry of the Monastery of the Sign. At 8a, in red brick, was the former cathedral of the monastery. The building similar to the English tavern used to house the monk's cells.

The monastery was built on the **Old State Court** *(Stary Gosudarev Dvor),* which was part of the estate of the Romanov family before Michael Romanov ascended the throne. Legend has it that he was born here. The Znamensky (Apparition of the Virgin) Monastery was founded on the old estate and enjoyed much royal patronage. The five cupola cathedral was built between 1679 and 1684 and the belfry in the eighteenth century. The Boyar's house at number 10 (late sixteenth and early seventeenth century) was also part of the Romanov estate.

The last church on Razin Street is the seventeenth-century **Church of St George** on Pskov Mount, characteristic of the ornamental architecture of its time.

Ipatyevsky Lane runs off the other side of Razin Street. At the end on the left at number 12, with its lovely facade, you will find the stone **House of Simon Ushakov.** He was a seventeenth-century painter who renounced traditional icon painting and adopted a more realistic style — this was his house and studio. Beyond it is the headquarters of the Communist Party and, legend has it, the famous canteen denounced by Boris Yeltsin.

In Nikitnikov Lane, which is at right angles to Ipatyevsky Lane, at number 3, is the **Trinity Church in Nikitniki,** considered to be one of the most beautiful churches in Moscow. This was built between 1631 and 1634 by a merchant, Grigory Nikitnikov, whose wealth enabled him, so it is said, to lend money to the Tsar. One of its most remarkable features is the number of beautiful *kokoshniki* (an architectural structure resembling a woman's traditional bonnet) around the domes. The walls within were frescoed by masters from the Armoury workshops. The lower tier of the iconostasis contains works by Simon Ushakov. Like many other churches, this one was turned into a museum by Stalin in the 1930s.

The end of Razin street is the end of Kitai Gorod. By turning right down Kitai Passage, towards the river, some remains of the wall may be seen. It is four metres thick with bevelling designed to withstand short, middle and long range firing.

Continue to the end of Kitai Passage, where on the corner next to the Rossia Hotel is the fifteenth-century whitestone **Church of the Conception of St Anne.** It has been restored to its original appearance and is one of the oldest churches in the city.

A walk in the centre

This walk will take you through the centre of Moscow, around the edge of Kitai Gorod and the northwest boundary of the Kremlin. It is based on Marx Avenue, the artery that links the main squares and avenues of central Moscow. You can start from Ploshad Nogina (nearest metro of same name), or shorten it by starting from Dzerzhinsky Square (metro: Dzerzhinskaya), and finish in Borovitskaya Square, by the river.

Ploshad Nogina (Nogin Square)
This square, which is really the lower part of Old Square, is named after Victor Nogin, another revolutionary. The principal building on it, on the corner of Kitaiski Passage and next to a church, is **Delovy Dvor** *(Business House),* which was built in 1912 to house banking offices. During the first years of the Soviet Union the Fourth House of Soviets was housed here, and a hostel for visitors. John Reed, the American author, stayed here. Later the building housed the Supreme Council on the National Economy of the USSR (V.

The Soviet Achievement. The titanium space monument, outside the Exhibition of Economic Achievements, is the most beautiful modern monument in Moscow (photo: Jim Helme).

Kuibyshev, after whom one of the principal streets of Kitai Gorod is named, worked here). Today it is occupied by the Ministry of Iron and Steel.

Next to the Delovy Dvor is the **Church of All Saints** on Kulishki, founded by Dmitri Donskoy in 1380, and built on the road taken by the Muscovite troops from the Kremlin to the battle of Kulikovo. It was rebuilt in the the sixteenth and seventeenth centuries, which style it retains.

With your back to the church, you face Ilyinsky Gardens (after the former Ilyinsky Gate), with **Staraya Ploshad** *(Old Square)* and Kitai Gorod on the left, and **Serov Passage** *(Proyezd Serova)* on the right. From Serov Passage you can observe the institutions on your left across the garden. You may care to stroll along Solyanka Passage, on your right by the church, which has existed since the fourteenth century and whose name derives from the royal salt factory that used to stand on Solyanka Street (which runs off it to the right) and then down to the Yauza River. Continuing along Solyanka Passage takes you up to Ivanovskaya Hill where ahead of you is a functioning church and on the right the remains of the **Ivanovsky Convent,** founded in the sixteenth century and used as a secret prison during the seventeenth and eighteenth centuries. The current buildings date back to 1861-78.

Back on Serov Passage, look across the garden to the huge building on the left of Old Square which houses the Central Committee of the Communist Party of the USSR. Along the passage you will notice a state cafe at number 25 and also a co-operative cafe called **Vecher** *('Evening'),* of some repute. Further up on the right is a tea house called **Chai.** Number 17, with big pillars and doors, not very old but in classical style, is a food shop. Next to it is a rather attractive nineteenth century building containing offices.

At the end of the gardens, left, stands a Victorian looking monument designed by the Englishman Sherwood; its inscription reads 'To our comrades who fell in the glorious battle of Plevna, November 28, 1877.' It was financed by subscriptions collected by Russian soldiers who took part in the storming of the Turkish fortress of Plevna. Beyond, left, the street is still dominated by the offices of the Communist Party.

On your right, by the underpass and entrance to the metro station, is Bogdan Khmelitsky Street. Its former name was Maroseika Street, or street of the Ukrainians, since there used to stand a Ukrainian hostel at number 11, where the Ukrainian government representatives used to stay. The present street name was given in 1954 in honour of an eminent seventeenth-century Ukrainian hetman. At number 5, left, is the seventeenth-century **Church of St Nicholas in Blinniki.** At number 17, blue, with classical columns and the old coat of arms, is the delightful former late-eighteenth century house that once belonged to Field Marshall Rumyantsev-Zadunaisky whose son's book collection formed the basis of the Lenin Library. Today the house is the Moscow offices of the Belorussian government. Almost opposite it is the fine 1795 Church of Saints Cosmas and Damian, designed by the same architect responsible for number 17.

Returning to Serov Passage, you will notice the large building that sits between it and New Square beyond. This is the **Polytechnical Museum,** devoted to the achievements of Russian and Soviet science and technology. The original exhibition opened in 1872 in another building. The basis of it was formed by material from the All-Russia Polytechnical Exhibition that took place during the celebrations of the 200th anniversary of the birth of Peter the Great. The present building was put up in three parts — the central part (1877) and the left part (1896) were built in imitation of seventeenth-century style, while the right wing (1903-7) includes art nouveau features. There are over eighty exhibition halls divided into a variety of sections: Electrification, Nuclear Energy, Chemistry, Metallurgy, Geology and Mining, Clockmaking, Telecommunications, Automobiles, Computers, Optics and some oddities, such as the world's smallest book (smaller than a poppy seed), a map inside a grape pip and so on. The museum is open from 10.00 to 17.30 (13.00 to 20.30 on Tuesdays and Thursdays), and closed on Mondays. Tel: 223 0756. One of the lecture rooms was used by Lenin to give his first speech in Soviet Moscow.

Beyond the museum, on the far side of New Square, at number 6 is the **Headquarter of the Young Pioneers** (a sort of politicised cub organisation) and at number 12 the **Museum of the History and Reconstruction of Moscow,** housed in the old Church of John the Divine (nineteenth-century Empire style). This museum contains plans, pictures and photographs of the development of the city until the present day.

The last building on the right, at the end of Serov Passage, with ornate windows, is the headquarters of the Komsomol, also known as the Young Communist League, which is soon quite likely to lose its pre-eminent position in Soviet society.

This brings you to Dzerzhinsky Square; bear right. Tucked away in a modern building almost immediately right is the **Mayakovski Museum.** Mayakovski lived between 1893 and 1930 and is considered one of the greatest of Soviet poets — he is much loved. Here are exhibited many of his notebooks and some of his poster paintings and drawings. The museum is open from 10.00 to 18.00 (on Mondays and Thursdays from 12.00 to 20.00) and is closed on Wednesdays. Tel: 221 9560.

Dzerzhinsky Square: the Black Heart of Stalinism

The square is named after the man whose statue has stood in the centre of it since 1958 (but is to revert to original name of *Lubyanka).* Felix Dzerzhinsky was a comrade of Lenin and became head of the Cheka (the All-Russia Special Commission for Combatting Counter-revolution, Sabotage and Speculation), effectively the secret police and the forerunner of the KGB. Dzerzhinsky summed it up himself: 'The Cheka is most important. The Cheka is the defence of the Revolution, just as the Red Army is. The Cheka must defend the Revolution and conquer the enemy even if its sword falls occasionally on the heads of the innocent.'

The grim building with the clock on the right of the square as you look at it from Serov Passage, was the headquarters of the Cheka and is now the most important of the buildings belonging to the KGB. It was built in the nineteenth century for an insurance company and enlarged in 1946. Note the plaque on the wall on the Dzerzhinsky Street side commemorating Yuri Andropov, President of the USSR in the early 1980s and before that head of the KGB. The black building on the other side of Dzerzhinsky Street also belongs to the KGB — perhaps it is the original 'black Lubyanka', the KGB prison. The word Lubyanka comes from the old name for the square, Lubyanskaya, which had been given by inhabitants of Novgorod who settled here in the fifteenth century, and named after Lubyanitsa Street in their own town.

The square has changed a lot over the years. In the 1930s the old walls of Kitai Gorod were pulled down to widen it. In 1946 the Church of Our Lady of Grebniev, which stood on the corner of Kirov Street, was pulled down and in the 1970s the square was further enlarged and the old buildings around the Polytechnic Museum demolished. Dzerzhinsky's statue stands on the site of the old drinking fountain for horses.

The large building that faces Serov Passage and New Square is **Dyetsky Mir** *(Children's World).* It was the first large modern shop to be built in Moscow (in 1957) and sells toys or anything to do with children. It is situated here because, bizarrely, Dzerzhinsky also headed the commission for children's welfare created after the Revolution. Russians adore their children.

Karl Marx Avenue *(Prospect Marxa)*
This is the wide road that descends away from Dzerzhinsky Square towards the Kremlin. Its old name, until 1961, was Theatre Avenue. It is to revert to original names and be divided into three — *Okhotny Ryad* (Hunters' Row), *Mokhovaya* (Mossy St.) and *Theatre Boulevard.* As you descend you will see, left, near an arch in what remains of the old walls of Kitai Gorod, the statue of Ivan Fyodorov, the first Russian printer.

Sverdlov Square *(Ploshad Sverdlova)*
Descending Karl Marx Avenue will bring you into this essentially nineteenth-century square. Formerly Teatralnaya Square, it takes its present name from the first resident of the Central Executive Committee of Soviets.

The square was entirely rebuilt following the fire of 1812. The River Neglinnaya, which used to flow through the square and caused frequent floods, was piped underground. In 1824 the Bolshoi ('Big') Theatre was built on the site of another theatre. Following another fire in 1853 it was rebuilt in its current form, with portico and quadriga. To the right of the Bolshoi is the **Maly ('Little') Theatre** (1821) which specialises in performing comedy and tragedy. The statue outside is of Ostrovsky, the Russian playwright. The façades of the other buildings in this part of the square were built in its likeness. Beyond the Maly, on the corner of Petrovka Street is the 1909 vintage **TSUM** or **Central General Store.**

To the left of the Bolshoi is the Central Children's Theatre, founded in 1921 in a building of 1821.

The Bolshoi can accommodate 2,200 people. It is most famous for ballet performances but the Bolshoi Theatre Company performs opera, choral and orchestral works. With a total of some 900 artistes it is the largest theatrical company in the world.

On the other side of Karl Marx Avenue is a public garden with a granite bust of Marx, sculpted in 1961. The rather more attractive fountain dates to 1835, the work of Vitali.

The distinctive building on the side of Sverdlov Square, the side nearest Dzerzhinsky Square, is one of the oldest hotels in Moscow, the **Metropole.** It was constructed in 1899-1903 in art nouveau style. The ceramic on the pediment is called 'La Princesse Lointaine'

(The Distant Princess) after a drawing by Vrubel. Before the Revolution it was one of the social centres of the city for the privileged classes. Fitzroy Maclean, who was a diplomat in Moscow in the 1930s, remembers overhearing an ageing retainer whisper to a foreign diplomat of pre-Revolutionary vintage: 'I can so well remember your climbing up those candelabras back in 1912, Your Excellency!' (*Holy Russia*, 1978). Following the Revolution the hotel was occupied by the All-Russia Central Executive Comittee headed by Sverdlov. Lenin spoke here many times and it was here that he held talks with the leader of the Mongolian People's Revolutionary Party, Sukhe-Bator. Mongolia was the first country in the world after the USSR to effect a communist revolution.

At the moment the hotel is being modernised in cooperation with a Finnish company.

The view from Sverdlov Square across the old walls to Kitai Gorod reveals the belfry of the Zaikonospassky Monastery, and the green building that used to house the Synod Printing Works.

Revolution Square *(Ploshad Revolutsi)*

The building that dominates the side of Sverdlov Square opposite the Metropole is the Moskva Hotel. Walking past that will take you into Revolution Square, formerly Resurrection Square. It was the scene of many battles between the Red and White Guards in late 1917 and is dominated by the Moskva Hotel. This was built in 1935 and was the first hotel built in Soviet Moscow. It incorporates part of the old Grand Hotel, built in 1879. Until the 1970s it was surrounded by older buildings later cleared away to provide two new wings.

On the Kremlin side of the square, opposite, is the red brick **Lenin Museum** (1890), the former **Duma** or Municipal Council of Moscow. It became a museum in 1938 and its three floors are dedicated to the life and works of Lenin. Many of his personal effects are on display, including the car he used from 1920-2; and there is a reproduction of his study in the Kremlin. It is open between 11.00 and 18.30 and closed on Mondays and the last Tuesday of each month.

On the other side of the square, which is actually just a continuation of Karl Marx Avenue, on the corner of Gorky Street, is the huge 1935 building of **Gosplan (State Planning Committee),** which attempts to control most aspects of state planning in the USSR. Next to it, on the corner of Pushkin Street, is what is now the **House of Trade Unions (Dom Soyuzov).** Built in 1785, it used to be the Nobles Club. The famous 'Column Room', surrounded by white marble columns, is perhaps one of the most elegant rooms in Moscow and is occasionally used for concerts. In 1924 Lenin lay in state there so that the population might pay their respects. In the 1930s it was used for a grimmer purpose: Stalin's State Trials, which continued for four years.

50th Anniversary of the October Revolution Square
(Ploshad Pyatidesyatiletiya Oktyabrya)
This is the large open space adjoining the Moskva Hotel. Before 1967 this was Manezhnaya Square and until 1934-9 was an old district of houses, shops with inns above them and narrow streets. These were demolished to create an open space for pompous parades and demonstrations.

The part of Marx Avenue which passes through the square used to be called **Okhotny Ryad (Game or Hunters Market).** It was here that hunters and fishermen used to bring their catch from the banks of the Moskva and Neglinnaya rivers and trade it for grain and flour.

On the corner of Gorky Street stands the National Hotel, another relic from the immediate pre-Revolutionary era, built in 1903. Lenin stayed here (in room 107) in March 1918 just after the government moved to Moscow from St Petersburg.

The building next to it, built in 1934, houses the headquarters of **Intourist.** It was formerly the American Embassy.

Next to it, on both corners of Herzen Street, is the 'old' University building. Moscow University was founded by Empress Elizabeth in 1755 with the help of the scientist and man of letters Lomonosov, whose name it bears. The building on the Intourist side of Herzen Street, containing the Arts Faculty, the **Anthropological Museum** and the **Zoological Museum,** was completed in 1793 and remodelled in 1812 following the great fire. The statues in the courtyard are of Herzen and Ogarev, two graduates of the university and 'revolutionary democrats'. The building on the other side of Herzen Street is the so-called 'new' University building (new compared with the old one across the road — the newest building is elsewhere). This houses the Faculties of Law and Economics and was completed in 1836. The rotunda on the corner used to be the chapel. The statue in front is of Lomonosov.

It was in front of this building in 1905, in what was then Mokovaya Street, that the Tsarist police fired on the crowd returning from the funeral of the revolutionary Bauman.

On the other side of the square, running the length of it from the corner of Red Square to the Trinity Gate, are the **Alexander Gardens (Alexandrovski Sad).** They were laid out in 1821-4 above the Neglinnaya River, which had been piped underground. At the foot of the Intermediate Arsenal Tower, Bove, who had designed the gardens, created an ornamental grotto, entitled 'Ruins'. The obelisk in the central avenue of the gardens commemorates certain socialist philosophers and revolutionaries — it is the first Soviet monument (actually an Imperial column originally erected in 1913 to mark 300 years of the Romanovs. The Imperial eagle and the names of the Tsars were removed and replaced with the others).

At the Kremlin end of the gardens is the **Eternal Flame** and the **Tomb of the Unknown Soldier.** The tomb had lain originally at the forty-first kilometre of the St Petersburg Highway (the point where the Nazis had been turned back) and was moved here in 1966 to commemorate the twenty-fifth anniversary of the expulsion of the Nazis from Moscow. A little further along is a row of ten blocks under which are urns containing earth from cities that had defended particularly bravely the Motherland during the WW II: Leningrad, Kiev, Minsk, Volgograd, Sevastopol, Odessa, Kerch, Novorossiisk, Tula, and Brest. It has become a tradition for newlyweds to pay their respects at the tomb and to lay flowers as a token of thanks.

On the side of the square nearest the river is the huge former **Manege** or **Riding School.** It was built in 1817 by the Frenchmen Betancourt and Bove, for the exercise of the horses belonging to the Court officers. At 170 m (557 feet) in length, with no intermediate pillar, it was regarded as a miracle of engineering in its time. Tolstoy was supposed to have learnt to ride a bicycle here. For a while, after the Revolution, it was used as a garage for Kremlin cars. It was restored in 1958 to become the **Central Exhibition Hall.**

To Borovitskaya Square

After Herzen you come to Kalinin Avenue. On the near corner is the reception hall where Kalinin (a comrade of Lenin and the first President of the Soviet Union) used to receive visitors. It now houses the reception rooms of the Chairmen of the Praesidium of the Supreme Soviet of the USSR.

On the far corner is the new part of the Lenin Library. This library, one of the largest in the world, has its origins in the elegant building (of oak faced with stucco) next door, the former Pashkov House. This was the work of the architect Bazhenov who built it for the wealthy landowner Pashkov in 1784-6. Then in 1862 it housed the Rumyantsev Museum and Public Library — Rumyantsev was an eminent collector of Russian books and manuscripts. In 1925 it became the **Lenin Library**; Lenin studied here between 1893 and 1897. Between 1928 and 1958 the new buildings on Kalinin Avenue were added. The library contains more than twenty-nine million books in various languages.

At the far end of the Manege there is a passage between it and the next building which is a spur of Kalinin Avenue. It has been cut off by Karl Marx Avenue and would have once been a splendid entrance to the Kremlin through the Trinity Gate. At the end of the building on the far side of this passage, in the nineteenth century mansion where he lived, is the **Kalinin Museum** dedicated to the life of the revolutionary Kalinin. It describes his early life, his participation in the Revolution, and his subsequent political career. Open Tuesdays, Wednesdays and Fridays, from 12.00 to 20.00; Thursdays, Saturdays and Sundays, 10.00 to 18.00; closed Mondays.

Beyond is the river and Borovitskaya Square. This square is named after the Kremlin gate of the same name, the site of the founding of Moscow. In the chronicles of 1493 it is written that Ivan III wished to protect the Kremlin from fire at this point by leaving a large gap between the Kremlin Walls and the residential area beyond the Neglinnaya. This is the origin of Marx Avenue.

A walk along Kalinin Avenue (Prospect Kalinina) and the Arbat

This is a circular walk that takes you along Kalinin Avenue, turns left at the Boulevard Ring and brings you back along the Arbat, one of the most picturesque parts of Moscow. Metro: Bilioteka Lenina.

Formerly Elevation Street (Vozdvizhenka Street), Kalinin Avenue begins across the road from the Troitskaya (Trinity) Gate of the Kremlin and continues to the west across the river, becoming Kutuzov Avenue, part of the route to Minsk. Because of the universally disliked modernisation of much of the avenue, Muscovites refer to Kalinin Avenue as 'the artificial jaw of Moscow'. It is named in honour of the revolutionary Kalinin.

The first part of Kalinin Avenue is one of the oldest streets of Moscow, for here lay the thirteenth-century road to Great Novgorod and later to Smolensk.

Beyond the **Lenin Library**, at number 5, is a town house built in 1787 by Kazakov for the landowner Talizin. It was rebuilt after the fire of 1812, although the staircase and frescos remained. It was later occupied by the hetman Kazumovsky and between 1920 and 1924 housed the Secretariat of the Central Committee of the Bolshevik Party. Since 1949 it has been the **Shchussev Museum of Soviet Architecture** (open from 11.00 to 19.00 every day except Mondays and Fridays). It contains models and photographs of past and present Soviet architecture and of reconstruction programmes in Moscow and throughout the country. This house was described by Tolstoy in *War and Peace* as belonging to Pierre Bezukhov. In the same work number 9 is described as the Volkonsky house — in fact at the beginning of the nineteenth century it did belong to Prince Volkonsky who was Tolstoy's grandfather. Today it is the headquarters of the Cabinet State Committee for Cultural Relations with Foreign Countries.

The enormous modern building that dominates this side of the street is a ministry and metro station.

The first building on the right, number 4, built in 1900, was Kalinin's reception room. It was also the home of Gorky (the revolutionary writer) in 1905, from where he took part in the insurrection of that year.

Number 6 was built in 1778. At the turn of this century it housed the Hunters' Club until after the Revolution when it became the Academy of the General Staff of the Red Army. Now it is a branch of GUM. Apart from an interestingly decorative ground floor, the shop is reasonably good for sports equipment and is particularly interesting on the top floor where military paraphernalia is sold. (Lavatories if needed.) There is a watch shop next door and a booth selling T-shirts on the corner.

Number 8 was built in 1780 and was the home of Praskoya Zhemchugova-Kovaleva, the serf-actress and wife of Count Sheremetyev (after whom the airport is named and whose former estate is at Ostankino).

Number 10 was the home of Bela Kun from 1923 to 1937. He was head of the short-lived communist government in Hungary of 1919, and was the mentor of the communist movement in Romania. The bronze monument to Kalinin is of 1978.

Number 14 dates back to the beginning of the twentieth century, when it belonged to a member of the Morozov family, the leading textile manufacturer of the time in Russia, and liberal intellectuals to boot. It now houses the Union of the Soviet Societies for Friendship and Cultural Relations with Foreign Countries. The neighbouring building, number 16, is now the **House of Friendship with Foreign Countries.** This was built in the nineteenth century, also for Morozov, in Portuguese-Moorish style. The Morozovs were an interesting family. In 1812 they were serfs; by 1880 they were Russia's leading industrialists. The first of them got on by exploiting his wife's skill at dyeing fabric — following the great fire of 1812 and the consequent lack of shops, he brought the cloth produced by her from his village to the city. By 1820 he had made enough money to buy his freedom and by the 1850s he was employing one thousand workers in his own cotton mill. His youngest son Timofei made the business into the biggest in Russia. Timofei's son Savva became a social democrat and a patron of the arts. It was he who provided the backing for Stanislavsky's Moscow Art Theatre and who also was in charge of the lighting for it. His house became a giant laboratory for theatrical lighting experiments. In 1905 he shot himself because, it is said, of opposition from his mother to a scheme to introduce profit sharing in the business. Others say it was because of the extreme direction his revolutionary friends were taking.

Soon you will come to the Boulevards ring. At this point Kalinin Avenue becomes, for the most part, severely modern, dominated by two rows of visually uninteresting buildings. (On your left, obvious from the lamps, and going away at an angle, is Arbat Street, along which you will return.)

Keep right of Kalinin and cross the ring road. The first building, right, is a post office. Across the road, at 13, 15 and 17, is what is left of old Kalinin this side of the ring road. They give some indication of what used to front lots of little streets and lanes between Kalinin and Arbat. They have been replaced by four 26-storey office blocks linked by a two- storey construction containing a food shop, a cafe and cinema, and at the end **Arbat** restaurant, the largest in the city. It is comparatively easy to get into but does not rejoice in a good reputation.

A diversion

On your right meanwhile, you come to Ul. Vorovskovo and a church on its corner — this is the seventeenth-century Church of the Stylite, which now houses the the **Exhibition Hall of the Municipal Society for Nature Protection.** You may wish to wander along Ul. Vorovskovo, and some of the streets between it and Gorky Street. Ul. Vorovskovo's former name was Povarskaya Street (Cooks Street) and there are examples of architecture covering 300 years of Russian history. In the first section there are a number of houses built at the turn of the century when detached villas with ornamental mouldings, in the art nouveau style, were fashionable. At number 25, in a town house built between 1817 and 1819 for Prince Gagarin, is the **Maxim Gorky Literary Museum,** which contains first editions, his manuscripts and some paintings by Soviet artists (his house- museum is in nearby Ul. Kachalova). Gorky is considered one of the great revolutionary Soviet writers. Moscow of the early twentieth century was portrayed in his four volume *The Life of Klim Samgin;* he was a playwright *(The Lower Depths)* and an organiser of the USSR Writer's Union. Curiously, he was a friend of Tolstoy, who admired some of Gorky's writing, although he hated Marxism.

Part of number 30/36 is the original nineteenth century building of **Gnesins Musical and Educational Institute** (the Gnesins were well known patrons of culture). Number 31, also nineteenth century, houses the **Institute of Folk Art.** At number 33, built in 1931-4, is the **Film Actor Studio Theatre,** where film actors are able to learn stagecraft. Number 48 was the home of the French writer Alexander Dumas during a visit to Russia and the large classical building with garden and statue of Tolstoy at the corner of the street, at 52, is the Writers' Union. Boris Pasternak (author of *Doctor Zhivago* amongst others, and a Nobel Prize winner) was denounced here in the 1950s, although he has since been rehabilitated. The house itself was built for Prince Dolgoruki in 1802 and was the model for the Rostov house in *War and Peace* (consent having been obtained by Tolstoy from the Dolgoruki family). It is recorded that in 1914 44 of the 54 buildings on Vorovsky Street were owned by aristocratic families.

Herzen Street (Ul. Gertsena, formerly Bolshaya Nikitskaya) runs more or less parallel with Vorovsky Street, and was the old road to Novgorod and part of the late medieval 'cooks' area — some of the street names (Stolovy meaning dining table, Khlebny meaning bread) testify to this. In the eighteenth century the area became more aristocratic and was the site of several estates.

Number 12 is a fine example of eighteenth century Moscow classicism. At number 13 is the **Moscow State Conservatoire,** where Tchaikovsky taught and where Rachmaninov, Scriabin and Kachaturian were all pupils. It is here that the International Tchaikovsky Competition is held. Opposite is the **Church of the Lesser Ascension** (eighteenth century). Number 18 is the Mayakovsky Theatre, founded in 1922 and one of the first Soviet theatres. Opposite, on the corner of Stanislavsky Street (Ul. Stanislavskovo), is the former residence of Major-General

Pozdiakov, where the Theatre-Français performed during the Napoleonic occupation.

On Stanislavsky Street itself, at number 7, is the **Museum of Folk Art** (open 11.00 to 17.00, except Tuesdays and Thursdays when the hours are 14.00 to 20.00, closed Mondays), which contains examples of ornamental household utensils, traditional folk costumes, embroidery, miniature painting, toys and carving. Number 23, now a cinema, was the meeting place in the 1830s of Herzen, the revolutionary thinker after whom the street is named, and his friends. Opposite is the TASS (News Agency of the USSR) building.

Nikitskiye Gates Square (Ploshad Nikitskiye Vorota) boasts two churches: the early nineteenth century **Church of the Greater Ascension,** where the poet Pushkin married Natalia Goncharova in 1831, and the squat **Church of St Theodore the Studious** of the seventeenth century. Herzen Street between here and the Sadovoye Ring is filled with the houses that were part of the mansions of the late-eighteenth and nineteenth century. Number 46 is a good example. Number 44, in Imperial style, once belonged to the Goncharovs. Number 53 is the Central Writers' Club.

Many of the small streets that run off Herzen Street (Sobinovsky, Lower Kislovsky, Kalashny and others) are most evocative of nineteenth century Moscow, with their wooden houses faced in stucco.

Kachalov Street (Ul. Kachalova, formerly Nikitskaya) runs off Nikitskiye Gates Square, parallel with the Sadovaya Ring end of Herzen Street. Number 6 is where Gorky lived and is a branch of the **Gorky Museum.** Number 12 is a state publishing organisation housed in a late-eighteenth century mansion built for Prince Naryshkin. Pushkin was a frequent visitor and wrote his *Stanzas* here. There are several stucco-fronted wooden houses in this street.

Two other streets worth exploring for their period charm are Alexis Tolstoy Street (Ul. Alexeiya Tolstovo, formerly Spiridonievsky Street) for its wooden houses; and Shchussev Street (Ul. Shchooseva, formerly Pomegranate Street). Close to here, near the Sadovaya Ring, is Vspolny Pereulok, with its array of restored wooden houses.

Back to Kalinin Avenue

Ahead on the right, beyond the church, are five 24-storey blocks of flats with shops and cafes on their lower floors, some of which are worth looking at.

In the first block there is a jewellers (two floors). Although the designs lack imagination, you may find the occasional prize and you can pay in roubles. Next is the largest bookshop in the city **Dom Knigi (House of Books),** where you can buy foreign literature, Russian literature in Russian and in other languages (limited supplies), second-hand books, posters and maps. A small section on the ground floor, with a separate entrance, is a foreign currency shop, where you can buy souvenirs, mostly American novels, magazines such as *Newsweek,* American newspapers and *Information Moscow,* the quarterly publication that contrives to give up to date information about the city. It is, for at least US $18, rather expensive.

In the next block there is a pleasant cafe (**Ivushka,** meaning 'little willow tree'). Beyond is a chemist, and beyond that **Melodya,** the main record shop in the city. Here you may find some bargains. The selection, these days, is surprisingly wide.

At the end, Kalinin Avenue meets the Sadovaya Ring and beyond it the river. Between the ring road and the river are two striking modern buildings. The nearest, upright like an open book, is the **CMEA** (Council for Mutual Economic Assistance or Comecon) building. This is the organisation for economic assistance between socialist countries. The lower, white building beyond is the **House of Soviets of the RSFSR** (the Russian Federation or the Republic of Russia, the largest republic in the Soviet Union), the central offices of the Presidium of the Supreme Soviet of the RSFSR. The river is crossed by the **Kalinin Bridge** built in 1957. Beyond it is the 168 m (550 ft) high **Ukraine Hotel,** one of seven Empire State lookalikes built by Stalin in the early 1950s.

The 'Stalin Empire Building'. The Ukraine Hotel, Moscow is a typical legacy of the Stalin years, grandiose in design but hopelessly impractical (photo: Jim Helme).

West of the river

Beyond the bridge Kalinin Avenue becomes Kutuzov Avenue, built between the 1930s and 1960s and named after the Russian General who defeated Napoleon. On this road you will pass two striking monuments: a silver-grey granite column crowned with a golden star, to commemorate the ending of WW II; and the **Triumphal Arch,** built to celebrate the ending of the Napoleonic War. (The original, of 1817, stood at the end of Gorky Street, at the Tver Gate, and was of wood, replaced in 1827 and 1834 by stone; moved here in 1968).

To the Arbat

By turning left at the end of Kalinin and walking along the Sadovoya Ring you will soon come to Smolensk Square, where the Smolensk Gate used to stand as part of the outer wall of the city, and which was a market place until the early twentieth century. To your left is Arbat Street, a pedestrian precinct. Ahead is another skyscraper, built in 1951, and the first of the seven that ring the city. This one is the **Ministry of Foreign Affairs.** To your right are the twin towers of the Belgrade Hotel and beyond them the Borodino bridge built in 1912 to commemorate the 100th anniversary of the Battle of Borodino.

Arbat Street (Ul. Arbat), left turn, is one of the oldest streets in Moscow. Its name probably comes from the Arab word *orbat,* meaning suburb and in the reign of Ivan the Terrible much of the court resided here. The end nearest the Sadovaya Ring was a settlement of icon-painters. During the eighteenth century much of the area became fashionably aristocratic, so much so that by the time of Paul I it became *the* place for noblemen when they tired of St Petersburg. It had to be rebuilt following the great fire of 1812 and many of the buildings represent the finest in late classicism, the so called Moscow Empire style. With the emancipation of the serfs and the decline of the nobility many buildings became the houses of the professional classes. In the 1880s there was still a rural flavour, with cattle grazing the streets, but by the end of the nineteenth century new apartment blocks began to alter the flavour of the area. Nevertheless its local commercial character has to a certain extent survived to this day. Many celebrated Russians lived on or near this street (it was known as the Moscow 'St Germain'); and it was along here that the Napoleonic army entered Moscow in 1812. In recent years Arbat Street has been restored and turned into a pedestrian precinct, popular among artists, who like to sell their work here.

As you enter Arbat Street, with the skyscraper on your right, there is a food shop on the corner, called **Smolenski**. This one differs from many in that it has a takeaway pizza service. Next to it is a kiosk outside a cafe **Russki Pelmeni**, which specialises in *pelmeni*, meat dumplings in broth, a dish that may well have its origins in the Mongolian steppeland. The first lane on the left is **Pereulok Troilniski** — a brief look here will lead you to an art gallery (entrance fee of a few kopeks) with pictures for sale by contemporary artists, as well as crafts and jewellery, for roubles.

The first lane on the right of Arbat Street is Ul. Vyesnina. Towards the far end of the street is the Italian Embassy and opposite it a **bookshop** which deals in foreign currency. Before, there are some fine examples of early Moscow architecture, not very grand but highly attractive with an almost rural flavour. Number 5 used to house the German Embassy immediately following the Revolution and number 9 is a wooden house dating back to 1822 when it was built for one Polivanov, a participant in the victory over the French in 1812. Number 12 belonged to the theatre director Vachtangov (whose theatre is further up Arbat Street) and to the architect Vyesnin, after whom this street is named.

As you enter Vyesnina Street, the first street on the left is Sievtsev Vrazhen Per., part of which formerly belonged to the Tsarina. Number 13 is an interesting forerunner of modern architecture, built in 1913 in art nouveau style. Number 19 was the house of the poetess Marina Svietayeva while 27 is a nineteenth-century stone mansion in Empire style that belonged to the writer and thinker Alexander Herzen. He was the illegitimate son of a wealthy man but managed to have himself expelled from France for supporting the Revolution of 1848. He was a gifted writer, dedicated to the cause of the oppressed, whose prose is highly considered. In London he founded an anti-establishment newspaper, *The Bell (Kolokol),* which became an important political force in Russia. The fact that it was prohibited did not prevent government ministers and the Tsar himself from reading it. He died in exile in 1870. This house, where he lived with his family between 1843 and 1846 and which was frequently visited by the writer Turgenev and others, is now the **Herzen Museum** (open 11.00-19.00 except Wednesdays and Fridays 14.00-21.00; closed Mondays and last day of month). Number 36 is the house where Tolstoy began his career and the church along here is the Church of the Apostle Philip built in 1688.

Back on Arbat Street the pale blue house in Empire style at 53 was the first home of the poet Pushkin and his wife following their marriage in 1931 and where he held his stag night. It is now the **Pushkin Flat Museum** dedicated to his life, the entrance to which is through the arch further to the right. Number 51, built in 1911, is where the poet Alexander Blok stayed in 1920 during his last visit to Moscow.

Left, at 44, is a basement video bar and cafe and on the right a small restaurant **Arbatskoe Bistro.** At 42, a low building in pretty traditional style, is the Georgian Club, which sells handicrafts from Georgia and which has a cafe serving Georgian specialities.

Plotnikov Lane is on the right. Number 4 bears a frieze with images of the writers Gogol, Pushkin and Tolstoy (because of his excommunication, this is the only pre-Revolutionary sculptured image of Tolstoy in Moscow). The first left off Plotnikov is **Krivoarbatsky Per.** ('Crooked Arbat Lane' and the old carpenters' settlement) where, at number 10, is a real curiosity. This is the futuristic house of the architect Melnikov. Built in 1927, it consists of two interlocking cylinders (he thought that a cylinder was the most perfectly spacious living area) built of brick covered in stucco, punctured with 60 hexagonal windows. On the front facade are the words 'Konstantin Melnikov Arkihitektor'. He was the darling of the avant-garde after the Revolution, but Stalinist denunciations barred him from continuing his work. He was still living here in the early 1970s. Now his house is being restored.

Further along Plotnikov Lane, on the left is Ul. Ryleva. Rylev was one of the Decembrists (see History section). The street was formerly Gagarinsky Lane and it was here that many of the court horses were stabled. At number 11 there is a building with unusual decor dating to 1895 and at number 15 a 'pearl' of Moscow Empire style, built in 1815 on the stone base of a house destroyed during the fire of 1812. In 1830 it was used by Turgenev's uncle Nikola and then by Schteingel, one of the Decembrists. Until 1913 it was in the hands of the Lopotin family, noted lawyers and philosophers.

Chertolsky Lane runs off Rylev Lane to the right — here is the oldest building in the area, a seventeenth century stone chamber with high basement, next to a school with a monument to the war dead.

Continuing along Arbat Street you will meet **Spasopeskovsky Per.** on the left, notable for the seventeenth century church (now something to do with the making of cartoons) of the same name ('Our Saviour in Peski'). Beyond it to the right, across the garden, is the residence of the American ambassador. This street is depicted in a painting called *A Moscow side street* by Polenev, in the Tretyakov Gallery.

41 Arbat is a **photographic shop** capable of developing western film (e.g. Kodak and Fuji) and also of making imprints from slides, for roubles. On the left there is quite a good souvenir shop — it sells jewellery, leather, laquerware, samovars and Matryushka dolls. There is also a kiosk inside that sells tickets for theatrical and sporting events. Beyond this shop there is another selling second hand books and a workshop that will make jewellery for customers who provide the raw materials. Number 35 was built in 1913 and is an early example of purpose-built flats. On the right is a specialist jewellery shop, one of the best in Moscow.

On the left is Ul. Vakhtangova (with public lavatories). At number 11 of that street is the **Scriabin Flat Museum** (open 10.00 to 18.00, closed Mondays, Tuesdays and the last day of the month), the former home of the great composer, which was opened as a museum in 1922. At 12a is the **Shchukin** (a famous actor) **Drama School and Opera Studio** of the Moscow Conservatoire.

Back on Arbat Street, at number 26, is the **Vakhtangov Theatre,** complete with colonnaded portico, named after the director who founded it in 1921. Number 31 Arbat is a lace embroidery shop and 29 a new co-operative cafe, the **White Horse Bistro.** At number 27 there is a plaque in memory of the Russian sculptor Andreyev, the man behind the basic study of Lenin that decorates squares all over the country. Number 25 is another claimant for the oldest pharmacy in Moscow which used, in the late-nineteenth century, to offer a discount to the poor. On the left at 22 is a cafe that sells *bubliki,* dough rings, delicious when well made. Number 20 is the **State Insurance Inspectorate.** On your right you then come to **Starukenusheny Per.** ('Old stables lane'). The striking lacy green wooden house down on the left dates to 1872, and a model of it won a prize at the International Exhibition in Paris. It came to represent, in international circles, the 'Russian' style. Now it is a **military museum.** Number 6 Arbat is called **Art** and as well as selling crafts it sells traditional samovars. Opposite is the **Ukrainian bookshop.** Number 4 deals in perfume and next door is the most famous poster shop in Moscow.

On your right is Ul. Myaskovskova, named after the composer. Number 8 was the meeting place of the Stankevich literary and philosophical circle during the 1830s, mentioned by Turgenev in his book *Rudin.* Number 12 was the home of Aksakov, the nineteenth-century writer and friend of Gogol.

On the corner of Arbat is the **Praga** (Prague) restaurant, specialising in Czech cuisine. It was built at the beginning of the century in Edwardian style and rebuilt in 1955 because of war damage. It is still considered one of the grandest restaurants in the city, retaining some splendid private rooms, so worth looking.

As you look across Arbat Square to the right, on the corner of Frunze Street stands an imposing building built in 1792 which acted as a theatre following the fire of 1812 when so many of the wooden theatres were destroyed. In the late-nineteenth century it became the Alexander Military School and during the Revolution it became the seat of 'counter revolution'. In the civil war that followed it became the headquarters of the Revolutionary Military Council of the Russian Republic.

A walk along Gorky Street (Ulitsa Gorkovo)

Gorky Street (formerly Tver Street and to revert to Tverskaya Street) used to be part of the main trading road to Tver (modern Kalinin). It was here that Muscovites built their first wooden houses. By the seventeenth century it was the whitestone street along which the Moscow rulers made their official entrances to Moscow. After St Petersburg became the capital it became part of the main route across the Empire. In the nineteenth century the road was widened to 18 m (59 feet). In the late 1930s it was widened still further to its present width of between 36 m (118 ft) and 41 m (135 ft). During the works the building in the courtyard of number 6, a block of flats weighing 23,368 mt (23000 tons), was moved overnight a distance of 49 m (160 ft). In art nouveau style, it resembles the Metropole Hotel on Sverdlov Square. Gorky Street is 3 km (1.9 miles) long.

Now Gorky Street is thought of as one of Moscow's principal shopping streets, although the shops are on the whole pretty dire. However, improvements are being made and the street is becoming livelier, if only because of the arrival of American fast food restaurants. Start on the right-hand side.

The **National Hotel** on the left corner of Gorky and Marx Avenue is discussed elsewhere.

Number 3, next door, is the **Intourist Hotel** built in 1971. This is, however, a convenient place for snacks, either from one of the kiosks outside, or from one of the restaurants inside. Between the National and Intourist is the largest Intourist service bureau in the city, for the purchase of tickets for foreign currency. On the other corner, at number 2, are the offices of Gosplan, the state financial planning committee, and at number 4 is one of the Stalinist buildings, complete with decorative sheaves of wheat and pillars in the upper storey, that marked the limits of the street when it was widened. The ground floor is taken up with shops, notable among which is the new **Christian Dior** shop where the French company's products may be bought for roubles. The **Kosmos** cafe is popular for its ice-cream.

The high arch in the middle of the building is also the entrance to Georgievsky Per. This is a short street, connecting Gorky Street with Ul. Pushkinska, but conceals, at the far end, behind a gate in the courtyard of Gosplan, an exceptionally fine example of seventeenth-century Russian architecture — the red **Chambers of the Boyars Troyekurov.** At the time wealthy Boyars liked to build their own palaces rivalling in beauty the old buildings in the Kremlin. Troyekurov was a commander of the Moscow military corps and built the palace for his family. Unfortunately it may only be viewed from outside the gate but is worth this short detour. Opposite it, on the left of Georgievski Per., is Moscow's first and rather modest **power station,** opened in 1881.

Beyond is Ul. Pushkinska. Number 6 of that street, a former mansion, now houses **Moscow Operetta Theatre.** Before the Revolution it had been a private opera house where Chaliapin, one of the greatest of opera singers, made his debut, and where Rachmaninov was a conductor.

At 5 Gorky Street, left, is the **Yermolova Theatre,** with its cafe, founded in 1937. It presents mostly modern plays. At this point it is worth turning back to look at the Kremlin, a splendid sight - it takes only a little imagination to visualise Tver Street as it was in its heyday.

The second street, left, is Ul. Ogareva. On the near corner is the **Central Telegraph Office** (1927), one of the first civic buildings of Soviet Moscow. Its art deco influences, with the obelisks in front and the railings at the top, are very clear. Looking down Ul. Ogarevayou you will see, right, at number 15, a former church, now a telephone office. On the corner of Gorky Street opposite the Central Telegraph Office is a branch of GUM. Both this and the building beyond were built in 1949. The second of them houses the State Committee for Science and Technology — the granite that faces its base came from Germany and was to be used, so it is said, for Hitler's victory monument on the capture of Moscow. In the middle of this building an arch on thick pillars leads to Ul. Nezhdanova, where many of the USSR's most prominent figures from the cultural world have lived. Number 8/10 is the **House of**

Composers where, in flat 23, the composer Shostakovich lived from 1962 until his death in 1975. Antonina Nezhdanova, the great Russian singer, after whom this street is named, lived at number 7, as did a former conductor of the Bolshoi, Golovanov. Famous actors from the Moscow Arts Theatre lived at number 17, and number 12 was the home of the eminent director Meyerhold. Down here too is a charming functioning church, most beautiful on a winter's night when the candles are burning in the windows.

On the other side of Gorky Street is **Khudozhestvennovo Teatr Proezd,** the home of one of the most respected theatres in the world, the **Moscow Arts Theatre.** It was founded in 1898, with Chekhov's seagull as its emblem, by Konstantin Stanislavsky and Vladimir Nemiro-Danchenko, after a discussion over dinner in the Slavyansky Bazaar restaurant. It was essentially an experimental theatre at first, but came to overturn the established acting norms and set an example followed the world over, not least in the West. Actors were expected to express themselves from their inner emotions, based on their own experience. Stage settings were made as real as possible; absolute concentration was required of the audience so that the special effects could be appreciated. It was said of Stanislavsky that he even bred crickets on his estate specifically to be used on stage when called for.

Following Gorky Street once again you will come to **Soviet Square,** with the statue of Yuri Dolguruki, the founder of Moscow, at its centre. This was sculpted in 1947 in honour of Moscow's eighth centenary. Behind it is the **Central Party Archive of the Institute of Marxism/Leninism** and on the right one of the best known of Moscow's restaurants, the **Aragvi,** which specialises in Georgian cooking. It stands at the beginning of Stoleshnikov Lane on which there is a good cafe at number 6 and one of the infamous beer cellars on its corner with Pushkin Street.

The building that dominates Soviet Square on the left of Gorky Street is the building of the Moscow City Soviet (Municipal Government) which was built between 1782-4 from bricks that had been taken from the old Bely Gorod wall, which stood where the Boulevards Ring is now. It became the three storey residence of Moscow's governor-general. Ten years later a parade ground was added in front — hence the square — and in 1938 the whole building was moved back and two more storeys added. A remarkable aspect of the proceedings within, and rather typical of the country in general, concerns the omnipresent Lenin. Following his death, Lenin was made a permanent deputy of the Moscow

Soviet and each time it holds a meeting, the deputy card number 1 is used in his name.

Gorky Street between here and Pushkin Square is mostly shops. On the right is the **Moskva bookshop,** in a building that was the former home of several prominent Soviet writers, including Ilya Ehrenburg. Opposite, on the left, is the **Druzhba (Friendship) bookshop,** which deals in literature from socialist (or formerly socialist) countries. You may find some interesting items in English. Beyond, on the left, is a shop selling crystal and glass, then cafe **Sever** and, at number 17, the former home of the sculpter Konenkov, whose memorial the **Konenkov Museum and Studio** (open 11.00-19.00, closed Mondays and Tuesdays) is clearly visible from Pushkin Square. It contains much of his work, including his bird-shaped armchair and his tree-stump armchairs. The former flat of the pianist Alexander Goldenweiser is also in this building. On the right of Gorky Street you come to Nemiro-Danchenko Street where at number 6 (the former Sever Hotel, later named 'Anglia' or 'England') the national poet, Pushkin, frequently stayed between 1828 and 1832 on his return from exile. Today this building houses the Soviet Women's Committee.

Number 10 Gorky Street is the **Tsentralnaya Hotel,** mostly used in the past by visiting delegations from socialist countries. There is also a **bakery** in the ground floor of this building which dates back more than one hundred years. Before the Revolution it was famous as Filippov's bakery. After this you will pass a jewellers and the new **Pizza Hut.** The attractive pink building at 14 was refurbished in 1875 but was occupied in the 1820s by Princess Volkonskaya, whose literary salon was regularly attended by the likes of Pushkin. The Princess ended her life in Siberia where she joined her exiled Decembrist husband. Her house was later converted into a luxurious foodstore, known before 1917 as the Eliseyev Grocery Store. It remains a food store, and although it is definitely worth looking in for the overpowering decor, do not expect to find much to eat there.

Pushkin Square is part of the Boulevards Ring. It was first laid out in 1780 on the place where the **Tver Gates Tower,** part of the defensive wall known as the **Bely Gorod,** had stood and where the roads to Tver and Dmitrov met. It was then called Strastnaya Square after a nearby convent (destroyed in 1930) and became a favourite place of recreation for the nobility as the city limit, previously marked by Bely Gorod, moved farther out. The monument to Pushkin was erected in 1880 at the end of Tver Boulevard, and moved here when the square was enlarged and a garden added in 1949. On the pedestal are lines from his poem *Monument:*

> And long the people yet will honour me
> Because my lyre was tuned to loving-kindness
> And, in a cruel Age, I sang of Liberty
> And mercy begged of Justice in her blindness.

On the left hand corner of Gorky Street, where it meets Pushkin Square, is the shop **Armenia,** which sells food from that republic, and where you are usually able to obtain Armenian brandy, which is very good, for roubles. Next to it is the aforementioned **studio-museum of Konenkov,** and beside it a good cafe. Opposite these is the largest **McDonald's** hamburger restaurant in the world. Also on the far side of the square, to the right, is the modern building that houses several major newspapers: *Investia, Trud* and *Moscow News.* A little way to its right is Ul. Chekova and at its beginning is the seventeenth-century **Church of the Nativity of the Virgin** in Putinki, built at the beginning of the old Dmitrov Road. It is built in the period monumental style and a particularly fine example of a pavilion or tent-roofed church. Number 6, dating to 1906, was the former **Merchants Club.**

The section of Gorky Street beyond Pushkin Square and as far as Mayakovsky Square, is shorter than the first part. It adjoins, on the left, the old **Armourers (Brunaya) district.** On the right, just beyond the newspaper building, is **Nastasinski Passage,** where there is an ornate pre-Revolutionary building marked 'Zdaniye Ssudnoi Kazney'. These were the money vaults of Moscow and judging by the armoured cars in the vicinity, still are.

The rest of the right hand side of Gorky Street as far as Mayakovsky Square is not very interesting — there is the **Minsk Hotel** of 1964, and the **Baku** restaurant which specialises in Azerbaijani dishes. For those interested in buying flowers or fishing tackle, you can do so at number 44.

The left hand side is of more interest. Number 21 was the **Razumovsky Palace** built in 1787, rebuilt in 1824, becoming the English Club in 1831. Now, inappropriately, it is the **Central Museum of the Revolution** (open 10.00-18.00 except Tuesdays and Fridays 11.00-19.00, closed Mondays and 31st of the month) which sets out with the help of documents, paintings, weapons and banners the history of 'the world's first socialist state'. The stone 'lions at the gates' were mentioned by Pushkin in his poem *Eugene Onegin,* as he describes the arrival of the heroine, Tatyana, in Moscow.

Number 23 the **Stanislavsky Drama Theatre** founded in 1935 as a studio for operatic and dramatic art; also a cafe and patisserie. Sadovskys Lane is worth a look for its prettily restored flats. Next to it at 25 is the **Exhibition Hall of the Union of Artists.** A little further at is **Pinguin,** a Soviet-Swedish venture, specialising in high quality ice cream. Beyond it there is a **souvenir shop** with a reasonable selection of articles and a promising looking bar. Next on the left is Blagoveshenski Per. — down it, past three junctions, on the left on the edge of Ul. Malaya Brunaya is the site of the former **Patriarch's Pond,** now a large pool in a square.

Gorky Street meets the Garden Ring at Pl. Mayakovskovo, named after the adored Soviet poet whose statue is found in the middle. Vladimir Mayakovski, born in Georgia, was the most famous of the radical group of artists and poets that, from about 1910, were known as the Futurists. He attempted poetic renditions of Cubist and neo-Primitive painting and in 1912 contributed two poems to the Futurist manifesto *A Slap in the Face of Public Taste.* He and his colleagues wandered the streets in outrageous clothes and declaimed his poetry in the cabarets 'with his flamboyant personal declaiming style, his tremendous feeling for rhythm, his brutal but effective use of slang and dizzying stylistic originality' (S. Massie, *Land of the Firebird).* The **statue of Mayakovski,** reading his poetry in a more sober manner, was unveiled in 1958.

Most buildings around the square date from either just before or just after WW II. On the right is the *Sofia* restaurant. On the near side of the square on the left is the **Tchaikovsky Concert Hall** and next to it the **Moscow Satire Theatre.** On the left is the **Peking Hotel,** built in 1951, which houses a much improved Chinese restaurant. An interesting literary phenomenon will be found by turning left out of Gorky Street, continuing along the Garden Ring to an arch in a white building (left), and going through into the courtyard to the second door on the left. Here the walls are covered in graffiti by lovers of Bulgarkov's book *Master and Margaret,* which was set in this building.

The end of the street

Gorky Street beyond Mayakovsky Square used to be called Tverskaya-Yamskaya. Most of the buildings are late-nineteenth or early-twentieth century and are tenement flats. Some smaller streets on either side of Gorky Street are more attractive. At its end is **Belorussia railway station** and **Belorussia Square,** on the site of the other set of Tver Gates (built to honour Russian troops returning from the Nápoleonic Wars). In 1870 Moscow was linked with Smolensk by rail and the square assumed a new importance. The present station was built in 1909 and 1912 in 'old Russian' style. It serves the west of the country and parts of Europe. The square itself was used to welcome Chkalov and Gromov when they completed a non-stop flight from the USSR to the United States over the North Pole in 1937. The **bronze statue** in the middle is of the writer Gorky.

Behind the KGB

Marx Avenue and Dzerzhinsky Square are lined by a wall of awesome institutional buildings that lead one to forget the streets behind. Some of them still retain a little of their pre-Revolutionary bustle.

The suggested walk covers Kuznetski Most, Petrovka and Razhdest Venka streets. Nearest metro, Kuznetski Most in Razhdest Venka.

Turn right from the metro station: the first junction is **Kuznetski Most (Blacksmiths Bridge).** Further to the right is Dzerzhinsky Street, once known as Blacksmith's Hill, where cannons and bells were made at the nearby **Cannon Foundry (Pushechny Dvor);** left Kuznetski Most used to cross the Neglinnaya River by bridge — hence its name. In the eighteenth century Catherine the Great decreed that trading no longer need be restricted to the trading rows in Kitai Gorod and many luxurious shops sprang up along Kuznetski Most. Although today's shops hardly warrant that description, a certain bustle prevails.

Just before Dzerzhinsky Street is Pl. Vorovskovo — number 21 was the Ministry of Foreign Affairs until 1953 and before that it housed the Russian Insurance Company. The statue is of Vorovsky, an early Soviet diplomat to Italy killed by 'counter-revolutionary agents', or a White Guard, in Lausanne in 1923.

Diversion

Some distance up Dzerzhinsky Street you will find at number 14 the baroque late-eighteenth century former residence of a Governor-General of Moscow, Count Rostopshin. Legend has it that it was he who ordered the burning of Moscow in 1812. One of the scenes in *War and Peace* takes place outside here. At the end of the street at number 19 are the remains of the seventeenth-century **Sretensky Monastery.**

Back to Kuznetski

Left of the junction with Razhdest Venka you will meet, left, the **House of Fashion** which moved here during the war. This street is often associated with books, and there is a **foreign language bookshop** further down on the left, outside which private sellers frequently tout editions that are hard to find. Opposite is the **Moscow Artists Club** and next to that **ATLAS,** specialising in maps. Where Kuznetski Most meets Neglinnaya Street there is a new shop, *Rifle,* which sells (for foreign currency) imported jeans and other clothes by the manufacturer of the same name; prices are reasonable.

Two hundred years ago the Neglinnaya river flowed where Ul. Neglinnaya is today. It would have crossed Sverdlov Square, borne right at Kitai Gorod and washed the walls of the Kremlin all the way to the Moskva River at the Bolshoi Kamenny bridge.

However because of frequent flooding it was decided in the eighteenth century to make the river bed part of a canal. In 1819 it was covered over and piped underground. Blacksmith's Bridge became redundant and was dismantled and the neighbouring streets were replanned, and became an important shopping centre in the 19th century. (The river continued to flood occasionally until finally channelled in a conduit directly to the Moskva.)

Number 12 Ul. Neglinnaya is the **State Bank of the USSR** in a

The backstreets of Moscow.

Renaissance style of the 1890s. Next door are the **Sandunovskiye Baths,** also built in the 1890s and luxuriously decorated with moulded ceilings, gilt and marble. Their name comes from a wealthy actor to whom they belonged. They remain in use and the experience of a Russian bath is recommended.

Kuznetski Most continues beyond Neglinnaya Street to Ul. Petrovka. (Kuznetski Most goes on to Arts Theatre Street and so to Gorky Street.) Petrovka Street bustles with shops. Left leads to the Bolshoi and Sverdlov Square, passing **TSUM,** the old department store. Right takes you past two places (on left) where you can get a snack — a **cafe** set back from the street and a kiosk selling *doner kebab* but whose hours are irregular. Opposite these is the old **Petrovsky Arcade,** one of the biggest stores of old Moscow, now part of TSUM. A little further is Stoleshnikov Per. (left) well known for its array of little shops. Number 11, **Stoleshnikov,** is famous for the two nineteenth century stoves that bake what are traditionally considered to be the finest breads and pies in Moscow. There is an interesting **second-hand bookshop** on the left and beyond it a jewellers. At number 9 there is a memorial plaque to Gilyarovsky, considered the 'uncrowned king of reporters', and a well-known commentator on Moscow social life.

Further up Petrovka is **Petrovskiye Linii** (right), a single nineteenth century architectural ensemble which was originally wholly in private hands. Opposite is the **Budapest Hotel.** Next is Rakhmanov Per. (right) which, at number 3, was the site of the old Moscow Labour Exchange. In line with Communist orthodoxy it was closed in 1930 when 'the last unemployed worker in our country has found employment'. Now it is occupied by the **Ministry of Public Health.**

At 15 Petrovska is **Intourtrans** the transportation arm of Intourist, where you may purchase tickets for travel within and without the Soviet Union. Beyond here the shops become fewer and the street takes on an air more reminiscent of an earlier existence when it was simply another road leading to the Kremlin. Before the Neglinnaya was channelled building was only possible on the left side of Petrovska, with one exception — the **Vysoko-Petrovsky Monastery** which stands on a hill close to the Boulevard Ring. Founded in the fourteenth century, it was of wood until Peter the Great rebuilt it in stone in the 1680s. At its centre is the whitestone **Church of Peter the Metropolitan,** built by Tsarina Natalya, Peter's mother; the main church served as a family mausoleum for Peter's maternal ancestors.

Petrovka forks here. To return via Razhdest Venka, turn right along the boulevard until Trubnaya Square. Number 25 on the left fork is one of the finest examples of Russian classicism in the city. It was built for the merchant Gubin in 1790 and now houses the **Institute of Physiotherapy.** A little way along the right fork, **Karietny Riad** (Carriage Street, because of the former coach works), brings you to another most attractive classical building (on the corner of Strasnoi). It was built between 1786 and 1790 for the courtier Gagarin and between 1802 and 1812 it housed the **English Club** (before it moved to Gorky Street). The dinner given in honour of the Russian general Bagration that is described in *War and Peace* took place in one of the rooms here. It is now a hospital. Beyond it is **Hermitage Park,** a delightful corner of Moscow with trees, statues, ponds and a summer theatre.

Pl. Trubnaya was once an animal and flower market. On the corner of Neglinnaya Street is the former **Hermitage Restaurant,** a convivial meeting place for Chekhov, Tchaikovsky, Turgenev and others. Razhdest Venka Street (Street of the Nativity) (right) is its recently-revived old name (replacing Zhdanov, after a Stalinist statesman) and taken from the **convent** a little way on the left. It was founded in 1386, in wood, but the stone cathedral (1501) is among the oldest monuments in Moscow. The rest of the buildings are seventeenth and eighteenth century. Number 11, (1778) is the **Institute of Architecture** which in the 1880s housed the Stroganov School of Fine Art. Eventually you will return to Kuznetski Most Metro Station.

Before finishing it is worth crossing the next street (Pushechnaya, where a cannon foundry was located by the side of the Neglinnaya River until the nineteenth century) to the **Savoy Hotel.** This is its original name from the time of its construction in 1912 when the Salamandra insurance company, having bought the land from Princess Turkestanova, was permitted to build a luxury hotel. In 1959 it was renamed the Berlin. It managed to retain much of its old charm — albeit rather shabbily — until refurbishments were begun with the help of the Finns and its old name restored. The work has been tastefully carried out and the Savoy is once again an elegant hotel.

South of the River — the Zamoskvorechye

Zamoskvorechye means 'beyond the River Moskva'. It is one of the oldest parts of the city and one of the prettiest — in fact it is a protected area. The atmosphere is in marked contrast to much of the rest of Moscow. Most of the area is made up of quiet residential streets lined by houses ranging from the palatial to the more humble. The old-fashioned suburban atmosphere is compounded by the calmness of the back streets — there is no pleasanter place for walking on a crisp winter's day or in the heat of the summer.

It was first mentioned in the fourteenth century, noted for its traders and artisans. It was cut off from the Kremlin by the river, the Kremlin wall, and its own wooden and earth wall, and acquired a separate identity. In the seventeenth century it was also the residential area for the *Streltsy* or Kremlin guards and the place where Tartar peasants from the southern regions brought their livestock to sell. The area was deserted shortly thereafter when Peter the Great disbanded the Kremlin guard. Most of the buildings are eighteenth and nineteenth century, when the area became residential for the bourgeoisie, with a large number of private houses and some elegant churches. The street plan remains mostly unchanged and bears some evocative names. There are three main streets: **Pyatnitskaya** in the east, **Bolshaya Ordynka** in the middle and **Bolshaya Polyanka** in the west.

Tretyakov (orange line) is the nearest metro station, and the walk begins there. (Alternatively, walk across the Bolshoi Moskvoretsky bridge from Red Square and join the walk wherever suitable. The advantage of this is that you can take the steps at the side down to the Maurice Thores Embankment — formerly Sofiiskaya Embankment — which was a milling area in the seventeenth and eighteenth centuries, for the most beautiful view across the river to the Kremlin. Walking further along will bring you to the British Embassy which is housed in a fine old mansion in a spectacular location. In doing so you will pass Falevski Lane — by walking along it and looking back you will have a beautiful and unusual view of the Kremlin.)

From Tretyakov metro station

Emerging from the metro station turn left and then immediately into Ul. Bolshaya Ordynka, which is the principal thoroughfare of the area. The name derives from the time when the road led to the Zolstaya Orda (the Tartar-Mongol Golden Horde). On your right, at 21, is a late eighteenth century mansion which had to be heavily restored following the fire of 1812. It was designed by the same architects responsible for the church further up on the left and belonged to the merchant Dolgov. This is the functioning **Church of the Icon of the Mother of God** 'Consolation of All the Afflicted', of which the belfry and refectory date to 1792, while the classical-style church is later, 1834. The floor is rather unusual — it is made of cast-iron plates. Immediately past the church stands the Laotian Embassy and then on the left the entrance to 3rd Kadashevsky Per., which you take.

This is a quiet residential street, highly evocative of old Moscow with, at its end, a charming, blue, late-eighteenth century mansion with a wooden telephone box before it. Turn right and follow the road to 2nd Kadashevsky Per. (right). A little way down it is the **Church of the Resurrection in Kadashi,** a fine example of late-seventeenth century baroque in red brick with whitestone lintels, portals and colonnade. Traditional details, such as *kokoshniks,* have been replaced by two levels of roof trees in a manner that is without equal in Russian architecture. This area used to form the **Kadashi,** one of the old artisan areas founded in the fifteenth century. Many of them were coopers who made *kadki* (barrels) for the Imperial court. Later the quarter became known for the production of canvas and table cloths.

You will meet Bolshaya Ordynka Street. Turn right and then almost immediately left into Chernigovsky Lane. A little way along is (right) a classical-style **mansion** in stunning pink, recently restored, now a kindergarten. In front of it is a seventeenth century **traditional Russian stone hall,** a rarity in an area which was mostly wooden houses at the time of its construction. Follow the road as it veers left and right, noting the attractive turn-of-the-century block of flats at number 4 (left) and passing a succession of churches: (right) the **Church of St. Michael and St. Theodar Chernikovsky the Miracle Workers** (1697), (left) the **Church of John the Baptist under the Wood** (1514). Next to the latter, on the corner of Ul. Pyatnitskaya, is a two-storey green belfry built in 1758 to accompany the churches behind. The walk continues right. (To see another **seventeenth century stone hall** — restored at 10 Middle Ovchinnikov Lane — take a short diversion left as far as the embankment, then right along it and right again into Middle Ovchinnikov Lane (Sheepskin-tanners' Lane).)

On Pyatnitskaya Street, number 12 has a plaque commemorating the fact that Leo Tolstoy lived there from 1857 to 1858 and wrote his novel *The Cossacks*. If you are hungry for Italian food the **Lasagne** (number 15) is one of the new co-operative restaurants with a very good reputation. Number 18, a mansion in classical Empire style, was built in the 1820s for Demidov, head of a rich mining family from the Urals. Number 31 also belonged to the Demidov family. Number 25 is **Radio Moscow HQ.** On the corner of Klimentovsky Per. is the most striking building on the street, and one of the finest of its kind in the city, the baroque **St Clements Church** built in 1758 by Trezzini. Further down, passing (left) the **Trinity Church in Vishnyaki** (1824-6) is (right) Alexander Ostrovsky Street, into which you turn. (Students of Revolution will not want to miss number 71, which belongs to a printing house founded in the late nineteenth century. Its printers went on strike in 1905 starting a wave of strikes thoughout the country.)

Ul. Alexander Ostrovskovo returns to Tretyakov metro station. It was formerly Malaya Ordynka Street but takes its new name from the great Russian dramatist (1823-86) who lived in the Zamoskvorechye for 20 years — indeed much of his work reflects his experience of living amongst the merchant classes of the area. At number 9 there is a **memorial museum** in the house where he was born.

The end of the street brings you to Klimentovsky Per. with **St Clements** (right) and the Metro station (left). Walk on to Bolshaya Ordynka Street and cross it to an alleyway opposite and slightly to the right. Follow it between the old apartment houses either side until you emerge into a small garden square. On the left, behind some beautiful wrought-iron railings which were made by Ural blacksmiths, is a lovely **mansion** of the late-eighteenth century, yet another that belonged to the Demidov family. It now houses the **Ushinsky Scientific and Pedagogical Library.** The other building, at the end of the square to the right, is the **Tretykov Gallery of Russian Art.**

The Tretyakov Gallery (open 10.00-19.00, closed Mon)

This gallery is devoted exclusively to Russian art and takes its name from one of the great patrons of art in the nineteenth century, Pavel Tretyakov in whose reconstructed house the collection is housed. Pavel and his brother Sergei came from that very merchant class so mercilessly lampooned in the plays of Ostrovsky. Their father, who had run a shop in the Moscow arcades off Red Square, had not been especially wealthy but the sons had made something of the business and while not among the richest classes of Moscow were certainly well off. Both loved art and from an early age Pavel vowed to form a permanent exhibition for their collections of Russian and European art. (Sergei's collection, mostly European art, became the basis of the Pushkin Gallery.) Pavel opened his collection to the public in 1874 and donated it to the city in 1892. He died in 1898. It was largely due to his influence that other important collections were begun in other cities in Russia, for example the Russian Museum in St Petersburg.

The façade of the museum was designed in the neo-Russian style by Victor Vasnetsv, some of whose paintings hang inside. The decorative detail, including the bas-relief of St George and the Dragon (which was the old Moscow coat of arms), is reminiscent of an old Russian *terem*. The inscription above the original entrance reads: 'The Pavel Mikhailovich and Sergei Mikhailovich Tretyakov Moscow Art Gallery. Founded by P. M. Tretyakov in 1856 and donated by him to the city of Moscow in 1892'. The museum has recently been renovated and extended, and efforts have been made to harmonise the modern part with the old. It contains over 55,000 exhibits.

To continue the walk, return to Bolshaya Ordynka Street and turn right. This part of the street, all the way to Dobrynin Square, is rather lovely, many of the charming houses are occupied by embassies. You will pass (left) a pretty white church (1647) — the **Church of St. Nicholas in Pyzhy.** It is heavily ornamented but one of those extravagances that gives Russia its fairytale image. Number 34, on the other hand, is a peculiarity that demonstrates the Russian love for their own lore and tradition. Go into the courtyard, pass under the bridge and follow the path to the left. Before you is a single-domed church with carvings. The first impression is of one of those pieces of old Russia tucked away and preserved oblivious to the changes around it. In fact it was built in 1908-12 in old style, part of the movement to revitalise Russian tradition, and was part of the **Mary and Martha Monastery.** Now, named after an eminent historian, it is the **Grabar Russian Art Restoration Centre.**

The path returns to the main street. Number 39 (left), the former **Church of Our Lady of Ivera** (1791-1802), is now the **Gallery Art Moderne,** which looks as if it is a co-operative venture. Nearby, also part of the Art Restoration Centre, is **St Catherine's Church** (1764-7). This stands next to Shchetininsky Per., home of the **Tropinin Museum** (open 10.00-17.30 except Tuesdays and Thursdays 13.00-20.30, closed on Mondays). Vasily Tropinin was a serf who obtained his freedom at the age of 47. Such were his skills as a portrait artist that a year later he was elected to the St Petersburg Academy of Arts. This museum shows mainly portraits connected with the cultural life of the eighteenth and nineteenth century by Tropinin himself, his predecessors and his contemporaries. There is also an exhibition of watercolours which show Moscow as it was before the Revolution.

Back on Bolshaya Ordynka the **Variety Theatre** is opposite number 72. At Pl. Dobryninskaya, where there is a metro station, turn right and right again into Ul. Bolshaya Polyanka. Many of the houses here are being restored and here too is one of the most delightful churches in the city.

On the left you will soon find a cooperative cafe called **Traktir**, distinguished by its large gates and the yellow writing above them. Soon, on the left is 2nd Spasonalivskovi Per., worth wandering along to see old and new Moscow merging.

Back on Bolshaya Polyanka (Road in the fields), number 45 (right), with a Transylvanian look, is **Dom Komsomoltsya**, an institution devoted to young communists. On the left is a long modern block of flats with shops in their ground floor. One of these shops (number 30, tucked behind a porch), sells some interesting souvenirs, and is next to a theatre ticket kiosk. Outside them is a good cake shop. On the right further on, opposite a clothes shop called **Sofia**, is a church, fairly uninteresting apart from its unusual belfry. Some way further on, however, is a seventeenth century masterpiece — the **Church of St Gregory Neokessarisky**, built 1667-9, with five domes and tented belfry. Opposite is **Polyanka** cafe and close by is Polyanka metro station (pale blue line).

The rest of the street contains modern houses and leads to the canal embankment. Ahead is the **Bolshoi Kamenni Bridge,** crossing the Moskva to Borovitskaya Square and the Kremlin.

A short way back along the embankment, on the right, in the ground floor of a large modern building, is a bakery that sells some unusually good Central Asian confections.

There are two last items you may wish to see close to the Bersenevskaya Embankment (*bersenia* is a type of currant bush and the whole area used to be occupied by horticulturists), along the Moskva River side of the island between the canal and the river on the other side of the island. Cross the Bolshoi Kamenni Bridge and take Ul. Serafimovicha (ahead, on the other side of the bridge, and left of the second bridge to the Kremlin). Turn left at Bersenevskaya Nab. Number 20 is a mid-seventeenth century **brick Boyar residence,** the Palace of the Secretary of the Duma Averky Kirillov, considered a fine example of Russian Baroque. The church behind is the graceful **Church of St Nicholas** (1656).

Right of the bridge is **Repin Square,** with a large garden and fountain. The statue is of the painter Repin.

Lenin — the most ubiquitous icon of them all.

Museums and other places of interest

There is an enormous number of museums in Moscow many of which are dedicated to former revolutionaries or to historical characters of interest peculiar to Russia. Some have been mentioned in the walks and are listed again here, as well as others not yet mentioned. It is worth pointing out that in the USSR disused churches and estates are frequently called museums.

Chekhov House Museum
6 Ul. Sadovaya-Kudrinskaya. Open 11.00-18.00, Wednesdays and Fridays 14.00-18.00; closed Mondays and last day of the month. Metro: Krasnopresnenskaya or Barrikadnaya.

Where the great playwright lived from 1886 to 1890.

Museum of Folk Art (see p. 167.)

Herzen Museum (see p. 170.)

Kalinin Museum (see p. 163.)

Konenkov Museum and Studio (see p. 175.)

Kuskovo Estate and Museum of Ceramics
2 Ul. Yunosti. Open 11.00-18.00; closed Mondays, Tuedays and last Wednesday of the month. Metro: Zhdanovskaya.

This is one of the few early classical estates in Moscow. It belonged to the Sheremetev family and was built between 1749 and 1792 as a summer house. The principal buildings (palace, church, bell tower and kitchens) surround a pond. Much of the interior decoration has survived — there are examples of seventeenth-century wallpaper and eighteenth-century portraits including two of Catherine the Great as well as a collection of English, French and German drawings from the eighteenth century and a collection of portraits of the tsars. The ballroom is particularly fine. The earliest building in the grounds is the **Dutch House,** a piece of eighteenth-century whimsy. The **Heritage** has a very elegant exterior. Note too the **Grotto** where a banquet was given for Catherine the Great.

The **Ceramic Museum** contains Chinese porcelain, Meissen dishes, Chelsea statuettes, Wedgwood china, Sevres china service, and Russian Soviet chinaware.

Central Lenin Museum (see p. 160).

Mayakovski Museum (see P. 158.)

Museum of Oriental Art
16 Ul. Obukha. Open 11.00-19.00; closed Mondays. Metro: Kurskaya.

Housed in the former Church of Elijah the Prophet, the museum concentrates on the art, past and present, of the peoples of Soviet Central Asia (The Uzbeks, Tajiks etc.) and the Caucasus.

Polytechnical Museum (see p.157)

Pushkin Museum of Fine Arts
12 Ul. Volkhonka. Open 10.00-20.00, Sundays 10.00-18.00; closed Mondays. Metro: Kropotkinskaya.

Opened to the public in 1912, this museum concentrates on Western art, ancient and modern. There are sections on Ancient Egypt, Byzantium, Renaissance and seventeenth- and eighteenth-century Italy (works by Botticelli, Veronese, Perugino, Tiepolo and Strozzi), Netherlands, Flanders, Spain, France (Sisley, Manet, Pissarro, Monet, Cezanne and Van Gogh) and twentieth century Europe.

Pushkin Flat Museum (see p.171)

Central Museum of the Revolution (see p.177)

Scriabin Flat Museum (see p.172)

Shchussev Museum of Soviet Architecture (see p.164)

Stanislavsky Flat Museum
6 Ul. Stanislavskovo. Open 11.00-18.00, Wednesdays and Fridays 14.00-21.00, closed Mondays, Tuesdays and last Thursday of the month. Metro: Gorkovskaya or Pushkinskaya.

The former home of the great director. Some of the rooms are as they were in his lifetime, others are dedicated to an exhibition about his life and work.

State History Museum (see p. 147).

Tolstoy Museums
There are two museums in Moscow concerning the great writer. One is his former winter residence at 21 Ul. Lev Tolstovo (open 10.00-16.30, closed Mondays and last day of month, individuals allowed in only at 11.00, 13.00 and 14.00. Tel: 246 9444. Metro: Park Kultury) and the other is basically an archive and contains manuscripts, portraits, photographs and a recording of his voice.

Tretyakov Gallery of Russian Art (see p. 185).

Tropinin Museum (see p. 186).

Novodevichy Convent
1 Novodevichy Proyezd. Open 10.00-17.00, closed Tuesdays and last day of the month. Metro: Sportivnaya. Tickets for the cathedrals are available from the Kassa near the entrance.

It was built as a fortress-convent on the old road to Smolensk to celebrate the recapture of that city in 1524. The nuns generally came from aristocratic families and the convent became one of the largest landowning estates in Russia. It played a role in Russian history, for the wives, sisters and mistresses of the Tsar sometimes ended their days here. The main building is the five-domed Smolensk Cathedral, with its magnificent iconostasis. Nearby is the later Church of the Dormition and the Bell Tower. In the grounds is the Old Cemetery where the Decembrists are buried. Next door is the New Cemetery where the former president Khrushchev is buried. Entrance seems to be restricted to relatives but check.

Ostankino Palace
Open 10.00-17.00 (10.00 to 15.00 in winter); closed Tuesdays, Wednesdays.

This is in the same area as the Exhibition of Economic Achievements, at 5 Ulitsa Pervaya Ostankinskaya. Metro: VDNK.

The estate dates back to the sixteenth century, although the palace itself is from the end of the eighteenth century. The Sheremetev family acquired the estate in the middle of the eighteenth century. It was decided to build a palace theatre, with, unprecedentedly, the theatre in the middle of the palace. The actors were to be serfs belonging to the estate. The theatre itself could be turned, by means of machinery, into the ballroom seen by the visitor today. The palace was built of wood, but both the exterior and the interior, beautifully decorated and restored, belie this fact. The carved and gilt woodwork of the decor is exceptional, the furnishings uncommonly fine. Smaller in scale than most, the palace is a delight to visit.

Andrei Rublyov Museum of Old Russian Art/Andronikov Monastery
10 Pl. Pryamikova. Metro: Pl. Ilyicha. Open 10.00-18.00. Closed Wednesdays and last Friday of the month.

Originally built in 1359 this fortress-monastery was named after its first Father-Superior. Monasteries were centres of artistic endeavour and Andrei Rublyov, considered the greatest of the icon painters, became a monk here. However, he did most of his work elsewhere, particularly in the Kremlin Cathedrals and in Zagorsk.

There are about 2,000 works of art from the fourteenth to the early-eighteenth century, mostly icons. In the grounds the **Cathedral of the Saviour** was built in 1420-7 and is one of the oldest surviving examples of stone church architecture in Moscow.

Botanical gardens and parks

There are two botanical gardens. The main one is in the north of the city (Metro: Botanicheski Sad. Tel: 219 5330) and is partially open in the winter (you can ski through it). The main entrance is on Ul. Vladykinskoye. The other garden is at Ul. Mendeleyeva. (Tel: 939 3293).

Izmailovo Park is in the eastern suburbs and has an interesting art market on a Sunday. Metro: Izmailovskaya.

Sokolniki Park where it is possible to hire bicycles and horses. Metro: Sokolniki.

More central are the **Hermitage Gardens.** (Metro: Novoslobodskaya.

Donskoi Monastery

1 Pl. Donskaya. Open 10.00-18.00 Closed Mondays, Fridays and last Thursday of the month. Metro: Shabolovskaya.

This was the last of the fortress monasteries to be built around Moscow, in 1591, on the place where the Russian army camped before their victory over the Crimean Khanate.

The **Great Cathedral** in the middle of the grounds was built in 1684-93 and has a magnificent wooden iconostasis. It now houses a branch of the **Russian Architecture Exhibition.** Elsewhere there is the **Church of the Tikhvin Icon of the Mother of God** built in 1713 above the Northern Gates. The bell tower was built between 1730 and 1753 by Trezzini and Shedel. The graveyard contains a number of eminent people including poets, architects, artists and scientists. The **Church of the Archangel Michael** contains the Monumental Sculpture Department of the Museum of Architecture, including a lot of beautifully carved gravestones.

Opposite: Winter in Zagorsk: colour and climate meet to show Russian architecture at its best.

Following page: A corner of Peterhof, now almost completely recovered from WWII.

The river

There are scenic river trips in the summer. There are several points of departure (one by the Rossia Hotel) but check with Intourist.

The zoo

Moscow Zoo at 1 Bolshaya Gruzinskaya has some very interesting and rare animals although the enclosures are not up to much. There are plans afoot to make improvements. Open 10.00-17.00 Metro: Barrikadnaya.

Cemeteries

The Novodevechy is mentioned under Novodevechy Convent. The cemetery where Sacharov is buried is called the Vostriakovskoya. Metro: Ugo Zapadnaya then bus 34 or Universitet and then trolleybus to Pl. Indira Gandhi.

The Exhibition of Economic Achievements
(open every day).

Often included on Intourist itineraries (to a chorus of groans), it is by no means as dull as it sounds. It is set in a huge park (part of the former Ostankino Estate) and consists of an array of pavilions dedicated to the various republics of the USSR and to different fields of endeavour in Soviet life. The most popular tends to be the **Space Pavilion** where models of all the Soviet rockets are exhibited but some of the others are not without interest (viticulture, flowers etc.). Unfortunately, some of them tend to close without explanation. Nevertheless, a visit in the summer is very pleasant, for the fountains are working and it is a favourite place to relax. In the winter Intourist organise Troika rides through the snowy woods.

Entrance costs a few kopeks. In summer, near the gates, there are trains to take you as far as the Space Pavilion (tickets available on board). There are several cafes, a cinema in the round and many kiosks selling books and postcards. Metro: VDNK

Kolomenskoye Estate

1 Proletarsky Pr. Open 11.00-17.00. Closed Tuesdays and last Monday of the month. Metro: Kolomenskoye.

The earliest records date back to the fourteenth century and in the fifteenth century it was a village belonging to the Grand Prince of Moscow. In the seventeenth century it became a summer residence of the tsars. The original centrepiece was the Royal Court, a masterpiece of wooden architecture which Catherine the Great destroyed; fortunately the plans survived and a model was made in the nineteenth century and is on display in the museum. There are several churches on the estate but the finest is the **Church of the Ascension,** overlooking the river.

Lenin Hills and the university
You cannot visit the university building (one of the Stalin skyscrapers) but on a clear day go for the view across the city from the nearby balustrade. Metro: Universitet then bus 119 or 684.

The metro
The metro system is not only a convenient means of transport (see 'Getting around') but is also worth visiting to look at some of the stations which are like underground palaces. The first line ran from Gorky Park to Sokolniki in 1935. A great deal of marble and precious and semi-precious stones were used in the construction and the great depth of some of the stations was to make them bomb proof. Many of the stations on and within the circle line are spectacular but the following route will take you to the most beautiful: Komsomolskaya, Novoslobodskaya, Byelorusskaya, Mayakovskaya, change at Ploshad Sverdlova to Ploshad Revolutsi, and finally Kievskaya.

Parks
There are many parks in Moscow. The most famous is Gorky Park though it was never anything like the book or the film. Still, it makes a pleasant place to visit, particularly in the summer. It is on the banks of the river and part of it was an eighteenth century pleasure garden (the Neskuchny). Metro: Park Kulturi or Oktyabrskaya.

Outside Moscow

Butildochny Domik (Bottle House)

This is a curiosity which might interest the intrepid explorer. Information is scarce but it seems that this is a house built, by an eccentric, of bottles. Take the train to Iksha (not far) from Savelovsky Station. Then ask.

The Abramtsevo Estate Museum

Approximately 65 km (40 miles) from Moscow, it can be reached by train from Yaroslavl station. Open 11.00-17,30; closed Mondays, Tuesdays and 30th of the month.

This estate with its large eighteenth century wooden house belonged to the writer Aksakov in the nineteenth century, and Turgenev and Gogol were frequent visitors. Later the estate was acquired by the industrialist Mamontov who was a patron of the arts — Repin, Serov, Chaliapin and Stanislavsky all lived and worked here. On display is a large number of works created by members of this circle. The small church was partly decorated by Repin and the fairytale 'Cottage on Chicken legs' by Vasnetsov.

Arkhangelskoye Estate Museum

Approximately 24 km (15 miles) west of Moscow. Open 1 May—30 September 11.00-17.00 and 1 October—30 April 11.00-16.00; closed Mondays, Tuesdays and last Friday of the month.

This beautiful estate as it is seen today dates back to the eighteenth century when it was built by Prince Golitsin. Later it was acquired by the Yusopov family and has remained unaltered since 1830. The garden is 14 hectares (35 acres) and contains a remarkable collection of statues and a number of pavilions. The palace itself, restored by the serf architect Strizhazov after Napoleon's army had ransacked it, contains some fine works of art, including works by Tiepolo, Lorrain and Van Dyck. There is also a fine collection of ceramics and furniture. The theatre was built separately and stands across the main road.

Yasnaya Polyana — the Leo Tolstoy Estate

About 120 miles to the south of Moscow. Open 10.00 - 17.30, closed Mondays and Tuesdays.

This is the birthplace of Leo Tolstoy and where he lived for almost 50 years from 1856. The house is much as it was in his day furnished with the desk where he worked and the divan where he was born. It was here that he wrote *War and Peace,* and *Anna Karenina.* The walls are lined with portraits of Tolstoy and other prominent writers, as well as photographs of his family. Tolstoy's grave is in the garden. During the war the Nazis wrecked the place and a great deal of restoration was required.

Holy Russia — the domes of Zagorsk.

Zagorsk

80.5 km (50 miles) north of Moscow. Trains from Yaroslavl Station. Open 10.00-17.00; closed on Mondays (the Sacristy closes Mondays, Tuesdays, and the last Friday of the month.)

This is a splendid ensemble of religious architecture, one of the finest in Russia. Founded more than 600 years ago, it quickly became an important fortress protecting Moscow and later a feudal estate.

The oldest building is the **Holy Trinity Cathedral** (1422-3). Rublyev worked on its decor. The centrepiece is the sixteenth-century **Cathedral of the Dormition** and next to it is a small extention which is the burial place of Tsar Boris Godunov. The Refectory dates back to the seventeenth century as does the Tsar's Palace. There are a number of other churches and chambers and all of the cathedrals and churches are functioning. The Sacristy, however, houses the **Exhibition of Old Russian Art** and the Governor's Chambers contain the **Exhibition of eighteenth and early nineteenth century Russian Art.** There is also a section devoted to folk art from the seventeenth century to the early twentieth.

The fantastical side of old Russia — Zagorsk.

Practical information

Shopping

Berioska and foreign currency shops

There are several. One of the largest is close to the Novodevechy Convent, almost opposite the entrance to the cemetery. Another large one is in the Rossia Hotel, on the side overlooking the river. There are other smaller ones in most of the hotels. There is a special food Berioska in the International Hotel (Hotel Mezhdunarodnaya). In the same hotel are a number of other foreign currency shops specialising in art and so on. The National Hotel has a Duty Free shop as well as a Berioska and a counter selling things such as condoms.

There are two Soviet-Swiss shops called **Sadko,** one at 9 Kutuzovsky (consumer goods) and another at 16 Ul. B. Dorogomilovskaya (food).

There is a Finnish equivalent called **Stockmann** on the ground floor of GUM on Red Square and another 4/8 U. Zacepski.

For other foreign currency shops, see headings below.

Art and craft

There is an art shop on Troili Per. at the Garden Ring end of Arbat Street. Paintings, jewellery and traditional Russian crafts are all sold for roubles. Artists sell their work all along the Arbat in the open air. Number 6 Arbat sells a variety of things including proper samovars (not the flowery ornamental kind). About half way along Arbat there is another shop (on the right walking away from the Kremlin) that sells jewellery, leather, lacquer and Matryoshka dolls for roubles.

Both the Intourist and National Hotels have shops specialising in contemporary art for sale for foreign currency. The Intourist hotel also has a couple of kiosks that sell some nice things for roubles.

Artists also sell their wares at Izmailovo Park on a Sunday.

Other galleries are at 5 Smolenskaya Nab. (closed Wednesdays and Sundays. Tel: 244 0183) and at 46b Ul. Gorkovo, closed Sunday.

Beauty shops
Mezhdunarodnya Hotel. Tel: 253 1789.
Zhen-Shen (Ginsheng), 32 Ul. Chernyshevskov. Tel: 227 1641.
OSA. 4 Ul. Semashko. Tel: 202 0282.

Books (Knigi)
There are two with books in foreign languages and Russian for
foreign currency. One is at 31 Ul. Kropotkinskaya, the other
opposite the Italian Embassy at the end of Ul. Veznina off the
Arbat.

Dom Knigi on Pr. Kalinin is the largest bookshop in the city
(roubles) — it has a counter selling imported foreign language books
and another selling Russian books in foreign languages. There is
also a new foreign currency section (separate entrance) selling
American paperbacks and newspapers, as well as the expensive but
very detailed *Information Moscow*. This, and a few paperbacks, are
sold too at a counter in the National Hotel.

There are two large bookshops opposite each other on Gorky
Street, by Pl. Sovietskaya. Second hand bookshops are good
hunting grounds — there are some to be found along Kuznetski
Most and along Stoleshnikov Per.

Clothes
Army surplus, 6 Pr. Kalinin.
Rifle jeans, shirts etc., corner of Neglinnaya and Kuznetski Most
(hard currency).

Department stores
There is not much in them in general but worth exploring for
interest. The most famous is GUM on Red Square. Another is
TSUM at 2 Ul. Petrovka. The Moskovsky is on Pl. Komsomolsky.

Foods
See also Berioska and foreign currency shops, and Markets.
Bakeries are usually good for a snack (one or two are specified in
the Restaurant section).

Pirozhki are sold on the streets.

Caviar may sometimes be bought from waiters for roubles or for
less foreign currency than in Berioskas.

There is a Russian Bread Coop at 1a Ul. Elektrozavodskaya.
Another specialising in cakes and pastries is Slastyona at 3
Krasnokazaarmennaya — orders by telephone possible on 261 0736.

Glass and porcelain
Berioskas and at 15 Ul. Gorkovo and at 8/2 Ul. Kirova.

Flowers
4 Arbat

Jewellery
Jewellery is found in most Berioska shops and in some of the shops mentioned in the Art and Craft section. Otherwise there are a few specialist shops:

Jewellery-Salon, 30 Grokholsky Per. Tel: 280 4706. Hard currency.
Berioska, 12 Ul. Gorkovo.
Malakhitovaya Shkatulka, 24 Pr. Kalinina.
Samotsvety, 35 Arbat.

There is another along Stoleshnikov Street at number 14 called Almas that looks promising but at the moment only people who live or work in the area are allowed in. Foreigners may perhaps manage entry.

Markets
The markets are good for fresh food (expensive but for roubles). You are often able to taste the produce. However they are often frequented by pickpockets, as well as sellers of fur hats and similar items.

   The main ones are: Centralny Rynok at 15 Tsvetnoi Bld. (the most famous); Cherymushkinsky Rynok at 1 Lomonovsky Pr.; Danilovsky Rynok at 74 Ul. Mytnaya; Dorogomilovsky Rynok at 10 Mozhaisky Val; Rizhsky Rynok at 94 Pr. Mira; and Tishinsky Rynok at 50 Ul. B. Gruzinskaya.

Posters
Dom Knigi on Pr. Kalinin.
21 Arbat.
2 Arbat

Records
Melodya, Pr. Kalinina.
Berioska shops.
Dom Knigi, Pr. Kalinina.

Entertainment

Bars, cafés, clubs

Cafes are mentioned under restaurants and in passing in the walks.

Bars are on the whole to be found in hotels, where the better ones usually deal in hard currency. There is a **pub (Red Lion)** in the Mezhdunarodnaya Hotel and a **German Beer Hall** in the **Intourist Hotel** and in the **National.** In the bigger hotels there are usually a couple of **buffyets** on the upper floors where cognac and vodka are sold for roubles but they are short on atmosphere.

Elsewhere the problem is rendered next to hopeless because of the draconian alcohol laws, but these are slowly being eased so the situation may change. There is a beer hall on the corner of Pushkinskaya and Stoleshnikov Street and a place called **Vecher** on Pr. Serova (Metro: Pl. Nogina) which is reputed to be good.

As for clubs the situation is almost as chronic. There is a jazz club called the **Bluebird (Sinyapititsa)** on Chekhov Street and legend has it that a club called **Olymp** has opened at the Luzhniky Stadium. Certain of the restaurants in the hotels offer variety/cabaret performances, e.g. in the Intourist and the Cosmos.

Baths

The traditional Sandunovsky Russian baths are on Petrovka Street.

Boating

In Gorky Park or on the river beach at Serebryany Bor.

Chess

The Central Chess Club is at 14 Gogolevski Blvd. Tel: 291 0641.

Horse riding

At Sokolniki Park (Metro: Sokolniki) or at the **Hippodrome** at 22 Ul. Begovaya (Metro. Begovaya). Tel: 945 4516 or 945 0437. Also in the Bitsa Forest Park.

Performing arts

There is no shortage of performances catering to all tastes — for a complete list speak to Intourist. The most famous theatre (for ballet and opera) is the Bolshoi but there are frequent performances given by the Bolshoi company elsewhere (for example in the Kremlin Palace of Congresses). Tickets for performances in the Bolshoi Theatre are hard to come by sometimes (Intourist is allocated some tickets for sale through Service Bureaux), but it is usually possible to get hold of tickets for foreign currency from touts outside the theatre — in fact this is true of all the theatres. Before parting with any money, check the validity of the tickets. Other theatres specialising in ballet, opera and music are mentioned below.

There are several drama theatres — listings are available from Intourist.

The famous puppet theatre provides an entertaining spectacle even if you do not speak Russian.

There are two circuses — the old one (being renovated) is the traditional one while the new one concentrates on a flashy contemporary style of showmanship. In the summer there is sometimes a tent circus in Gorky Park and there is a children's circus (acts presented by children) not far from Prospect Mira.

Traditional folk dance performances or recitals by groups such as the Red Army Choir or the Balalaika Orchestra are often given in the Tchaikovsky Concert Hall. There are often performances of choral music given in churches and occasional concerts in the Ostankino Palace or the Hall of Columns in the House of Trade Unions on the corner of Pushkin Street.

There are plenty of cinemas (there is a magazine called *Kino Nedelya* which tells you what is on in Russian — ask someone in the Service Bureau to translate), but films are usually in Russian. Old films can be seen at the Povtornovo Filma, 23/9 Ul. Gertsena.

Addresses

Bolshoi Theatre, 2 Ploshad Sverdlova. Bookings — Tel: 292 0050.
Palace of Congresses (Box Office). Tel: 227 8263.
Stanislavsky and Nemirovich-Damchanko Musical Theatre, 17 Pushkin Street.
Operetta Theatre, 6 Pushkin Street;
Maly Drama Theatre, 1/6 Ploshad Sverdlova.
Puppet Theatre, 3 Sadovo Samotechnaya. Tel: 299 3310.
Tchaikovsky Concert Hall, Ploshad Mayakovskaya. Tel: 299 3487.
Old Circus, 13 Tsvetnoi Blvd.
New Circus, 7 Vernadsky Prospect. Tel: 930 2815.

Snooker

15 Ul.Karl Marx.

Sporting events

Athletics, soccer and ice hockey are all popular and can be seen in the Lenin Sports Complex (Tel: 201 0955) at the foot of the Lenin

Hills (Metro: Sportivnaya). The Dynamo Stadium (Tel: 212 7092) is on Leningradski Prospect (Metro: Dynamo). Horse Racing can be seen at the **Hippodrome** (see Horse Riding). Tickets are obtainable on the spot or from the various ticket kiosks scattered around the city.

Swimming
The most famous pool is the huge open-air one not far from Kropotkinskaya metro station. It is heated and open all year — beautiful in the winter. Entrance is 50 kopeks plus 30 for the hire of a towel. There is a beach on the Moskva river at Serebryany Bor (Tel: 199 4619) for use in the summer.

Tennis
Chaika Tennis Courts, 3/5 Kropotkinskaya Nab, Tel: 202 0474.

Winter sports
For the brave there is a practise ski jump near the university on the Lenin Hills. Otherwise you can usually hire cross country skis and skates at Gorky Park.

Services

Airlines
Aeroflot. Tel: 928 8791; flight info: 155 0922. **Air China (CAAC).** Tel: 143 1560. **Air France.** Tel: 237 2325. **Air India.** Tel: 237 7494. **Alitalia.** Tel: 923 9840. **British Airways.** Tel: 253 2492. **Bulgarian Airlines.** Tel: 921 0267. **Czechoslovak Airlines.** Tel: 250 4571. **Finnair.** Tel: 292 8788. **Japan Airlines.** Tel: 921 6448. **Jugoslavian Airlines.** Tel: 921 2846. **KLM.** Tel: 253 2150. **Lufthansa.** Tel: 921 9293. **Malev (Hungarian Airlines).** Tel: 292 0434. **Mongolian Airlines.** Tel: 241 0754. **Pan-American.** Tel: 253 2658. **Lot (Polish Airlines). Tel: 238 0003. Sabena Belgian Airlines. Tel: 248 1214. SAS.** Tel: 925 4747. **Swissair.** Tel: 253 8988.

Banks
Bank of America Tel: 253 7054. **Banque National de Paris.** Tel: 207 5888. **Banca Commerciale Italiana. Tel: 209 6518. Barclays.** Tel: 209 6452. **Deutsche Bank.** 201 2988. **Lloyds.** Tel: 253 8174. **Midland.** Tel: 253 2144. **National Westminster.** Tel: 207 5739.

Car hire
Cosmos Hotel. Tel: 215 6191. Troika, 12 Krasnopresnenskaya Nab.
Tel: 253 2255.

Car spare parts
Tel: 288 9056 or 243 0555.

Chemists
24 hours: 32 Ul. Kirova. Tel: 923 1388. 71 Pr. Mira. Tel: 281 1124.
10 Pl. Smolenskaya. Tel: 241 9882.

Church services
Protestant and **Anglican** services (Tel: 143 3562 for info.).
Catholic: 12 St Louis Malaya Lubyanka (every day at 08.00) and
Chapel of Our Lady of Hope (Tel: 243 9621).
Russian Orthodox: There are several but two are the Troitsky
Cathedral (Danilovsky Monastery) and the Uspenskaya Church
(Novodevichy Convent) (Tel: 245 3168). There is also a small
functioning church next to the Cosmos Hotel. Services are usually
at 08.00 or at 18.00 (Sundays 07.00 and 18.00).
Old Believers: 29 Rogozhsky Per.
Mosque: 7 Vypolzov Per. Tel: 281 3866.
Synagogue: 8 Ul. Arkhipova. Tel: 923 9697.

Co-operatives
For general information for co-ops, entertainment and sport try
TOPAZ, 28, Ul. Rechnikov. Tel: 115 1001.

Cultural organisations
House of Friendship. Tel: 203 7073 or 290 6085.
Shalom Jewish Cultural Society. Tel: 110 3758.

Doctors
Tourists Clinic, 2 Gruzinsky Proyezd. Tel: 254 4396.
LIK - medical Coop. Tel: 305 1212.
Swiss Medical Interline in Intourist Hotel (particularly dentistry).
  Tel: 203 9496.
Europ Assistance. Tel: 254 6927.
Alternative medicine. Tel: 157 6855.

Embassies
Australia, 13 Kropotkinskaya Per. Tel: 246 5012.
Canada, 23 Starokonynshenny Per. Tel: 241 5882.
China, Leninskiye Gory, 6 Ul. Druzby. Tel: 143 1543.
Great Britain, 14 Nab. Morisa Toreza. Tel: 231 8511.
Ireland, 5 Grokholsky Per. Tel: 288 4101.
Japan (visas), 5a Sobinovsky Per. Tel: 202 8303.
Mongolia (consul), 7/1 Spakopeskovsky Per. Tel: 241 1548.
New Zealand, 44 Ul. Vorovskovo. Tel: 290 3485.
USA, 19/23 Ul. Chaikovskovo. Tel: 252 2451.

Emergencies
Ambulance Tel: 03; Fire 01; Police 02.

Gayline
Tel: 240 6086

Intourist
Head Office: 16 Prospect Marxa. Tel: 203 6962.

Libraries
Lenin Library. Tel: 202 5790.

Lost property
Metro Tel: 222 2085 Taxi 923 8753 Tram and buses 233 4225

Post offices
International Post Office, 37a Varshavskoye Chaussee. Tel: 114 4648.

Shipping agent
Mosvneshtransexpeditsa. Tel: 975 4284.

Taxis
Ordering by telephone Tel: 927 0000.

Visa office and registration for foreigners (UVIR)
10 Kolpachy Per. Tel: 924 9349.

206 St Petersburg

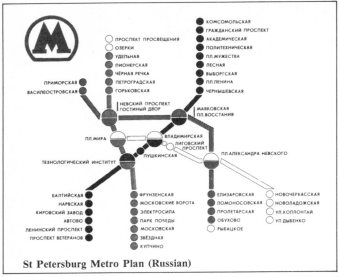

St Petersburg Metro Plan (Russian)

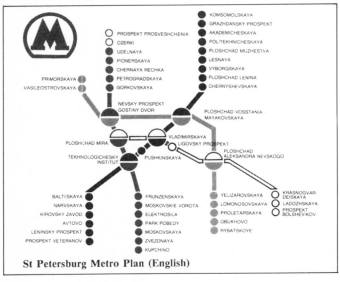

St Petersburg Metro Plan (English)

Arrival and departure

By air

St Petersburg airport is very small and is the only one serving the city. International arrivals first go through passport control, then to the small baggage claim section. There, if you have not already filled in a declaration form, you will be able to do so. When you have your bags, proceed to customs, where you will have to present bags and form. After the check, proceed into the hall where your contact will be waiting. Intourist guides frequently come into the baggage claim area to offer help.

There are very few trolleys.

To and from the airport

St Petersburg airport, (Pulkovo Tel: 293 9021, 293 9031), lies 15 km (9.3 miles) south of the city. It is twenty minutes' drive from the city limits and a further twenty minutes from the centre. Most visitors are likely to be met by a representative of some sort but for those who are not there are two options - taxi or bus. The bus is run by Aeroflot and takes passengers for a few kopeks to and from Gertsena Street, close to Nevsky Prospect, but quite a walk from the nearest metro station. The bus will drop you, if required, at Moskovskaya metro station. Departures theoretically run every twenty minutes. Taxis are thin on the ground but when you get one try and ensure that you are not ripped off. The taxi should be metered and should not cost more than ten roubles. However, many drivers are likely to try and force you to pay more. Do not go beyond what you can afford because you will eventually find one for a reasonable fare. Some will accept, illegally, foreign currency.

By rail

The international train service to the USSR is described on pp. 00. While it is possible to go directly to Moscow from Hoek van

ST PETERSBURG

Scale 1:50 000

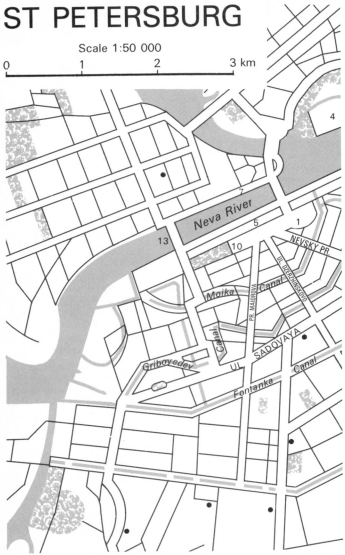

KEY : UL. = ULITSA (STREET)   PR. = PROSPECT (AVENUE)   ●= METRO

Places of Interest
1. Dvortsovaya Square
   (Winter Palace)
2. Alexander Nevsky Monastery
3. Vosstanya Square & Moskovski Station
4. Peter & Paul Fortress
5. The Admiralty
6. Smolny
7. University Embankment
8. Finland Station
9. Summer Garden
10. Decembrists Square & St. Isaacs
11. Iskusstv Square
    (Arts Square)
12. Merchants Court
    (Gostinny Dvor)
13. Lieutenant Schmidt Bridge
    (Most Leitenant Shmita)
14. Field of Mars

Holland or Ostend, to reach St Petersburg requires changing trains in Berlin. There are five major railway stations in St Petersburg. Information tel: 168 0111.

Moskovski Vokzal is the one which you are most likely to use, since it serves Moscow. Centrally located on Vosstanya Square, half way down Nevsky Prospect. The duration of the journey to Moscow is roughly eight hours but it can be longer or shorter depending on the service, of which there are at least three a day. The taxi queue is always long but being a foreigner willing to pay over the odds will shorten it. Metro: Ploshad Vosstanya or Mayakovskaya.

Finlandski Vokzal, made famous by Lenin's arrival here from exile (the train that brought him is still here), serves Helsinki and towns north of St Petersburg. Metro: Ploshad Lenina.

Vitebski Vokzal, centrally located on Zagorodni Prospect, serves areas southwest of the city, Belorussia and the Ukraine. Metro: Pushkinskaya.

Varshavski Vokzal is the principal station serving northern Europe, Poland and Germany. Coming from Ostend, you arrive here. Metro: Baltiskaya or Frunzenskaya.

Baltiskii Vokzal, next door to the Warsaw Station, serves the areas to the south of the city as well as the Baltic Republics. Nearest metro: Baltiskaya.

By sea

Should you come by sea your ship is likely to dock on Vasilevsky Island near the end of Bolshoi Prospect but this may vary according to circumstances. Sea port tel: 355 1902.

By river

It is extremely unlikely that you will arrive or leave on a riverboat. For the record, the river port is at 195 Prospect Obukhovskoi Oborony. Nearest metro: Lomonovskaya.

Getting around the city

The metro
The St Petersburg metro is more modern than its counterpart in Moscow. While not as striking as some of the Moscow stations, many of the stations here are also decoratively laid out. The standard of service is just as high, although the gaps between stations seems to be greater. The flat fare is 5 kopeks. There are a couple of elements that are different. Many of the stations have sliding doors along the platforms which will open only upon the arrival of a train. Here the announcements telling you the name of the next station are made as you pull into the preceding station. Remember also that, as in Moscow, some stations where two lines meet have a single name while others have two names, and that the two lines may be a substantial distance apart.

Trams, trolley buses and buses
The flat fare for each is 5 kopeks.

Taxis
Not always easy to find. Bargain hard if you think the price is high and try to flag down any vehicle if desperate. To order a taxi tel: 10 0022.

Accommodation

The situation is even worse than in Moscow, although individual tourists or businessmen who are willing to spend money will soon be able to book directly with the newly restored Astoria or Europa. For the record:

Evropeiskaya: 1/7 Ul. Brodsky.
Excellently located on a small street that connects Nevsky Prospect and Arts Square (Ploshad Isskustv). This is a rather beautiful old hotel with period features which seem to have survived intact. It is currently closed for complete refurbishment. When that has been accomplished it is unlikely that it will be used for the tourist groups but for individuals with money to spend. Metro: Nevsky Prospect or Gostinny Dvor.

Astoria, 39: Ul. Gertsena.
Again with a fine location, next to St Isaacs, this is the most famous
old hotel of St Petersburg, where H. G. Wells and others stayed.
Much period charm but currently under restoration. Unlikely to be
used for tour groups. Nearest metro: not really close to any, but the
nearest would be as for the Evropeiskaya. Trolleybuses 5 or 14 will
take you to it.

Moskva: This hotel is often used by Intourist and has a good
location at the monastery end of Nevsky Prospect. The quality of
service is not high but of a typical standard. Its location
compensates. Nearest metro: Ploshad Alexander Nevskovo, in the
same building.

St Petersburg: 5/2 Pirogov Embankment.
Another Intourist hotel, located across the Neva from the Winter
Palace, not far from the Aurora and the Peter and Paul Fortress.
Standard sort of accommodation. Nearest metro: Ploshad Lenina.

Sovietskaya: 43 Lermontovsky Prospect.
Standard Intourist, nearest metro: Technologicheski Institut, which
is a short tram ride from the hotel, and then only a couple of stops
to the centre.

Pulkovskaya: Moskovsky Prospect.
A comfortable Intourist hotel on the edge of the city in the direction
of the airport. However, the metro will take you directly to the
centre without changing lines. Nearest metro: Moskovskaya.

Pribaltiskaya: 14 Ul. Korablestroitel.
Although this is the most comfortable of the Intourist Hotels, it is
not conveniently located for the user of public transport. However,
its position on the edge of the Gulf of Finland, on Vasilievski
Island, is spectacular. The nearest metro is Primorskaya, which is
five bus stops from the hotel (buses 44, 151 or 152).

Restaurants

While the situation has vastly improved recently, the choice remains
small. Nevertheless, it is possible to eat well, although there is no
guarantee of quality. Some information is hard to find — details
welcome. Metros in brackets.

Cooperatives and joint ventures

Aist Kafe: 79 Karl Marx Prospect. (Lesnaya)
Aktyor Kafe: 4 Pl. Lenina. (Vyborgskaya)
Azherbaijani Kafe: Ul. Gavanskaya, close to the Pribaltiskaya Hotel. (Vasileostrovskaya)
Brik Kafe: 22 Ul. Kolokolnaya. (Vladimirskaya)
Iveria Kafe: 35 Ul. Marata. (Mayakovskaya)
Jazz Club: Tel: 164 8565. Champagne and Cognac, snacks, music, fashionable.
Karina Kafe: 28 Ul. Kuibysheva. (Petrogradskaya)
Klassik: 202 Ligovsky Prospect. (Ploshad Vostanya)
Lagidze Vody: 29 Ul. Belinsky. Specialises in flavoured mineral waters and Georgian snacks such as *Hachapuri:* which is a hot cheese bun. (Mayakovskaya)
Na Fontanke: 77 Naberezhnaya Fontanki. Tel: 310 2547. (Mayakovskaya)
Poliyessye: Tel: 224 2917. Belorussian cooking.
Ritsa: 17 Ul. Bratev Vasilyevik. Tel: 232 8413. Georgian. (Gorkovskaya)
Shabski Domik: Tel: 528 2211. German food and beer. (Krasnogvardeiskaya)
Sofia Kafe: 4 Ul. Blokhina. (Gorkovskaya)
Tbilisi: 10 Ul. Sitninskaya Tel: 232 9391. Georgian. (Gorkovskaya)
Tet à Tet: Tel: 232 1035. (Gorkovskaya)
Troika: Zagorodni Pr.; supposed to be good.
V Gostyakh u Skazki: 46 Ul. Tchaikovskova. (Chornyshevskaya)
Victoria: 24 Kirovski Prospect. Tel: 232 5130. 'Kitch and popular with the nouveaux riches'. (Petrogradskaya or Gorkovskaya)

Others:

Admiralteski: 27 Ul. Gertsena. Tel: 315 5661. (Nevsky Prospect)
Austeria: Petropavlovskaya Krepost. In the Peter and Paul fortress, quite good reputation. (Gorkovskaya)
Baku: 12 Ul. Sadovaya. Tel: 311 2751. Azerbaijani.
Chaika: 14, Canal Griboyedeva Embankment. Tel: 312 4631. Ordinary restaurant with beer hall for foreign currency. (Nevsky Prospect)
Fortezza: Tel: 233 9468. No other information.
Kafe Literaturnaye ('Literary Cafe'): 18 Nevsky Prospect. Tel: 312 8536. A recently restored St Petersburg institution. Formerly a gathering place for litterati, where Pushkin had his last meal before his duel, and where Tchaikovsky is said to have eaten the food that

led to his death. There are sometimes music recitals and every evening a rather formidable woman interrupts your meal to recite the history of the place. Food not bad, quite entertaining. (Nevsky Prospect or Gostinny Dvor)

Kavkazski: 25 Nevsky Prospect. Tel: 311 4526. Georgian and good. (Nevsky Prospect or Gostinny Dvor)

Metropol: 22 Ul. Sadovaya. Good food. (Gostinny Dvor or Nevsky Prospect)

Neva: 46 Nevsky Prospect. Tel: 210 3466. Not bad. (Gostinny Dvor or Nevsky Prospect)

Okhotnichii Dom: 28a Engelsa Prospect. Tel: 244 5544. Specialises in game. (Udyelnaya or Pionerskaya)

Okolitsa: 15 Primorsky Prospect. Tel: 239 6984. (Chornaya Riechka)

Palanga: 127, Leninski Pr. Tel: 255 6417. Floor show of not outstanding quality ('Like physical exercise in underwear — not sexy just repellant'). Food quite good. (Leninsky Prospect)

Troika: 27 Zagorodni Prospect. Tel:113 5343. With variety show. Good. (Vladimirskaya or Pushkinskaya)

U Prichala: Bolshoi Pr. Tel: 217 4428.

The Theatre of Arts Square, St Petersburg. The details of old St Petersburg have miraculously survived the rigours of the twentieth century.

Exploring the city

Introduction

Leningrad, really St Petersburg, its original name is in total contrast to Moscow. It is the product of the will of one man, Russia's greatest Tsar, Peter the Great, but its astonishing beauty is a mix of Russia and western Europe and represents that curious ambivalence of Russians towards the western world. It is not a city that has grown and expanded with time but was the result of Peter's decision to build a new city that would bring Russia closer to the influences of the outside world. Its site is in fact preposterous, on a marshy delta, but Peter wanted a city by the sea.

He chose an area that had formerly belonged to the city of Lord Novgorod the Great but which had been in the hands of the Swedes for most of the seventeenth century. Peter, like his predecessors always dreaming of the sea and anxious for a fine port to serve the country, took the area back in 1702 and laid the foundations a year later. On 16 May 1703, on the Island of Hares, Peter cut the earth with a bayonet and said 'Here shall be a town.' This was followed by the first stone of the Peter and Paul Fortress. The new city was called St Petersburg, after Peter's patron saint and it became capital in 1712.

The proposition was very impractical and wholly Russian. The city would be difficult to defend, it was next to useless as a port and although it straddled a good network of waterways the presence of the court would make it too expensive for merchants. Geographically (close to Sweden) and climatically (the river froze for several months each year) it was a bizarre choice but such objections were waved aside by Peter. The result was one of the most beautiful cities of the world and one which produced the most romantic and glittering court in Europe.

Architects, little known in their own countries (Cameron, Trezzini, Rastrelli) found themselves here and achieved immortality. The greatest flowering of Russian art took place here, for Pushkin,

Lermontov, Turgenev, Dostoyevsky, Glinka, Mussorsky, Tchaikovsky and Repin all lived in Leningrad. Yet its history is punctuated by violence and suffering, for riot and revolution here were eventually to bring changes that affected the world and during the WW II the city withstood siege by the Nazis for 900 days. There was no electricity and water only from the canals. During the winter of 1941-2 hundreds of thousands of Leningraders died of starvation. After this extraordinary feat of endurance Leningrad was awarded the Order of Lenin.

Much had to be rebuilt after the war. Now it is a busy, thriving city but one, like Venice, in possession of a particular beauty that reflects a unique history.

Facts and figures

The Neva is only 80.5 km (50 miles) long. It freezes from November to April. There are some 700 bridges in the city. The population is five million. It was called Leningrad until 1914 and Petrograd until 1924.

The Griboyedev Canal and a distant church: perfectly preserved pre-war Russia.

Walking the city

The beauty of St Petersburg is concentrated into a comparatively small area and the only way to know the city is to discover it on foot. Here are walks which cover most of the historical centre and which touch on all aspects of St Petersburg life.

The first takes you along the most famous street in Russia: Nevsky Prospect. Metro: Ploshad Alexander Nevskovo.

This, the main street of St Petersburg, is 4 km (2.5 miles) long, stretching from the Admiralty to the Alexander Nevsky Monastery. The territory upon which St Petersburg stands was part of the domain of Lord Novgorod the Great. Nevsky Prospect was originally built to link the shipyard, where the Admiralty now stands, with the Great Novgorod Road, which was the old road that linked the villages of the Novgorod empire. All the materials for construction of the shipyard and for its work had to come by way of this road (which ran where Ligovski Prospect runs now) and then along a variety of indirect tracks that made the business of transportation rather tiresome. To facilitate this it was decided to build Nevsky Prospect. Its original name was 'the Great Perspective Road' (owing to the fact that it opened up new vistas). In 1738 it was renamed the 'Nevsky Perspective Road' and in 1783 it became Nevsky Prospect. It very quickly became the city's principal thoroughfare, along which churches, palaces and markets were built. As the years passed so banks and hotels were added, most notably in the section beyond Vosstanya Square. Indeed the contrast in styles of the buildings is explained by the fact that the original southern boundary of the city lay along the Fontanka Canal. Thus the section between the Admiralty and the Fontanka is somewhat older.

Although it has remained the principal thoroughfare of the city, to which all other roads lead, do not expect the shops to resemble those of Oxford Street. Many of them are of interest, and indeed improvements are being made, but glittering emporiums they are not.

It would make chronological sense to start the walk at the Admiralty but it is more practical to begin at the other end since there is a metro station there (Alexander Nevskvo). Apart from a few items such as the Alexander Nevsky Monastery the part between that end and Vosstanya Square is less interesting. If you wish to confine your walk to the more spectacular part, then start from either Ploshad Vosstanya or Mayakovskaya metro station.

The walk

Outside the Alexander Nevskovo metro station, the Moskva Hotel is left behind you; opposite and right is the **Alexander Nevsky Monastery.** This monastery, founded not long after the foundation of the city, held the highest rank, *lavra,* of which there were only four in the country before the Revolution. In the old days the Winter Market took place near the entrance, specialising in cattle, horses, peasant carriages and sledges. The rural atmosphere was enhanced by the traditional wooden houses that lay scattered hereabouts.

Occasionally events in the monastery macabrely reflected the politics of the day. After Peter III, husband of Catherine the Great, was murdered, he was interred in the cemetery. When Paul, supposedly Catherine's son by Peter, came to the throne, he had his father exhumed and reburied next to Catherine (who had instigated the events that led to Peter's murder and who had never liked her son), with a crown placed on his coffin. Furthermore he made Alexei Orlov, the man who had murdered Peter and the brother of Catherine's lover Grigori Orlov, carry the crown on a golden cushion. The church at the entrance dates to 1783.

Left of the main entrance is the eighteenth-century **Lazarevskoye Cemetery.** In this cemetery lie buried the sister of Peter the Great, the greatest of Russian scientists Lomonosov and the architect Carlo Rossi, many of whose buildings help to give St Petersburg its character. Right of the entrance is another cemetery, the **Tikhvinskoye.** Here lie some great souls indeed — the composers Glinka, Tchaikovsky, Mussorgsky and Rimsky-Korsakov, and the writer Dostoyevsky. As for the monastery itself, the oldest part is the tower to the left of the main gate (from 1722), in which there are two churches. In the lower of them is buried the great Field-Marshall from the time of Catherine the Great, Suvorov. Here too is the **Museum of Urban Sculpture** which houses, for example, the original models for the equestrian statues on the Anchikov Bridge.

The **Cathedral of the Trinity** (1778-90) is one of the finest examples of Russian classicism and the Metropolitan's residence (1756-9) is a marvellous work of Russian Baroque. Sunday services here are spectacular.

Beyond the Cathedral is another cemetery filled with graves of Revolutionaries.

The drawbridge spanning the Neva beyond the monastery, at 906 m (2972 ft), is the longest in St Petersburg.

At 139 Nevsky Prospect there is a plaque commemorating the

fact that the composer of the popular tune *Moscow Nights* (known as Midnight in Moscow in the West) lived here as a child. Further along, on the left, is Ul. Poltavskaya. Down there you will see what looks like a Kremlin wall. It was never intended to be a fortress but was built in 1914 as a decorative screen around the railway marshalling yard. Just before arriving at Pl. Vosstanya you will notice a good **second-hand bookshop.**

Ploshad Vosstanya

The translation is 'Uprising Square' and is the point where the original Great Perspective road (Bolshaya Perspektivnaya Doroga) met the Great Novgorod Road, which is now Ligovsky Prospect. For a long time there was nothing here, until the **Church of the Sign** was built where Ploshad Vosstanya metro station stands now. The square thus acquired its first name — the Square of the Sign, or Ploshad Znamenskaya. However, until the construction of the railway line between Moscow and St Petersburg in 1851, the square remained remote from the main town. In that year the Moscow railway station, on the left as you look at the square coming from the monastery, was built and is identical to the St Petersburg station in Moscow. The façade has remained unaltered but the interior was wholly changed in 1951. Opposite it is its twin, the mid-nineteenth century hotel now known as the **Oktyabrskaya,** only rarely used by Intourist. However, there is a cocktail bar and restaurant in the part facing the square.

The square acquired its modern name because, inevitably, of Revolutionary connotations. It was the site of frequent demonstrations and meetings during 1917 and in the same year one was fired upon by the police. Several people were killed and the ensuing strike became an uprising. The Tsar was overthrown soon afterwards. Hence Uprising Square. The obelisk in the middle, not much liked by St Petersburgers, was unveiled in 1985 to commemorate the fortieth anniversary of the end of WW II.

(There are public lavatories behind the metro station pavilion.)

The section of Nevsky Prospect from Ploshad Vosstanya to the Anichkov Bridge was built up in the nineteenth century, at a time when the capital was emerging as one of Europe's cosmopolitan centres. Many of the buildings were used as banks and company offices, which have become flats and shops.

On the corner of Nevsky Prospect and Ul. Vosstanya, by the metro station, is a rather good shop, **Heritage,** which deals in arts and crafts. You may find some very interesting items here, for roubles. The first **cinema** that you meet (right) was the first in St Petersburg to show 'talkies'. Beyond it, at 104, is a confectioner's specialising in food from Central Asia. Opposite is the entrance to Ul. Marata, down which, at 24a, is the **Museum of the Arctic and the Antarctic,** devoted to exhibits about the nature and history of polar exploration. Marat Street was also the home, at number 14, of the aristocratic thinker Alexander Radishchev (1749-1802) who was the author of *A journey from St Petersburg to Moscow* which denounced serfdom. The result was that he was stripped of his title and exiled to Siberia. (If you have walked around Red Square in Moscow you may have noticed the plaque outside the old Yama prison, where Radishchev was incarcerated on the way to Siberia). On the corner of Marat and Nevsky is the **Nevsky** restaurant which is several restaurants in one, one on each floor. It has a reputation for being something of a 'railway station' but you are likely to get a seat. A little beyond, left, a **jeweller's shop,** one of the better ones in the city.

Number 88-90 is a **stereo cinema,** with a reasonable cafe. Just after it, at 86, is one of the more elegant buildings in this part of the city, the **Stanislavsky Centre for Workers in the Arts,** which is a theatrical society, exhibition hall and cafe. Originally built in the eighteenth century in classical style, in 1830 it was rebuilt and until the Revolution was one of several mansions which belonged to the eminent Yusupov family. With its high central colonnade and luxurious bas-reliefs it dominates this part of the street.

You will then cross Litenii Prospect (Foundry Avenue), its name and width deriving from the fact that this was the foundry centre of the city. There is nothing of much interest to the right (although there are several bookshops), but the dome to the left of Nevsky belongs to **St Vladimir's Church,** which has recently been handed back to the church. Further up Nevsky on the left is the **Titan cinema,** which in the nineteenth century was the fashionable Toulon restaurant.

Just before the Fontanka Canal there are two attractive buildings. One, painted in vermillion oil (rather unusual in this climate for it deteriorates quickly and has to be replaced every year), and eighteenth-century in style, was built in the middle of the nineteenth century by the architect Stakenschneider, whose buildings made quite an impact on the character of St Petersburg. It was built for Prince Beloselsky-Belozersky and now houses the administrative committee for this district. Opposite is a building in classical style dating from the early-nineteenth century. For many years the great critic Belinsky lived here in a flat, regularly visited by the likes of Goncharov and Dostoyevsky (whom he championed when others, including Turgenev, ridiculed him). Turgenev also lived here during 1851.

Next door at number 70 is the St Petersburg branch of the **Union of Journalists (Dom Journalisti)**. Built in the 1820s by Domenico Quadri, in the nineteenth century it was the residence of General Sukhozanet, a hero of the Napoleonic wars. It has a classical façade with an impressive wrought-iron balcony. If you are able to have a look inside you will see a hall decorated with columns faced with artificial marble and a frieze with military motifs.

The **Fontanka canal** is so-named from the fact that its water supplied all the city fountains. Originally the canal was a small creek with a water tower but as the city grew larger so did the need for water and the creek became a canal. Here was the southern boundary of the original city. Although the two preceding sections of Nevsky grew up to meet the demands of a growing commercial city in the nineteenth century, this older section was also of commercial importance, with a total of 28 banks along it before the Revolution. This section was also the most fashionable part of Nevsky — it was close to the Winter Palace and it was known as the 'sunny' part for which shopkeepers paid higher rent for their premises.

The **Anichkov Bridge** is named after Lieutenant-Colonel Mikhail Anichkov, who led the team which built it. Before crossing the bridge you may wish to walk along the canal to the right — number 34 is the **Institute of the Arctic and Antarctic** with, in front of it, the bust of the great explorer Amundsen, presented by the Norwegian government. The land on which it stands was presented to Field-Marshal Sheremetev and the present building erected in 1750 by Russian architects. It is a fine example of early Russian baroque, with traditionally simple lines, but rather ornate decoration. In the mid-nineteenth century it was still occupied by a Nicolai Sheremetev, one of the richest men in Russia and a patron of the arts. Glinka was a regular visitor here.

The Anichkov Bridge

The bridge, built in 1839-41, replaced an earlier drawbridge with granite towers. Its fame rests with the marvellous bronze equestrian statues sculptured by Pyotr Klodt. Originally there were two of each statue (a man leading a horse and a man containing a rearing horse) but Nicholas I ordered that two of them be presented to the King of Prussia, to be replaced by plaster moulds. Bronze ones were erected again in 1843. Three years later the Tsar wanted to present two of them to the King of Naples. Plaster moulds were put up again. Klodt was asked to cast them again but expressed a preference to cast two entirely new ones. Thus the third figure became a youth kneeling and placing a bridle around the horse's head, the fourth of a man thrown under a rearing horse.

Just beyond the bridge on the left is the **Anichkov Palace,** which takes its name from the bridge. Its front looks over the Fontanka, while its sides extend along Nevsky to Ostrovsky Square. It was built by Rastrelli in 1750 for Count Razumovsky. The story of Razumovsky is one of the most charming in Russian history. The Empress Elizabeth was an exuberant and loving woman. When she heard the singing voice of Alexei Razumovsky, the son of a Ukrainian shepherd, she was captivated. He, to paraphrase Catherine the Great, was 'one of the handsomest men she ever saw' and became Elizabeth's lover, remaining thus for the rest of her life. Whether they secretly married or not is a moot point. He never became involved in politics, but was intensely religious and both he and his brother Kyril were great patrons of the arts and despite their sudden elevation to the highest society are reputed to have remained entirely unspoilt. Generosity was in the family, for Beethoven dedicated the Razumovsky Quartets to Alexei's nephew Andrei in gratitude for his patronage. In later years Catherine the Great was anxious to know whether Alexei had married Elizabeth and sent a messenger to find out. He, faithful to Elizabeth to the end, burnt all the documents that could have given any sort of answer. It is alleged that he afterwards said: 'I have never been anything but the late Empress's most faithful slave. Now you can see for yourself that I have no documents of any kind.'

In later years the Anchikov palace was used by Catherine's favourite, Potemkin. Now it houses the **Zhdanov Palace of Young Pioneers** where children come to pursue their hobbies.

Opposite the Anichkov Palace, right, is a **glass and china shop** where bargains are sometimes to be found. Beyond it is the **St Petersburg Academic Comedy Theatre** at 56, the ground floor of which is a grocer's shop dating back to the early part of the century (when it was known as Yeliseyev's) and which has recently been restored to its original gaudy splendour. The **State Puppet Theatre** is at 52, founded in 1918. On this side is also **Morozhnenoe cafe,** which specialises in dairy products like yoghurt.

Ploshad Ostrovskovo

On the left is Ostrovsky Square (Pl. Ostrovskovo). Restful and spacious, it is surrounded by some fine buildings and is a favourite haunt of artists. Left is the Anichkov Palace, with its gardens and wrought iron railings. The two pavilions and the railings were designed by Carlo Rossi in 1817-18. At the back of the square is the **St Petersburg State Theatre Museum** which tells the history of Russian drama and musical theatre from the beginning to the present day.

The street that leads from this building behind the square is **Architect Carlo Rossi Street (Ul. Zodchevo Rossi),** formerly Theatre Street, created by Carlo Rossi between 1828 and 1834. The width is the same as the height of the buildings (22 m, 72 ft) and the length of each building is ten times its height. The perspective of the street is therefore perfect and it is considered one of the most beautiful streets in the world. Rossi, born in St Petersburg, was the illegitimate son of an Italian ballerina and went on to become Tsar Alexander's favourite architect, having a hand in many of the fine buildings of the city. The ground floors of the buildings were originally to house shops, but the merchants of the nearby Gostinny Dvor, afraid of losing custom, put a stop to it.

Next to the Theatre Museum, is the former **Imperial Ballet School** which moved here in 1836. The name has changed (it is now the **Vaganova School of Choreography,** after the ballerina who taught here from 1921-51) but it continues to produce stars. Pavlova, Fokin, Balanchin and Ulanova all studied here.

On the square across the front of the entrance to Carlo Rossi Street is the **Pushkin Academic Drama Theatre.** This was built in 1828, also by Rossi, on the site of the garden that had been there before. The theatre was christened the Alexandrinsky in honour of Alexandra, the wife of Nicholas I and was host to some great theatrical moments, such as the premiere of Gogol's *The Inspector General,* before the Emperor himself. Depsite the fact that the Tsar was lambasted, he appeared to enjoy it. Later, Bakst designed some of his most marvellous sets for performances here.

In front of the theatre, in the small garden, is a **statue of Catherine the Great,** from 1873. On the front of the monument is her favourite, Potemkin, and next to him General Suvorov. On Potemkin's other side is Field-Marshal Pyotr Rumyantsev Zadunaisky and behind him Dashkova, the director of the Russian Academy of Sciences. Amongst others are the poet Derzhavin and the admiral Chichagov.

The rather dour building on the right of the square, indeed dominating it, is the **Saltykov-Shchedrin Public Library.** The oldest part is on the corner of Nevsky and the road behind it, Ul. Sadovaya, and was built to the design of Sokolov between 1796 and 1801. Between 1828 and 1832 Rossi added the part that overlooks Ostrovsky Square, crowning it with a **statue of Minerva,** the goddess of wisdom. It was opened as a library in 1814 and by now is one of the largest in the world. When it opened there were 238,000 volumes for a reading room that could hold only 46 people. Now there are 25½ million volumes including works in more than 250 languages, ancient manuscripts, the personal library of Voltaire, the earliest extant example of Russian printing, the letters of Erasmus, ancient Chinese scripts and the autographs of Byron, Rossini, Napoleon and many others.

Gostinny Dvor

Nevsky Prospect crosses Garden Street (Ul. Sadovaya) and comes to the huge **Gostinny Dvor (Merchants Court),** left. This is now the largest department store in the city, but was built in 1761-85 by De la Mothe as a lodging house and market for the merchants coming to do business in the city. The building covers an entire block, with a length of more than a kilometre (0.6 mile). All cities had a Gostinny Dvor (although not on this scale), with their echoes of the Eastern caravanserai. These markets were wholly Russian in character, as different from the fashionable stores of St Petersburg as Portobello Road market in London is different from Harrods. Russian custom was to group shops or stalls selling the same things in rows *(ryady),* and in St Petersburg there were some ten thousand merchants in Gostinny Dvor, all dressed in the traditional costume of Russian shopkeepers — blue kaftan and blue cap. In winter, since fires were not allowed, the merchants wrapped themselves in furs. Naturally each shop had its icon and the whole place resounded to the sound of birdsong and the rattle of the abacus. The air was moist with the steam of samovars and thunderous with the call of the merchants.

The Gostinny Dvor, which sold the highest quality goods, was not the only merchant quarter in the area. Along Ul. Sadovaya, beyond, were two more areas frequented by the peasant community. These were so densely packed with buyer and seller that wooden bridges were thrown across the streets that connected them. Between these three markets there was nothing that could not be bought and the whole area took on the atmosphere of a bazaar.

During the WW II the Gostinny Dvor was seriously damaged, providing an opportunity to redesign the interior. It now houses some 300 shops. During the reconstruction eight gold ingots weighing a total of 128 kg (282 lb) were discovered, apparently concealed there by a jeweller at the time of the Revolution.

Opposite the Gostinny Dvor is another large department store called **Passazh** (meaning passage or arcade), which has entrances on Nevsky and on Rakov Street behind it. Within the store is the **Komissarzhevskaya Drama Theatre** where Gorky's plays were staged in the early part of the century, next to which is the **Neva Restaurant** (reasonable) and the cafe **Sever,** which is in a building that was once a bank. Here too is the former Armenian church of St Catherine built in the 1770s in strictly western classical style. Originally it was endowed by an Armenian merchant called Lazarev who had come across an enormous stolen diamond smuggled out of India. He sold it to Catherine the Great's lover Orlov who gave it to Catherine. She had it set in her sceptre.

Further up, right, is Brodsky Street (named after the artist) which leads to Arts Square and the Russian Museum (described in another walk). On its corner with Nevsky is one of the oldest and most elegant hotels in the city, built in 1910 in art nouveau style, the **Evropeiskaya.**

On the other side of Nevsky, just past the Gostinny Dvor, in the middle of the road is a small **decorative pavilion** designed by Luigi Rusca between 1802 and 1806. When the metro was being constructed it was dismantled and then reconstructed. Now it is a ticket office.

Nevsky: the old Singer (sewing machine) building, now the 'House of Books'

Next to it is the pentagonal tower that sits atop the old **City Duma (City Council)** building. The Duma building was built by Quarenghi in 1784, while the tower is a later addition by Ferrari in 1804. The tower, built as a fire observation tower, was later adapted for sending sight communications between St Petersburg and the Tsar's other residences in the area, and also to Warsaw. On the roof of the Winter Palace there was a large T shaped frame with lights at its tips. It could be rotated into different positions which corresponded to certain signals. In this way messages could be passed to Warsaw within 24 hours.

In the arcade beneath the tower there used to be, until the Revolution, a jewellers shop, which is now an art salon.

On the other side of Nevsky is the former Roman Catholic **Church of St Elizabeth,** designed by De la Mothe in the late eighteenth century. Here the last Polish king, Stanislaw Poniatowski, who spent his remaining years in St Petersburg lies buried. Here too is the grave of General Moreau, a Frenchman who 'defected' to the Russian side during the Napoleonic War.

Next to the church, on the banks of the Griboyedev canal, is the **Lesser Hall of the St Petersburg State Philarmonia,** a building of the second half of the eighteenth century that belonged to a close friend of Pushkin, V. Engelhardt. During the nineteenth century many great musicians gave concerts here, amongst them Liszt, Berlioz, Wagner and Strauss. On the other side at number 35, is the **Balkan** cafe, which is not bad.

The Kazan Cathedral

The Griboyedev Canal is named after the Russian writer and diplomat. It was originally the Catherine canal. Crossing the Kazansky bridge (built by the father of the great Russian general, Kutuzov), will reveal, left, a spectacular view of the Kazansky Cathedral, built between 1801 and 1811, designed by one of the most interesting of the architects to have made a mark on St Petersberg, Andrei Voronikhin. He had been a serf of Count Stroganov who had noticed his artistic talents and and sent him to Moscow to study painting. He was more drawn to the study of architecture, however and enrolled in the St Petersburg Academy of Architecture. He also studied in Paris. Meanwhile Tsar Paul had decided to build a new cathedral to house the miraculous icon of Kazan, which had been brought to St Petersburg from Moscow. It was to be a wholly Russian effort and a competition was held to choose the architect. Voronikhin won. The cathedral with its half circle of Corinthian columns dominates this beautiful square and would seem to take its inspiration from St Peters in Rome, which the architect had seen on his travels around Europe. The **bas-reliefs** at the top of each end of the colonnade display two biblical scenes: on the left is Moses Parting the Waters and on the right the Brazen Serpent. The **bronze doors** are an exact copy of the fifteenth century doors by Giberti in the Baptistry in Florence.

After the defeat of Napoleon the cathedral became a sort of shrine to military glory and the 103 banners and flags taken from the French army were placed here. In the vault of the chapel to the right of the entrance is the grave of the commander of the Russian forces during the Napoleonic War, Kutuzov, buried where he prayed before he left for the front. A statue of him with his sword drawn, along with that of Field Marshal Barklai de Tolli, is in front of the cathedral. The overall effect of the interior, with its 56 red granite columns and mosaic floor of Karelian marble, is rather striking. The Kazan Cathedral has been the **Museum of the History of Religion and Atheism** since 1932. This is likely to be done away with fairly soon.

The area where the garden is now was the scene of several demonstrations before the Revolution, notably on Bloody Sunday in 1905.

A short diversion is recommended here. Take the embankment street left of the cathedral (Naberezhenaya Kanal Griboyedeva), passing **Kolos** beer hall and a booking office for airline and train tickets (also lavatories). A little beyond is a rather striking bridge, with a pair of gryphons at either end. This is the **Bankovsky Suspension Bridge,** so named because it led directly to the large building on the left, built as a bank in 1783-90 by Quarenghi. (Gryphons in ancient Greece were considered to be guardians of gold.) Today this is the **St Petersburg Finance and Economic Institute.**

Back on Nevsky, opposite the Kazan Cathedral on the corner of the canal, is the **House of Books (Dom Knigi).** Faced with granite and surmounted by a glass tower with a globe, it was built in 1907 for the Singer Sewing Machine Company. It had been planned as an 11-storey building, but a decree that nothing should be higher than the Winter Palace reduced it to six. Although the selection of books in English remains small, you may find some interesting maps and posters here. Near it, set back a way, is the Romanesque **Lutheran church** built between 1833 and 1838, used originally by the many German artisans who lived in St Petersburg at the time.

On the other side of the street, near the corner of Ul. Plekhanova, is the **Kavkasa** restaurant which specialises in Georgian food and is quite good; next to it is the **House of Fashion**. Just before it, with its entrance in Ul. Plekhanova, is a cafe where you can get good coffee and snacks in clean and pleasant surroundings.

Next to the Kafkasa restaurant is the baroque-style **palace** built by Rastrelli in 1753 for Count Stroganov. The arch over the gateway is surmounted by the Stroganov coat of arms, made up of features of Siberia where the family owned vast lands. The windows of the ground floor are one third their original size because of the raising of the level of Nevsky Avenue.

The tree-lined street on the other side of Nevsky is Ul. Zhelyabova. Number 21/23, the **House of St Petersburg Commerce,** is one of the largest stores in the city. It was built between 1907 and 1913 and was the first building in Russia constructed with ferro-concrete, although the style is the old Empire style.

Next to this street, at 20 Nevsky, is the former Dutch church. This was built in 1837 and now houses the **Alexander Blok Library.** Blok was a member of that literary movement, the Symbolists, for which art was everything and which tried to create a mystical world of metaphor — at one point he was paid five gold roubles for each line he wrote. His poetic dramas were performed in the experimental theatre on Offitserskaya Street in a new attempt to convey purified extracts of emotion. He described St Petersburg as 'a point of departure into infinity'.

Cross the Moika canal (described in another walk). On the other side, at number 15 (left), is a building, now housing the Barricade cinema, which is known to St Petersburgers as the **House of Columns.** It was built in the 1760s for the Chief of Police. The architect Quarenghi lived here when he first came to St Petersburg in 1800. Later, in 1858, the building became the property of the wealthy merchant Yeliseyev (whose grocery shop you saw earlier in the walk).

You now come to Ul. Gertsena, most of which extends away to the left and which, with Gogol Street, was the site of many banks and insurance companies. The little bit on the right leads to an arch of the General Staff building and then out to the Winter Palace (both of which are described in the next walk). This part of the street was built by Carlo Rossi along the Pulkovo Meridien — at noon watches can be checked here, for the buildings cast no shadow on the pavement. The section on the left leads to **St Isaac's Square,** (described in next walk) passing a bookshop (which sells ballet shoes) at number 9. The grey grim building on the corner is the **Kirov Technical Institute;** Aeroflot is at 13; and the fortress-like building is the **St Petersburg Building Committee.** Then, on the left a minor gem, is a jeweller's shop called **Yakunt.** Outside however, by the entrance, is emblazoned the name of the former owners: Fabergé. On the right is the **Amiralskaya** restaurant and at number 22 on the left a small Berioska shop.

Number 14 Nevsky Prospect has an interesting throwback to WW II and the siege of Leningrad. Some white letters are stencilled on a blue background, preserved, according the plaque next to it, in memory of the courage of the citizens during the siege. Soviet intelligence had established that Nazi artillery was positioned in such a way that the northwestern sides of streets were the more dangerous. This sign was one of many put up to warn citizens of the danger. The building itself is a rather new one, erected as a school in 1939.

The building at 8 and 10 are the oldest on Nevsky Prospect, with some very attractive friezes decorating their exterior. Number 8 is now a salon where St Petersburg artists sell their work. It is also possible to buy some high quality souvenirs.

Opposite is Gogol Street, named after the great Russian playwright, who lived at number 17 from 1833 to 1836. Here he created perhaps his most famous work, *The Government Inspector.* Number 13 was the home of the composer Tchaikovsky until his death (after a meal at the Literary Cafe on Nevsky Prospect, so it is said) in 1895.

Numbers 1 to 10 were well known as fruit shops before the Revolution. The most interesting building now is number 9, built in 1912, which is a sort of imitation of the Doge's Palace in Venice. Most of the building materials were brought from Sweden by a banker called Wawelberg. Now it houses the Aeroflot office and a Berioska shop.

The Admiralty

Opposite the end of Nevsky, the Admiralty was originally the site of the first city shipyard as well as a defense system secondary to the Peter and Paul Fortress — hence the open spaces in the area. The first fortress was made of earth, the second of stone. In 1738 all was rebuilt, with a tower and a golden spire. And at the beginning of the nineteenth century (1806-23) it was rebuilt again, to become one of the symbols of the city, marking the point of convergence of three main thoroughfares. The plan of the eighteenth century building was retained, as was the spire with the bronze caravelle at its tip. The theme of the sculptures on the façade is the glory of the Russian navy. Above the main entrance is a relief devoted to the founding of the navy by Peter the Great. Neptune, with the goddess of wisdom, Minerva, at his side, hands his trident to Peter. Under a tree is Russia in the guise of a woman resting on Hercules' club of strength. She holds the horn of plenty, which is being touched by Mercury the god of commerce. Other statues along the colonnades represent the four elements, the four seasons, and the four winds. The remaining depictions also have marine and military connections.

St Isaac's, St Petersburg. An impressive exterior, but an interior of unparalleled magnificence (photo: Jim Helme)

Merchant's Lodging to St Isaac's Square

Metro: Gostinny Dvor
From Gostinny Dvor metro station: Arts Square and the Russian
Museum, Church of the Resurrection, Field of Mars, Summer
Palace Embankment, Millionaires Row, Winter Palace and St
Isaacs Cathedral.

From the metro station walk across Nevsky Prospect and down
Ul. Sadovaya (public lavatory on left and a **Chasnaya** (Teashop) on
right). There is a cinema in an elegant mansion at number 12. At
Ul. Rakova turn left for Arts Square.

(You may like to make a short diversion, right where number 25
Ul. Rakova is a beautiful **baroque house** painted in blue, now an
academic centre. Number 42 Rakova (1771), was the home of the
statesman Speransky where Turgenev was a frequent visitor and
where the Decembrist Batenkov also lived. Then retrace your steps
towards Arts Square (Pl. Iskusstv).

Arts Square is as old as St Petersburg itself. The current ensemble
is another Rossi creation, most of the buildings dating to the early
nineteenth century, when owners of land in the area of the square
were asked to ensure that their palace façades conformed to Rossi's
design. It is one of the loveliest squares in the city, dominated by
the **Mikhailovsky Palace** on the right. In some ways this might be
thought of as the cradle of St Petersburg creativity since so many
famous artists have lived or performed here.

As you enter the square the **Musical Comedy Theatre** is on the
left at number 13, formerly a music hall; then, on the corner of
Brodsky Street, is the **St Petersburg Philarmonia building,** formerly
the assembly building of the aristocracy, and now named after the
Soviet composer Shostakovich. Even in its days as an assembly
room it was frequently used as a concert hall because of its excellent
acoustics. Tchaikovsky conducted his own *Sixth Symphony* here,
although it was only politely received. More recently, in 1942 during
the Nazi blockade of the city, Shostakovich's *Seventh Symphony,*
which he had written while working in the city's air defence unit,
was performed here. On the other corner is the **Evropeiskaya Hotel.**
The artist Brodsky used to live at number 5, in the basement of
which was the **Stray Dog cafe,** a meeting place of the litterati. It
opened in 1911 — lectures on avantgarde theatre were given, music
by avantgarde composers played, Mayakovski declaimed his poetry
here and the ballerina Karsavina danced to the music of Couperin
surrounded by flowers. On the site there once stood a hall where

both Berlioz and Lizst played; and next to it, at number 1, is the famous Maly ('Little') Opera House. Before the Revolution it was known as the Mikhailovsky Theatre, where performances were given to the nobles — ballets were frequently performed here in the early nineteenth century by the resident French company of which Sarah Bernhardt was a regular visiting member. Next is the Mikhilovsky Palace or the **Russian Museum.**

The Russian Museum (Mikhailovsky Palace)

It was built for Mikhail, the brother of Nicholas I, by Rossi between 1819 and 1825, although the wing on the left as you look at it was added by the architect Benois in 1912. The wrought iron work of the railings is particularly fine and the opulence of the building is enhanced by the ramp on either side of the central portico that would have allowed carriages to drive right up to the entrance. A park was created at the back. Much of the original interior decoration has survived and is considered one of the best examples of Russian classicism. In 1898 it was opened as a museum dedicated to Russian art. Works are displayed dating from the eleventh century to the present day.

On the first floor, **Rooms 1-4** contain mostly icons, including some by Rublyev. **Rooms 5-14** have paintings and sculptures of the eighteenth century (e.g. the *Field Hetman* by Peter the Great's court painter Nikitin). In **Room 6** note the mosaic portraits by Lomonosov (e.g. of Peter I's daughter Elizabeth). **Room 7** has a staue by the great architect Rastrelli's father Carlo. **Room 8** is dedicated to the portraitist Rokotov. In **Room 9** are busts of several of the emperors and the beginning of the trend of historical realism in painting. **Room 10** is dedicated to the charming portraits of the students at the Smolny Institute. Room 11 is the Room of White Columns by Rossi.

Rooms 15-17 display art of the early nineteenth century. In **Room 15** there is the famous picture of the destruction of Pompeii according to the description by Pliny the Younger, and the seascapes by Aivazovsky. **Room 16** has landscapes by Shchedrin, many of Italy. **Room 17** has portraits by Kiprensky.

The ground floor, in **Rooms 18-24,** is dedicated to the first half of the nineteenth century. **Room 19** has the peasant portraits by Venetsianov. Ivanov's *Christ before the People* takes up much of Room 21 and Room 24 contains the 'social comment' paintings of Fedotov (e.g. *A marriage of convenience*). **Rooms 25-74** deal with second half of the nineteenth century. The themes are a mixture from preceding eras — Perov, in **Room 25,** is a social commentator, and the continuing vogue for historical subjects is shown in **Room 26** with Ghe's *Peter the great interrogating Tsarevich Alexei at Peterhof.* In **Room 27** are works by Kramskoy, who started the 'Happy Wanderers' group of itinerant artists. **Rooms 33-5** are devoted to the works of the other 'wanderers'. **Rooms 36** and **37** contain work by Vereshchagin, his pictures from around the world and his war scenes from the Russo-Turkish War. Kuindji specialised in moonlit scenes, shown in **Rooms 38** and **39.**

The art of the late nineteenth century continues on the first floor of the Benois building. The work of Repin, perhaps the greatest of Russian painters, is exhibited in **Rooms 47-50.** The theme of Russian folklore was a favourite of Vasnetsov whose work hangs in **Room 51.** The portraits of Serov are in **Rooms 56-7. Room 60** contains works of Diaghilev's 'World of Art' group from the turn of the century — Benois, Bakst and others. In **Room 61** look for the portrait of Chaliapin. The ground floor of the Benois wing is devoted to Soviet art based on 'Marxist aesthetics . . . a civic approach on the part of the artist . . . fidelity to realism . . . produce a new type of harmoniously developed person with higher intellectual and spiritual requirements'.

To the right of the palace is the **Ethnography Museum,** built in 1911. This is the principal museum of its kind in the country and is dedicated to the ways of life of the many different nationalities that live in the USSR. It was founded in 1901 as part of the Russian Museum and for 'ideological' reasons became independent in 1934. Despite the fact that the country's nationality policy has been a transparent failure, it is extolled here. However, the exhibits dedicated to the traditions of the various peoples, from Turkmen carpets to Tajik paintings, and their national costumes, are of considerable interest.

Next to it is **Secondary School 199** built in the 1930s on the site of the house of Poland's national poet, Adam Miskevich.

In the centre of the garden is a **monument** to the poet Pushkin, erected in 1957.

To continue the walk go between the Maly Opera Theatre and the Benois wing of the Russian Museum to the Griboyedev Canal, and turn right. Ahead is a church with traditional Russian church features, but without the grace and balance. This is the **Church of the Resurrection,** completed in 1907 on the spot where Alexander II was assassinated in 1881 with a bomb, by members of a revolutionary organisation called 'People's Will'. Alexander constituted something of a threat to these extremists for the veryreason that he was trying to introduce reforms, and indeed had on his person the text of a speech he was to make the next day outlining some reforms. The assassination had a curious side effect. Alexander's daughter-in-law was inconsolable following his death and the Tsar her husband asked the court jeweller, Fabergé, to find something to cheer her up at Easter. Fabergé suggested a 'surprise' egg made of precious stones and thus a tradition was born that was to last until the Revolution. Follow the road right of the church, with the garden and its exquisite wrought-iron railings to the right. Follow the road around the church to **Konuzhanaya Square** on the left. The two large buildings here used to house the Imperial horses and carriages.

Turn right from the church until you reach the garden, then left, crossing the Moika canal, to the Field of Mars (Marsovo Polye), right, and a very large building that extends all the way ahead of you on the left of the street. The **Field of Mars,** received its name at the turn of the nineteenth century, imitating the plain near Rome used for military manoeuvres and taking its name from the god of war. The name was given to this ten hectare (25-acre) piece of land in honour of the two military leaders, Suvorov and Rumyantsev, whose monuments stood nearby, and was used for military exercises and parades. In 1919 a gravestone was laid in honour of all the Revolutionaries who died for the cause, and in 1920 the field was landscaped. The eternal flame was added in 1957 to commemorate 40 years of the USSR.

The huge building spanning the length of one side of the field, at number 1 Marsovo Polye, used to house the barracks of the Pavlovsky Regiment and was built between 1817 and 1820. The attic above the main entrance is decorated with Imperial military insignia.

The end of the street meets Ul. Khalturina. Before turning left here you may wish to visit the nearby **Summer Garden** (walk resumes p. 236). Turn right and walk until you reach a square. In the middle of it is a statue of the eighteenth century military leader Alexander Suvorov, after whom the square is named. Turn left here (Kirovski Bridge — originally the Trinity Bridge — ahead of you and an eighteenth-century building right), then right again along the embankment (lovely views across the Neva to the Peter and Paul Fortress and, further along, of the battleship Aurora) until you come to the Summer Garden, right, behind some beautiful railings.

The Summer Garden

The railings, and the embankment, were designed by Yuri Felten, the son of Peter the Great's chef, and were excecuted by artisans from Tula. They are elegance itself and are considered one of the finest examples of wrought-iron work in the world. The story is told of an Englishman who travelled by ship to St Petersburg, anchored by the Summer Palace, admired and sketched the railings and promptly hoisted anchor and left.

The little bridge at the end of the railings, crossing the Fontanka where it meets the Neva, is the oldest stone in the city, from the 1760s. The Royal Laundry was nearby: thus its name Laundry Bridge (Prachechny Most).

The Garden, the most beloved in the city, was laid out by Peter the Great, who wanted a garden greater than that of Versailles and 'open to all the people'. Its location is very typical of him, surrounded on three sides by water (the Neva, the Lebyazhya Canal and, then forming the southern boundary of the city, the Fontanka) and work on it began in 1704. Its designer, Leblond, was a Frenchman and the style is very French, a series of *allées* with many fountains, statues, bushes and flower beds. The fountains have gone (damaged by floods in 1777), but the garden is essentially as it was for although the original ideas were forgotten during the nineteenth century, the eighteenth century plan has since been re-established. In winter the flower beds were packed with straw and the statues housed where they stood in little wooden sheds, much as is done today. Pushkin loved to stroll here in the early morning and Tchaikovsky's opera *The Queen of Spades* opens here. Throughout the month of May there were a series of fêtes, and until 1917 Whitsunday was given over to the parading of their marriageable children by the wealthy merchants of the city.

Peter's **Summer Palace** was built in the garden. It is a construction of surprising simplicity, built in 1710 to the design of Trezzini and in the style that Peter had decreed appropriate for all nobles. It sits by the Fontanka, with a small dock for Peter's boat. Both floors are identical in layout, seven rooms plus a room for the servant on each. All the rooms are airy with large windows, very much in contrast with the comparatively stuffy rooms that had suffocated Peter in Moscow. The upper floor belonged to his wife Catherine, whose rooms were decorated in Chinese silk, woven with gold and silver and parquet floors inlaid with ivory and mother of pearl. Flemish and German tapestries hung here and there, as did Venetian and English mirrors. Peter's floor was spacious but furnished very sparingly with wooden panels, Dutch tiles and some of Peter's favourite scientific devices.

Behind the palace there are some of other small buildings: the **Tea House,** built in 1827 and the **Coffee House** of 1826. Close to the central *allée* is a statue of the writer of fables Ivan Krylov from 1855. Elsewhere the garden is dotted with **sculptures** from the era of the garden's creation. Just in front of the Palace is a group by Pietro Baratta called *Peace and Abundance,* executed in 1722. Nearby is one of the oldest pieces in the garden — a bust of the Polish King Jan Sobieski from 1680. The bust of the Roman Empress Agrippina, in baroque style, is unmistakable for the octopus that peeps from between the folds of her mantle. Finally, the Cupid and Psyche that stands near the terrace by the Swan Ditch (Lebyazhaya Kanavka), on the other side of the garden from the Palace, is a fine baroque sculpture.

The red brick structure with the spire behind the garden is the **Mikhailovsky Palace** built on the orders of the paranoic Tsar Paul I in 1797-1800, to replace the wooden palace that had been designed by Rastrelli. It is riddled with passages and protected by a moat and ramparts to foil the conspiracies, imaginary or otherwise, at court, yet within 40 days of moving in he was strangled by his peers. Later, the Central Engineering College, where Dostoyevsky studied, was housed here, earning it the name 'The Engineers' Castle'. Each of the four façades is different (e.g. the side overlooking the garden is floral and ornamental). Outside the main entrance is a statue of Peter the Great by Carlo Rastrelli. The castle now houses the **Science and Technology Library** of the St Petersburg Scientific and Technical Information Centre.

To resume the walk, return to the junction of the Field of Mars and Ul. Khalturina. You can walk to the Winter Palace along the embankment, but the view of the palace is better from the other side of the river. (By walking along Khalturina Street you will be able to absorb more of old aristocratic St Petersburg and approach the Winter Palace from a more intimately evocative angle.)

Khalturina Street was, before the Revolution, known as Millionaires Street for here, close to the Winter Palace, lived some of the richest citizens of the Empire. Opposite this junction, at number 5 (right), is the **Marble House.** This was built between 1768 and 1785 to the design of Antonio Rinaldi and was the home of the nobleman and lover of Catherine the Great, Grigory Orlov. The architecture is typical of the transition period from baroque to classicism. The Corinthian pilasters of the first and second floors are of pink marble. Today this elegant mansion houses the St Petersburg branch of the **Central Lenin Museum** with an armoured car in front bearing the inscription 'The Enemy of Capital'. From this vehicle Lenin made a speech upon his arrival at the Finland Station.

On the same side, on the corner, is a **beautiful house** with wooden window frames, stained glass windows and a fine balcony. At number 10 the great French writer Honore de Balzac lived and met his future wife Evelina Hanska. At number 11 there is a public lavatory. Number 19 has a rather attractive courtyard. Number 22, with its marble pillars, is now the **Committee for Physical Culture.** The courtyard of number 27 is of interest with its **chapel** of 1887. In here too is a hotel used by visiting academics.

Soon you will cross a small canal known as the **Winter Ditch (Zimnaya Kanavka)** which links the the Neva with the Moika. Its name derives from the fact that the original Winter Palace was built just here and is now very picturesque, a sort of Venetian corner with the aerial covered bridge on the right. On the corner just before the bridge is the **Hermitage Theatre** built by Quarenghi in the style of the theatre in Vicenza, and completed in 1787. The auditorium is in the round and the walls are decorated in pink and yellow artificial marble and striped with Corinthian columns, in between which are statues of the muses. It was the private theatre of Catherine the Great (some of her own works were performed here) and is now used as a lecture hall.

On the other side of the bridge is the rather overpowering entrance to the **New Hermitage,** built between 1839 and 1852 on the orders of Nicholas I. The ten statues are *atlantes* based on models by the Sculptor Terebenev. This was the first building in Russia to be purpose-built as a public art gallery and admission was free. The Neva side of this building is the **Old Hermitage** built by Felten and De la Mothe between 1775 and 1784, a commission from Catherine the Great who wanted a sort of townhouse to which she could retire (hence the name) away from the vastness of the Winter Palace. It was also built to house her library and her growing art collection. Boatloads of paintings, mostly from Western Europe, were often seen to be unloaded at the dock in front of the Hermitage, for she bought wholesale. She did not encourage native painters but instead bought foreign art by the batch (e.g. 15 Van Dycks from Sir Robert Walpole). She acquired more than 4,000 pieces, which became the basis of today's collection.

Although matters of state were dealt with in the Winter Palace, Catherine liked to hold her own more informal soirees in the Hermitage, where it was not necessary to rise every time the Empress did and where all formality was banned. Plays were read, paintings discussed and games, such as charades, played. This came to a halt only with the death of her favourite Potemkin, who had also lived in the Hermitage for a while.

Opposite the Hermitage, at number 38, is an apartment block with a canopy over the entrance. This was the Guard's Headquarters.

Khalturina Street ends at the Palace Square.

The Winter Palace: a powerful symbol of imperial splendour.

The Winter Palace

The square is dominated by the extraordinary aquamarine and white Winter Palace, a Russian Baroque masterpiece by Rastrelli, built between 1754 and 1762, that is a fairy tale in itself.

The plans for the original Winter Palace were drawn up by Trezzini in 1711. Two were built by him, one of wood and one of stone. They were originally located, as you have seen, on the other side of the Winter Ditch by the Neva, close, as Peter the Great required, to the shipyards and the Admiralty. The Winter Palace as you see it now was the fifth and was built for the Empress Elizabeth by Rastrelli.

Francesco Bartolomeo Rastrelli was the son of the Italian sculptor Carlo who was recruited by Peter the Great and who executed several busts of the men of his time. He brought his 16-year-old son with him to St Petersburg and taught him to love sculpture, which is evident from the architectural style of his son. The young Rastrelli was to become the court architect during the reign of Elizabeth and the genius behind the particular beauty of St Petersburg. He developed what came to be known as Elizabethan Rococo. Certainly it owes something to West European architecture but its inspiration is quite Russian. Rastrelli's creations are best seen beneath a coverlet of snow.

Rastrelli himself had built a third wooden palace for Anna and a fourth for Elizabeth. He started work on the fifth in July 1754 and it was to be lower but even more massive than the Catherine Palace at Pushkin (Tsarskoe Selo). It has 1,050 rooms, 1,786 windows and 117 staircases. Within, enormous halls were designed to hold thousands of people, their wooden doors over 12m (40 ft) high and covered in gold. It was not truly completed until 1817. Despite its size it can be regarded as a triumph, for it has a grace and elegance that somehow diminishes its massiveness but not its grandeur. It was the home of the most splendid court in Europe and still exudes grandness. The magical quality of the palace in its heyday is best shown by contemporary paintings where its lights burn through the windows out into the frosty air.

The dazzling nature of the festivities and balls that took place within is hard to imagine. It was of a majesty that belongs to another era, at least to another century. Yet, the rituals of court life remained unchanged for generations and lasted until the Revolution.

The 'season' opened on New Year's Day with a reception, given in the St George's Hall, for the Diplomatic Corps. However, it was the invitations to the court balls that were most sought after. For as many as ten thousand guests at any one time it was an entrée to another world, where they could mingle in the splendour of the **Golden Salon,** which was filled with mosaics, or the **Malachite Room,** which was decorated with furnishings in distinctive green. At each door a befrocked footman stood guard and equerries in capes and ostrich plumed hats were at the service of the nobility.

The balls took place in the **Nicholas Hall.** A ball would begin at 9 p.m. with the heralded entry of the Tsar and Tsarina. Then there was dancing, the ladies in their magnificent gowns and sparkling gems, the subalterns in their tight elkskin trousers which had to be heaved on by two batmen. Supper was at 11.00. The guests, preceded by the Tsar, went to another salon where thousands of candles, connected by string soused in quick-burning oil, burst into flame simultaneously. An orchestra played at either end. Then there was dancing again until 13.30 the next morning, when the Imperial couple took their leave.

Certainly the events within the Palace were far from the lives of ordinary people. Yet in some ways the gap between ruler and ruled was comparatively small. At Easter ice slides, surrounded by temporary booths, restaurants and theatres, were erected stretching from the square before the Palace all the way to Decembrists Square. The Emperor used to like to walk along the Palace Embankment and the Palace itself was open to foreigners who deposited their passports at the door. In 1839 the poet Zhukovsky, who was tutor to the Imperial children, shared his palace apartments with the writer Gogol, whose plays were not exactly pro-Government.

Nevertheless, palace life belonged to another world. The 6,000 inmates have gone but they have been replaced by the millions of exhibits that make up one of the greatest museums in the world, the Hermitage.

The Hermitage

The Winter Palace and the Hermitage are really two distinct entities. However, the museum has come to be known as the Hermitage.

To describe the collection in detail would require a separate book — there are 19 km (12 miles) of corridors and exhibits. The intention here is to give the visitors a rough idea of what there is to see and where to find it. It should be born in mind that exhibits are sometimes moved around.

The Intourist entrance is on the square. The roubles entrance is on the Neva side. By entering the latter you will see the famous **Grand Staircase,** designed by Rastrelli. As with a good deal of the interior decoration, it was partially destroyed in the fire of 1837 but it remains magnificent. At the top you can proceed through the **Field Marshal's Hall,** through the corridor hung with tapestries, to the **Pavilion Hall** with its columns and chandeliers, which is part of the Old Hermitage. There is the extraordinary **Peacock Clock** built in London by James Cox in the late-eighteenth century. From here you can go down to the ground floor, where the antiquities departments are. **Rooms 106 onwards** deal with **Roman** antiquities, **from 111 Greek** antiquities, and nearby are the rooms devoted to **Egyptian** antiquities.

The painting section is on the second and third floors:
Italian (Second floor): Room (Martini), 211 (Lippi), 214 (da Vinci), 217-18 (Giorgione), 219 (Lotto, Titian), 221 (Titian), 222 (Veronese), 232 (Carraci), 235 (Guardi), 236 (Tiepolo), 237 (Veronese, Tintoretto, Sustris, Caravaggio, Carraci), 238 (Giordano, Tiepolo, Canaletto, Bellotto). (Third floor): 337 (the twentieth-century art of Morandi and Guttuso).

Spanish (Second floor): Room239 (Goya, Murillo, Velazquez, Ribera, Zurbaran), 240 (El Greco, Pantoja de la Cruz). (Piccaso's works are found among the French on the third floor.)

The **Low Countries** are divided into Flanders, Holland and the Netherlands:
Flemish (Second floor): Room 245 (Brouwer, Teniers the Younger, de Vos, Snyders, Jordaens), 246 (Van Dyck), 247 (Rubens), 248 (Wildens).
Dutch (Holland) (Second floor): Room 249 (Hals, Steen, de Hooch, Janssens Elinga, Terborch, van Ostade, Heda, van der Ast, van Beyeren, Porcellis, Potter, van Ruisdael), 254 (Rembrandt).
Dutch (Netherlands) (Second floor): Room 261 (Campin), 262 (van der Weyden, Gossaert, Jacobsz, van Leyden, Breughel the Younger). (Van Gogh is among the French on the third floor.)

German (Second floor): Room 263 (Unknown artist fifteenth century *Last Supper*), 264 (Ambrosius Holbein, Cranach the Elder, Schultz, Pesne, Mengs). (Third floor): 342 (Caspar David Friedrich).

British (Second floor): 197 (Dawe). 299 (Reynolds. Romney), 300 (Gainsborough, Wright of Derby, Morland), 301 (Lawrence).

French (Second floor): Room 275 (Vouet), 276 (Le Nain), 279 (Poussin), 280 (Lorrain), 284 (Watteau), 285 (Lancret, Boucher), 287 (Chardin), 288 (Fragonard). (Third floor): 314 (Gros), 316-320 (Impressionists and Post-Impressionists including Van Gogh), 321 (Millet, Corot), 322,323 (Barbizon School), 331 (Delacroix), 332 (David, Ingres), 344, 345 (Picasso), 347, 348 (Matisse), 349 (Marquet, Dongen), 350 (Derain, Leger).

Other exhibits worth seeing: Room 315 (sculptures of Rodin), 243 (West European armoury), 128 (Kolyvan vase, made of Jasper), 162 (mosaics from the workshop of the scientist Lomonosov and a portrait by him of Peter the Great), 189 (the Malachite Room), 190 (tomb of Alexander Nevsky), 198 (St George's Room).

The rest of Palace Square (Dvortsovaya Ploshad)

Opposite the Winter Palace is the **General Staff Building.** The Tsar wanted the square to harmonise with the Winter Palace, and so bought all the houses on the south side of the square in 1819 and asked Carlo Rossi to create a new building to house the General Staff of the Russian army. Two buildings were erected in a sort of arc linked by a triumphal arch leading to Ul. Gertsena and to Nevsky Prospect, and which coincidentally celebrated Russia's defeat of the Napoleon) crowned by horses bearing the winged figure of Glory. It eventually housed the Ministry of Finance and the Ministry of Foreign Affairs as well, and was completed in 1829. It is the longest building in Europe.

In the centre of the square is the **Alexander Column,** supposedly the tallest monument of its kind in the world. It was designed by Auguste Montferrand (architect of St Isaac's) and is another celebration of the defeat of Napoleon. The basic material was extracted from a cliff in one of the bays of Finland and brought by boat to St Petersburg in 1832. Weighing 715 mt (704 tons) it was a demanding item to lever into place and the fact that it was done without damage to it or to the workmen is considered an engineering miracle. It is 47.5 m (156 ft) tall and not cemented to its base. The angel on the top symbolises the peace over Europe following the defeat of Napoleon. The bas-reliefs on the pedestal symbolise Peace and Justice, Wisdom and Plenty, Victory and Peace and, in the one facing the palace, the crossing of the Rivers Niemen and the Vistula by troops in pursuit of the French army.

The Palace Square is famous in more recent history for the deaths of workers who were fired upon while trying to hand a petition to the Tsar in 1905. More than a thousand were killed on 'Bloody Sunday'. In October 1917 the Palace was stormed by the Bolsheviks in an attempt to bring down the Provisional Government established following the fall of the Tsar.

To continue the walk, cross the square to the gap between the Admiralty and Nevsky Prospect. Walk past the entrance to Nevsky, keeping the Admiralty (described in the preceding walk) right and St Isaacs Cathedral ahead of you. This is **Admiralteisky Prospect.** At number 6 is a testament to the recent ignoble past — this was the first home of the CHEKA (All Russia Extraordinary Commission for Struggle Against Counter-Revolution and Sabotage), effectively the forerunner of the KGB. You will pass Dzerzhinsky Street, left (public lavatories, right, in front of the Admiralty), and then come to Maiorova Street, left. Number 4, just around the corner from Admiralteisky, is the **Gril Sal** and which serves some very passable snacks.

Continue along Admiralteisky to the former Senate Square, now known as **Decembrists' Square (Ploshad Dekabristov),** passing (left) number 12, a huge wedge-shaped building, built in 1817-20 by Montferrand, the architect of St Isaac's, for Prince Alexei Lubanov-Rostovsky. The lions in front, playing with balls, one of which has rolled away, are symbols of alert guardianship. Beside it is St Isaac's Cathedral (see below), to which you may return after a quick look at Decembrists' Square, scene of the attempted aristocratic uprising in December 1825 (see History section).

In front of you, at the end of Admiralteisky Prospect, is the porticoed **Manege** (stables) built by Quarenghi in 1804-7, now the **Central Exhibition Hall.** In front of it are two marble statues of naked **Dioscuri** (in Greek mythology, offspring of Zeus and a mortal woman; they spent alternate days on Mount Olympus and amongst the dead of the underworld). They are copies of those in front of the Quirinale in Rome and were placed here in 1817. But their nakedness was deemed inappropriate so close to the cathedral and they were removed and returned only in 1954. Next door is the former **Horse Guards Boulevard** (today's Bulvar Profsoyuzov), marked at its beginning by two Ionic columns erected in 1845 to commemorate the feats of the Horse Guards (whose barracks extend along the right side of the Boulevard) in the war against Napoleon.

Next to the Boulevard is the former **Synod** building linked by an arch to the former **Senate** building by the Neva. The Senate, which was the highest organ of government before the Revolution, was originally on Vasilyevsky Island, and was moved here in 1763. The little street next to it was known as Galley Street (now Krasnaya Street). In the early nineteenth century Rossi was asked to rebuild the Senate and to create something similar for the Synod (the administrative organ of the Russian Orthodox Church). Thus the merchants house on the corner of Galley Street was purchased and the current ensemble created. Today the **Central State History Archives of the USSR** are housed here.

In the centre of the square is one of the great sculptures of the world — the equestrian **statue of Peter the Great,** created by the Frenchman Falconet. The base is a huge block of granite from a cliff some 19 km (12 miles) away. It was rolled on castors, all 1,625.6 mt (1,600 tons) of it, to the coast and brought here by boat. Falconet took 11 years to complete this project, spending long hours studying horses and riders in the nearby stables. Peter looks out across his beloved water leading his country on to progress, unbowed by obstacle or opponent. The bronze lettering says: 'To Peter I from Catherine II. 1782.', the year of the statue's unveiling.

St Isaac's Cathedral

There is something particularly right about this cathedral. Its colouring of bronze and gold stands resplendent against the colours of the skies typical of St Petersburg and is one of the symbols of the city. The first church was a wooden one built in 1710 hard by the Admiralty, also called St Isaac's in honour of the saint whose feast day coincided with Peter the Great's birthday. This was followed by a stone version which by the end of the eighteenth century had become rather dilapidated.

At the beginning of the nineteenth century Alexander I decided to replace it with something new, monumental and permanent. The commission went to Auguste de Montferrand, a Frenchman whose only claim to fame was to have assisted in the building of the Madeleine in Paris before enlisting in the Imperial Guard. Work started in 1818 and was completed only 40 years later.

On the pediment of the southern façade (overlooking the square) the **bronze high-relief** is the story of the 'Adoration of the Magi'. On the north it is the 'Resurrection of Christ', on the east the meeting of Isaac with Emperor Valens (a symbol of union of church and state) and on the west the meeting of Isaac with the Emperor Theodosius (in the left hand corner of this one there is a partially

Opposite: Peter I, the Great: a visionary who brought Russia closer to the West, and in doing so created one of the most beautiful cities in the world. **Following page:** The Venice of the North. A view across the Fontanka Canal to the vermillion Beloselsky-Belozersky Palace.

naked man, Montferrand, holding a model of the cathedral.)

The interior is 'a symphony of gold, marble, lapis lazuli, malachite and porphyry'. The walls and vaults are decorated with paintings and mosaics by the leading artists of the day, and the walls and floors are lined with marble from Russia, France and Italy. The columns of the iconostasis are faced with malachite and lapis. There are altogether 112 columns of polished granite holding the building up, of which 24 support the dome. There are 562 steps up to the top. It can hold 14,000 people. It doesn't take much imagination to visualise such a congregation, their faces brightened by thousands of candles lit simultaneously by guncotton fuse soused in inflammable oil. Indeed it is encouraging to note that the Cathedral, having been deconsecrated in 1931, has recently been reconsecrated and will no longer simply be a museum.

The Cathedral is 101.5 m (333 ft) high and the dome (for the making of which 100 kg (220.5 lb) of gold was used) is 26.5 m (87 ft) in diameter, making it one of the largest in the world.

Montferrand died a month after it was completed and when his request to be buried in its vaults was refused his body was returned to Paris and the obscurity whence he came.

St Isaac's Square (Isaakiyevskaya Ploshad)

There are several buildings of interest here. Directly ahead (from the Cathedral) is the **Mariinsky Palace** (not unlike Buckingham Palace) built in 1839-44 by the architect Stakenschneider for Maria the daughter of Nicholas. In 1884 her family sold it to the government and it became the seat of the State Council, which was the highest legislative body in Tsarist Russia. Following the Revolution of February 1917 the provisional government was set up here, until it was forced out by Lenin and the Bolsheviks. When the capital moved back to Moscow, it became the office of the city Soviet (Municipal council) and so it has remained.

In front of it is the **Moika Canal** and the **Blue Bridge,** the widest in the city (100 m, 328 ft).

There are two identical buildings on either side of the square, dating back to 1844-53 and built for the Ministry of State Property. Today they both form part of the **Vavilov Institute** of Plant Breeding. Number 11 (right) is a building of dark red granite, built in 1911-12. It became the German Embassy but now houses the offices of the St Petersburg branch of Intourist.

Ul. Soyuza Svyazi runs off the square and is noticeable for the arch that spans it.

Number 7 Ul. Soyuza Svyazi houses the **Popov Communications Museum,** exhibiting the history of communication in Russia and the state collection of postal stamps. Number 9 is the old **General Post Office,** dating back to 1782-9. The arch was added later to enable the post office director to commute to work from his flat across the street. It remains a post office.

Number 5 St Isaac's Square houses the **Museum of Musical Instruments,** one of the largest in the world. The remaining building, on the left of the square, is the **Astoria Hotel,** an elegant piece of pre-Revolutionary high life built in 1912, with mock-Louis XV bedrooms. H.G. Wells was one of the many eminent people who have stayed here. It has recently been restored.

In the centre of the square is the **equestrian statue** (1859) of Tsar Nicholas I, rather more pompous than that of Peter the Great. He was a lover of things military and that is how he is portrayed. The pedestal is decorated with figures representing Faith, Wisdom, Justice and Power, with the faces of his wife and daughters.

The walk ends here; nearest metro station is a third of the way down Nevsky Prospect — buses 3, 22 and 27 go there.)

The Moika Canal and the University Embankment

The moika is in some ways the epitome of St Petersburg. 5 km (3 miles) long from its beginning near the Field of Mars to its end at the Neva beyond St Isaac's Cathedral, it cuts through many of the most interesting parts of the city and yet remains comparatively tranquil. Here was the meeting point of aristocrat and artist, revolutionary and hotelier. The canal waters were filled with brightly painted houses on rafts called *sadki,* which were effectively fish restaurants. On two sides there were rooms, one for the crew and one for the customers. The main room in the middle was festooned with salted and smoked fish, illuminated by icons in the corner with lamps burning underneath.

To walk along the canal on a crisp winters day, or under the white night sky of July, is to see St Petersburg at its most typical.

The nearest metro stations are the linked Gostinny Dvor and Nevsky Prospect. (If you arrive at the first, follow the first part of the last walk i.e. Sadovaya, Ul. Rakova, Pl. Iskusstv and the Griboyedev Canal across the bridge to the corner of the Field of Mars. If you arrive at the second follow the Griboyedev to the same point.)

(The Field of Mars and the huge building at number 1 Field of Mars on the corner of the Moika Canal are described in the preceding walk.)

Walk from the Field of Mars along the Moika. The mass of the former **Imperial Stables** is on the other side, built by architect Stassos in 1823. Pushkin's body, after his death, was brought to a chapel that stands in the middle of the stables. On the right, at number 3, is the former eighteenth-century covered market known as the **Round Market.** Number 9 is reputed to have been the house of Stakenschneider, one of the principal architects of nineteenth century St Petersburg, although there is nothing there now. It was one of the social centres of the city, the meeting place of many eminent and artistic figures such as Dostoyevsky and Turgenev. Number 15 is a charming building which now houses the **French consulate.** You cross a small bridge and pass at number 8 (left) the former home of the nineteenth-century satirical writer Saltkinof Schedrin — he was arrested here and exiled to the town of Viatka. Number 23 (right), which looks older, was only built in 1913-14 for Prince Lazarov and is now the **Committee for Physical Culture.** Opposite, at number 12, is the house where the poet Pushkin lived, where he returned after his duel and where he died early on 29 January 1837. His body was quickly moved to a chapel for fear of the rumpus that might ensue should it be moved in daylight. His flat is now a **memorial museum** — it included the waistcoat he wore at the duel, his death mask, some of his personal effects, and his personal library.

Next door at 14 lived the Decembrist Ivan Pushin, who was also the close friend of Pushkin — they studied together at the Lyceum at Tsarskoe Selo. Further up, at 24 lived the friend of the tyrannical Nicholas I, the reactionary and enemy of Pushkin, Aracheev.

Soon you reach the 70 m (230 ft) **Singing Bridge,** so called because of the concert hall (the capella) to its left (right is the Winter Palace and its square, and the wedge of the General Staff Building). Valinsky Street, first left after the bridge, is named after a former resident of the 1730s who led an unsuccessful plot against Buhren, the unpopular German lover of the Empress Anna. Number 40 (back on the Moika), with the canopy over its main entrance, was a fashionable hotel in the nineteenth century where Pushkin,

Griboyedev and Turgenev stayed.

Crossing Nevsky Prospect to continue along the Moika you come to the **Stroganov Palace** (left). The buildings all belong to the **Herzen Pedagogical Institute,** one of the largest teacher-training schools in the country. The most palatial of the buildings, with the statue of Ushensky who was a famous teacher in front of it, was built by Rastrelli for a nobleman by the name of Stegelman. At the end of the 19th century, it became the St Petersburg orphanage.

Continuing along the Moika will bring you to Dzerzhinsky Street, named after the first leader of the CHEKA (forerunner of the KGB). In the other direction, at 62 Dzerzhinsky Street, Rasputin lived. The building to the right, on Dzerzhinsky at the corner of the Moika on the far side, was started in 1915 by Benois, to be a bank. It was only completed in 1929, with the addition of a few ideologically correct Soviet features. It then became a textile institute, where former President Kosygin studied.

Continue to St Isaac's Square, passing (left) the Mariinsky Palace and (right) the Cathedral. (What seems to be part of the square in front of the Mariinsky is in fact the Blue Bridge. The buildings on the square are described in the preceding walk, but the twin buildings, right, on the banks of the canal facing each other across the square, were built in 1844-53 for the Ministry of State Property.)

Back on the Moika, 72 (left) used to belong to the poet and leader of the Decembrists, Ryleev, and became the HQ for the movement. He was hanged when the uprising failed. In fact the house belonged to the Russian-American Trade Company, but Ryleev lived in a flat there. Number 86 was the house of the architect Montferrand, who designed St Isaac's Cathedral.

There are a number of beautiful houses on this part of the Moika but one of the most impressive is at number 94, past the footbridge. it is a grand edifice with huge pillars, large wooden doors and lanterns. This is the former **Yusopov Palace,** built in the 1760s by the French architect De la Mothe for one of the wealthiest families in the country. In the private theatre here Glinka sang in the premiere of his opera *Ivan Susanin* and in the basement Rasputin was shot before being thrown into a nearby canal. Now it is a **Palace of culture** for teachers but is occasionally open to the public for tours of its splendid interior. Sometimes performances in English or French are given in the theatre. (To find out about tours or performances ask someone at an Intourist service desk to telephone on your behalf, or go yourself, armed with your questions written in Russian.)

Cross to the right bank of the Canal and continue forward, to a point where the Moika is met by another canal on the right. This canal, the Krustein Canal (formerly the New Admiralty canal) forms a loop and rejoins the Moika further up, creating an island known as New Holland. Turn right here, keeping New Holland to your left. The island was used for the storage of inflammable goods, such as wood. In 1763 it was decided to replace the old wooden storage sheds with stone ones. Furthermore, it was decided that logs were to be stored vertically, at a slight incline, rather than horizontally and so the height of the sheds varied according to the lengths of timber.

The circular building on the banks of the Krustein Canal is the old naval prison, built in the 1820s.

Continue to Trud Square, where the first part of the walk finishes. (A number 6 bus will return you to a metro station).

Trud Square (Labour Square) was originally on the edge of the city and came into being after the construction of a permanent bridge between Vasilyevsky Island and the Admiralty. The canals that used to flow across this area were piped underground and the square became an integral part of central St Petersburg, with the name of **Annunciation Square.** To show the importance of the square a huge palace was built between 1853 and 1861 by Stakenschneider for the first son of Nicholas I. Later it belonged to Xenia, the daughter of Alexander III. Subsequently, in 1895, it became the Xenia Institute for Noble Young Ladies (a school for the daughters of the aristocracy). In 1917 it was given to the Petrograd Trade Union Council and named the Palace of Labour, now the **St Petersburg Trade Union Council.**

(The Synod and Senate building on this square are described in the previous walk.)

Ahead is the bridge which crosses to the University Embankment. On the embankment on this side, number 44 (left) is the **State History Museum of St Petersburg.** It is mostly dedicated to the history of the city under Soviet rule — the most interesting part tells of the 900-day siege during the WW II.

Formerly the English Embankment (now Krasnova Flota Embankment), the **English Church** was at 56.

The bridge was formerly the Nicholas Bridge, opened in 1850. and is now the Lieutenant Schmidt Bridge (after a Revolutionary). When Nicholas I commissioned the bridge by Stanislav Kerbedz, the architect was told that he would be elevated a rank for every buttress that was built. Naturally he added a few extra buttresses and ended up an engineer-general. Kerbedz's bridge was dismantled in the 1930s (it apparently could not cope with the traffic) and moved to the town of Kalinin. The current bridge was finished in 1938.

Vasilyevsky Spit and the University Embankment

(Visitors exploring this section as a separate item are likely to start with the Spit and should therefore follow the walk in reverse.)

Vasilyevsky Island is the largest in the estuary. Left of the bridge is Lieutenant Schmidt Embankment; right is Universitetskaya Embankment. The most famous and elegant part is to the right but there are a few buildings of some interest to the left. For example on the corner of the embankment and the 7th Line (Street) (Sedmaya Liniya) is the house where the physiologist and Nobel Prize winner Pavlov lived. Also left, towards the end of the embankment, is the **Mining Institute and Mining Museum** between Lines 21 and 23. This building (1806-11) is considered one of the finest in the city. It contains one of Peter's boats.

Turning right after crossing the bridge brings you soon to the **Academy of Arts** with its long façade and three colonnades, built in 1764-88 by De la Mothe and Kokorinov. It is one of the finest examples of early classicism in Russia. The Academy was founded in 1757 and has produced an enormous number of eminent Russian artists, amongst them the painters Serov, Shishkin and Repin and the architect Voronikhin. Today it is the largest art school in the world and houses an art museum with works by former students and graduates.

In front of the Academy there is a pier designed by Ton in 1832-4. It is rendered rather distinctive by the pair of **Egyptian sphinxes,** made of pink granite, at either side. They bear hieroglyphic inscriptions in honour of the Pharaoh Amenhotep III (1455-1419 BC), and were brought to St Petersburg in 1831. Here too are granite benches bearing images of gryphons and girandoles, which were recreated in 1954 after they had disappeared at the beginning of the century.

Next to the Academy is a garden with a **1799 obelisk** commemorating the victory of Russia over Turkey in 1768-74.

Number 15 is the **Palace of Alexander Menshikov** (a close friend of Peter the Great), one of the most interesting buildings in St Petersburg. At the beginning of its construction by Fontana and Schadel, at the beginning of the eighteenth century, it was the most luxurious palace in the city and the first large stone building. In fact the palace was so much more palatial than Peter's that government assemblies were not infrequently held here. originally the whole island belonged to Prince Menshikov, although Peter later retrieved his gift. The palace succeeds in combining European features (the gables are Dutch influenced) with Russian in the exterior. The interior is of considerable interest, rather more satisfying in its noble simplicity than the gaudy and overpowering palaces outside the city. Note that the railing of the main staircase with the monograms of both Menshikov and Peter fashioned into it. Here too are some fine Dutch landscapes, Dutch decorative tiles, a portrait of Menshikov, Russian tiled stoves, sixteenth- to eighteenth- century furniture, and the walnut room overlooking the Neva, with marvellous views across to St Isaac's Cathedral, the Admiralty and the aristocratic palaces that line the embankment to the right. Note too the 1713 lathe, placed here to please Peter who was a lover of such things.

Although the palace has been restored to its seventeenth-century state, in the second half of the eighteenth century it became the **Imperial Cadet School** until the Revolution.

In order to obtain tickets you should go first in the morning to reserve a place on one of the afternoon tours.

Number 13, next door, was the original cadet school of St Petersburg, built by Burkhardt in 1740.

Adjacent at number 11 (built in 1727 for Peter II), is the **Philological Department of St Petersburg Zhdanov State University.** The main university building next door is one of the oldest in St Petersburg. Peter had considered constructing the city centre on Vasilyevsky Island and thus the 'think tanks' that he initiated in 1718 as part of his campaign to civilise the country were to be housed here. There were to be 12 such groups and Trezzini was commissioned to design a building to house them — each group was to be evidently separate yet at the same time under one roof. The result went up in 1722-41 and as you look along its immense length you can see the 12 divisions quite clearly. Eventually it was clear, before the era of bridges, that placing the city centre on an island separated from the mainland by a wide tidal river was not a good idea and so most of the government institutions were moved to the other side. Thus in 1819 Trezzini's building became **St Petersburg University.** Between it and number 13 is the little red building that is the rector's office — the poet Alexander Blok was born here.

After the main building is Mendeleyevskaya Liniya and then, at number 7, the main building of the **Academy of Science.** The St Petersburg Academy of Sciences had its beginnings in the building next door but in 1783-8 these premises were built to alleviate the Academy's cramped conditions. Another classical design by Quarenghi, this is considered to be one of his masterpieces. After the Revolution it became the Academy of Sciences of the USSR and moved its headquarters to Moscow, although a great deal of its work continues in St Petersburg. The statue in front is of Lomonosov, the greatest of Russian scientists.

A quick look across the Neva to the Admiralty shows you how the original E-shaped plan of its buildings has been ruined filling the giant courtyard thus created with office blocks.

Next door, number 3, originally the home of the St Petersburg Academy of Sciences, is the **Kunstkammer** (German for 'art chamber'). Peter the Great had accumulated a considerable private collection of curiosities (housed first in the Kikin Palace near Smolny), which became the first Russian natural history museum (free to the public). When the collection outgrew Kikin Palace, the Kunstkammer was constructed in Russian Baroque by Novi in 1734. Lomonosov worked here for over twenty years in the middle of the eighteenth century and the lecture hall where he taught has been preserved. The upper storey was an early astronomical observatory and the country's first public library was housed here. Today the Kunstkammer houses several museums under its roof. The **Institute of Ethnography** and the **Peter the Great Museum of Anthropology and Ethnography** specialises in the lives of the indigenous peoples of Africa, the Americas, Asia and Australia — particularly interesting is the section on North American races collected in the eighteenth and nineteenth centuries when Alaska belonged to Russia. Here too is the collection of human and animal 'freaks' that belonged to Peter.

The **Mikhail Lomonosov Museum,** also in the Kunstkammer, is dedicated to the scientist's life, Russian astronomy and the Great Academic Globe (with a world map on its surface and a map of the heavens on its inner surface: several people could stand inside and follow the movement of the stars as the globe rotated).

Next to the Kunstkammer, number 1, is the **Zoology Museum and Zoology Institute.** This is housed in one of the warehouses that made up the Spit around the corner. On display here are more than 40,000 species of animals from all over the world, including many that are extinct or very rare. One of the highlights must be a stuffed mammoth discovered in 1901 and a baby one discovered preserved in the ice of Siberia in 1977.

The so-called **Vasilyevsky Spit** was the St Petersburg port between

1733 and 1885. The old **Customs House,** the old **Stock Exchange** and the **warehouses** were built here. The southern warehouse, which houses the Zoological Museum, and the northern warehouse, on the other side of the old Exchange, were built in 1826-32 by Giovanni Lucini. The northern warehouse today houses the **Central Soil Science Museum.** Between the two is the former Stock Exchange, built in 1805-10 by de Thomon in the style of a Greek temple. The façade is adorned with a figure of Neptune. It now houses the **Central Naval Museum,** founded by Peter the Great elsewhere in 1709. It contains one of Peter's boats, an ancient dugout and material devoted to the feats of the Russian and Soviet navy.

In front of it is the Spit itself, a granite embankment and dock constructed on piles at the start of the eighteenth century. To either side of it stand two **Rostral Columns** (a rostrum in Ancient Rome was a column decorated with prows of captured galleys), each of which is 32 m (105 ft) high. The metal prows on the columns are symbolic of Russian naval victories and at their bases are personifications of the four great Russian waterways — the Dnieper, the Volga, the Volkhov and the Neva. Atop each column is a bronze bowl which would have been filled with oil. As the oil burned the flame acted as a sort of beacon for arriving ships.

Along the embankment beyond the northern warehouse (number 4) is the old **Customs House,** built by Lucini in 1829-32. The dome above its portico was an observation tower from which was sounded a signal on the arrival of a ship — calm though the spit is today only a hundred years ago it was one of the liveliest parts of the city and the Customs House was kept endlessly busy. Today it houses the **Institute of Russian Literature of the USSR Academy of Sciences,** known as Pushkin House. Here many manuscripts of the great men of letters of Russian history are stored. There is an exhibition devoted to the lives of Gogol, Turgenev, Tolstoy and Dostoyevsky and others.

(Here the walk ends — nearest metro is distant; you are advised to take a bus over the Palace Bridge, to Nevsky Prospect — Buses 7, 10, 44, 45 or 60.)

The Peter and Paul Fortress and Petrovsky Island

Nearest metro station is Gorkovskaya.

You may choose to walk this area in several ways: the Peter and Paul Fortress alone; the Fortress combined with Peter's cottage and the Aurora; Fortress, cottage, Aurora, plus the walk along Kirovski Prospect; or Peter's cottage, the Aurora and the Kirovsky walk, excluding the Fortress.

The Peter and Paul Fortress

Here, on Hare's Island (Zayachi Ostrov) is the beginning of the city, a fortress built to defend the outlet to the Baltic. It was an excellent choice for it overlooks three waterways — the Neva and the Greater and Little Nevkas. The original was built of earth and wood but it was decided in 1706, after Peter had decided to build his new city, to construct a permanent fortress of stone, designed by Gaspard Lambert. It took 35 years to construct the 12-m (39-ft) high brick walls, later faced with granite slabs in the 1780s.

Before visiting the fortress proper you may wish to visit the **Artillery, Engineering and Signals Museum.** This is on a piece of land surrounded by a moat beyond the Kronwerk Straight — the stretch of water that separated Hare's Island from the mainland: from the metro station turn right along the Kirovski Prospect to the Kirovski Bridge; right again before the Kronwerk Straight and just after a monument to a bridge across the moat. The monument is to the crew of the torpedo boat Steregushchy who, during the Russo-Japanese War of 1904, scuttled their damaged boat, preferring death to dishonour.

The museum stands on the earthwork that used to protect the fortress from the north and is the biggest military museum in the world. The display ranged from ancient arquebuses to recent ballistic missiles. There is also an exhibition dedicated to the capabilities of the Soviet Army and its relations with the armies of the rest of the world. Outside the museum, in the park, is a tall obelisk to mark the spot where the Decembrists were executed.

Retrace your steps back to the Fortress. Enter through St John's Gate (1740) and proceed to St Peter's Gate, built by Trezzini in 1717-18. Trezzini, an Italian from Lugano who had been in the service of the Danish Court, was one of the first architects to imprint his stamp on St Petersburg. The gate us the one part of the Fortress that is completely original. There are two **bas-reliefs** in wood — one depicts armour and the god of Sabaoth in the clouds, the other a pagan priest overwhelmed by the prayer of the Apostle Peter, an allegorical representation of Peter the Great. The two-headed eagle was the symbol of Imperial Russia. (Originally this was the symbol of ancient Rome — the early Tsars believed that Russia was fated to assume the role of Byzantine and thus it became the symbol of Russia for 420 years.)

Proceed to the **Cathedral,** passing (left) the **Engineers' House** built for the engineers constructing the Fortress in the 1740s and today housing the **Museum of eighteenth to early twentieth Century Architecture of St Petersburg and Petrograd** and (right) the early nineteenth century **Artillery Arsenal.**

The foundations for the Cathedral were laid in 1712 by Trezzini and the Cathedral itself jointly designed with Ustinov. The spire, 122 m (400 ft), until recently remained the highest building in the city. It is one of the great symbols of St Petersburg and in fact was built before the main body of the church in order to allow the ground beneath it to settle. The design owes a lot to Trezzini's sojourn in Denmark, but the original was more baroque and more Danish — the original wooden spire was burnt by lightening in 1756 and replaced by a still slimmer spire.

The Cathedral was the burial place for most of the Tsars from Peter the Great onwards and the sarcophagi are splendidly arrayed. **Peter's sarcophagus** is the right of the south entrance; amongst the others those of Alexander II are rather fine — they took 17 years to carve from jasper and rhodonite. The inconostasis was carved in the 1720s.

The **old prison, Alexeyevsky Ravelin,** is at the western end of the Fortress, beyond the Cathedral. As you leave the Cathedral you will pass (right) the pavilion where one of Peter the Great's boats is kept and come to the **Mint,** which runs almost the width of the Fortress. The original mint, founded in 1724 was elsewhere — this one was built in 1802 and from 1876 became the only place in the country where money was legally coined. Soviet coinage has been produced here since 1921.

Behind the Mint is the original wall and its **bastions,** the Trubetskoi (left) and the Zotov (right). In the middle is the **Vasilyevsky Gate.** The Peter and Paul Fortress soon became a prison; indeed Peter had his own son Alexei imprisoned here, accused of treason; he was tortured and eventually died. As time

The National Hotel, Moscow. Pre-revolutionary style is much in abundance and new attempts are being made to return it to its former magnificence (photo: Jim Helme).

passed anyone deemed subversive was incarnated here, including several of the Decembrists. The Alexeyevsky Ravelin prison was demolished and another built inside the Trubetskoi Bastion in 1870. The writer Gorky was one of the many radicals to languish in the latter, in cell number 60.

On the south (river) side, back towards the Cathedral sits the former Commandant's House now the **Museum of the History of St Petersburg and Petrograd 1703-1917.**

The wall near here forms the **Naryshkin bastion** (to the right of the Commandant's House looking at it from the Mint). On its summit is the flagpole on top of which a lamp burned as the signal to the cruiser *Aurora* to fire the shots that launched the storming of the Winter Palace.

A little further along the wall is the **Neva Gate** of 1787, considered one of the finest pieces of architecture in the Fortress. It leads to the **Commandant's Pier,** from which a cannon is fired every day at noon.

(To continue this walk to Peter's cottage, return to the metro station.)

Peter's Cottage and the Cruiser Aurora

(metro: Gorkovskaya)

From the metro station you will see the **mosque** built in 1912, a copy of the Tamberlane Mausoleum in Samarkand. Turn right and follow Prospect Gorkovo, crossing Kirovski Prospect. At its end, as you approach Revolution Square, is (left) the **house of Matilda Kshesinskaya** (1902), a ballerina and the mistress of Tsar Nicholas II. It now houses the **State Museum of the Great October Socialist Revolution.**

The square was originally **Trinity Square,** and is one of the oldest parts of the city with the first buildings of St Petersburg — shops, the Senate and a church.

Turn left into the square, then right past the huge becolumned block that houses flats for Revolutionary veterans and the *Nomenklatura*. At the end of the building, where it meets the Neva, turn left to a small square on the left. Within the enclosure in the middle is **Peter the Great's original log cabin,** the only edifice to survive from the very earliest days of St Petersburg. (The stone building covering it was built in 1844.) It was built at the end of May 1703 of pine logs, painted to look like bricks. Its simplicity of construction is matched by the simplicity of its furnishings — there is a bedroom, study and dining room. The roof originally carried carvings of mortar cannon and blazing projectiles to show that the house was an interim war camp. Peter lived here in the summer of 1703 while the city was built and while a war was being fought in the Baltic — he moved out only when the Summer Palace was built. Towards the end of the eighteenth century the dining room was turned into a chapel and so it remained until 1929. In 1930 it became a museum and was the first to reopen at the end of the WW II. Note the little plaque as you enter that indicated the level of the flooding in 1975. The boat within is said to have been built by Peter himself.

On the quay in front of the cabin there are two **sculptured Chinese lions,** traditional guardians of palaces, put here in 1907.

Turn left from the cabin to the corner, passing a glorious example of 'socialist realism' and left again towards the battleship *Aurora,* which is moored on the Bolshaya Nevka (the Big Nevka). It was built in 1903 in St Petersburg and fought in the Russo-Japanese War, but it is most famous for another reason: moored by the Lieutenant Schmidt Bridge, opposite the Winter Palace, a shot from one of its cannons signalled the storming of the palace by the Bolsheviks. *Aurora* fought later in WW II and was afterwards moored permanently here.

The older building by the ship is the **Makhimov military Naval College.**

To Kirovski Prospect

Continue towards the bridge spanning the Bolshaya Nevka (the modern building on the other side is the Leningrad Hotel), passing public lavatories on the left. On the left is Kuibyshev Street leading to Kirovski Prospect. (All trams go back to the beginning of Prospect Gorkovo but the 6 or the 26 take you to near the metro station and Kirovski Prospect.)

Kirovski Street differs from many of the other principal streets of the city — the buildings are generally more recent, it is unusually narrow, there are no tramways and there are many tall buildings with small open spaces. Part of the explanation is that many of the architects involved in its construction were much influenced by Parisian architecture of the turn of the century; at the same time, at the turn of the century the city was expanding fast and ways had to be found to accommodate this.

In front of the metro station on Gorkovo Prospect is a **statue** of the writer Gorky. Behind the statue is the block in which the writer had his flat until 1921. Turn right and then left into Kirovski Prospect (previously known as Kamino Ostrovsky, meaning 'Road to Stone Island') where most of the buildings are from the turn-of-the-century, and often in neo-Renaissance style.

Number 1 (right) is a very interesting example of art nouveau style, with its array of animals around the entrance. Soon after, right, is Ul. Bratyev Vassilyevek, on which there are several restaurants or cafes: a co-operative, left, called **Troitsky Most;** further up on the right a reasonable state-run cafe called **Flora;** and Number 17, a co-operative restaurant, **Ritsa,** serving Georgian food for roubles.

Back on Kirovski, number 10 (left) is the colonnaded building of **Lenfilm studios,** founded in 1918. Next to it is the building that stands on the site of an entertainment garden where the first film in Leningrad was shown and where Chaliapin gave his first concert. Number 14 (left) was built in the 1930s by Benois, specifically to house artists. Chaliapin lived here for a while as did the painter Vodkin, famous for his paintings of peasants.

The junction with Peace Street (Ul. Mira) is octagonally shaped and the buildings around it are reminiscent of Scandinavian architecture. Further up on the right, number 21 (behind a garden and a bust of Lenin) is the **oldest building** on Kirovski — the former **Lycee.** The Lycee was a school for the sons of nobles, founded in Tsarskoe Selo (the village today called Pushkin) at the end of the eighteenth century. Pushkin, amongst others, studied there. In 1843 it was transferred here and is now an artistic vocational college. Opposite it is the pink building that houses the **Victoria,** a new co-operative restaurant, frequented by the new Russian rich.

Number 26/28 is a block of flats designed by Benois in 1911-12. Kirov, the head of the St Petersburg Regional Party Organisation, whose assassination (probably carried out on the orders of Stalin) was the excuse for the purges of the 1930s, lived here in flat 20. It is now open as a **museum.** Most of these flats, before becoming communal, belonged to eminent military and party members, who lost their lives during the purges of the 1930s.

(St Petersburg has one of the worst housing problems in the country — by passing through the arch near the 26/28 sign, you can see how these once luxurious flats have been turned into communal flats, the lowest on the scale of housing in Soviet cities. A communal flat basically involves having one's own sleeping quarters but sharing the kitchen and bathroom with several other families. Inevitably, squalor is the result.)

Continue along Kirovski to Pl. Lev Tolstovo (Leo Tolstoy Square). Here is **House of Towers,** one of the last examples of pre-

Revolutionary architecture, completed in 1916. (Here too is the Petrogradskaya metro station where you may choose to end your walk.)

(On sunny, dry winter days, or on warm summer days, you could continue to walk around the other islands.)

Apothecary's Island, Workers' Island, Yelagin Island, Krestovsky Island

(Nearest metro stations: Petrogradskaya or Chornaya Riechka)

Apothecary's Island (Aptyekarski Ostrov) is divided from Petrograd Island only by the narrow River Karpovka. The name comes from the **Apothecary's Garden** that was created here in 1713-14 to grow medicinal herbs. A century later the **St Petersburg Botanical Gardens** were opened here.

The entrance to them is on Ul. Professora Popova. Plants, bushes and trees from all over the world grow here. There is also a **Botany Museum,** with one of the largest herbariums in Europe.

Workers' Island (Ostrov Trudyashchikhsya) is connected to Apothecary's Island by bridge. It was the former Stone Island, owned by contemporaries of Peter the Great who dug canals and built hunting lodges. It is a popular holiday place (lots of sanatoriums). On the east of the island is the **Stone Island Palace,** built by the future Tsar Paul I.

Yelagin Island (Yelagin Ostrov) lies just to the west of Workers' Island and became the site of the Tsar's summer residence. On its eastern side is the Yelagin Palace, the first important commission by Rossi and one of the most important achievements of Russian Classicism.

Krestovsky Island (Krestovsky Ostrov) is the largest of the four islands and the most modern in the sense that most of the building took place here after the Revolution. The **Dynamo football stadium** was built in 1925 and the large **Esplanade Victory Park** created after WW II. The **Kirov Stadium** was built in 1950.

One unexpected nearby feature (on the mainland to the north of Workers' and Yelagin Islands,) is a **Buddhist Temple** (at 91 Primorski Prospect), built in Tibetan style at the beginning of the century with the help of a scholar from Lhasa.

Smolny

(This walk includes Smolny Cathedral and Institute, Voinova Street, the Taurida Palace, to the Embankment from where you will have several choices: visiting the Summer Garden; backtracking slightly to Foundry Bridge and crossing to the Leningrad Hotel near Ploshad Lenina metro station; continuing along the embankment to the Hermitage and Winter Palace; or simply walking along the Fontanka Canal to Nevsky Prospect.)

There is no metro station close to Smolny, the nearest being Chernyshevskaya. Alternatively, you could use Ploshad Vosstanya metro station, walk to Suvorovski Prospect and take bus 26 to the Smolny Institute or the number 5 trolleybus which will take you close by. Or you could walk along Suvorovski Prospect. Although there is not much of particular interest on Suvorovski it shows you another aspect of turn-of-the-century St Petersburg with pretty streets running off it, tree lined and tranquil, rather Edwardian in flavour. As you walk up the street you will have a fine view of the Smolny Cathedral.

Once you are in Dictatorship of the Proletariat Square (Pl. Proletarskoe Diktaturi) you will see the grand entrance to the former **Smolny Institute**, with its imposing porticoes (added in 1923) crowned by slogans about the proletariat. You are able to walk along the drive to the palatial building at the end.

The early history of this building is closely linked to that of the beautiful **Smolny Convent** next door. The name Smolny comes from *Smolyanoi Dvor* which means 'tar yard' — there was a tar yard here in the early years of St Petersburg, producing tar for the shipyards. In 1723 the tar yard was moved elsewhere and the Empress Elizabeth built a convent in its place in 1744, where she aimed to live out her last days. Construction of the **baroque Cathedral** was started by Rastrelli in 1748, and most of it was finished by 1764. It is considered by many to be his masterpiece — the model he made shows that he had intended his creation to resemble medieval Russian monasteries. The domes and its decoration in blue and white and silver were to have given the impression of a church behind older monastery walls. Around the cathedral a quadrangle was built for the nuns' cells and for the refectory. Because of lack of funds the convent was never finished, although Rastrelli had wanted to add a 137-m (450-ft) bell tower. Unfortunately the Cathedral was deconsecrated and now houses the permanent exhibition of **St Petersburg Today and Tomorrow.**

Catherine the Great decided that a useful addition to the convent would be an **Institute for Noble Young Ladies.** This was the first state school for daughters of the nobility and it was closed only at the time of the Revolution. The architect was Quarenghi, who in 1806-8 left a rather austere building both outside and in. Indeed the school regime was rather austere. There were 500 girls at first, half of whom were daughters of the nobility and half daughters of the bourgeoisie. Their course lasted six years. The curriculum emphasised languages, but the girls also studied geography, religion, ancient and modern history, and science, the study of which made these Russian women's education the most advanced in Europe. Before dinner psalms were sung in harmony and the girls were taught Russian dances which, according to observers, they executed with considerable panache. Their only free time was for one hour after dinner when they were allowed to wander the corridors. There were long summer holidays but in term they were allowed to go for drives only twice a year. There was one additional time when they were allowed out — at carnival.

Carnival was one of the most truly picturesque times in pre-revolutionary Russia. It lasted the eight days before Lent and was known as Maslenitsa, or Butter Week, because of the traditional absence of butter during Lent. It was a time of great gaiety and great consumption. It began on the Sunday eight weeks before Easter and among the many events taking place, which included theatrical performances all over the city and the erection of temporary restaurants, was the parade of sleighs and carriages. An enormous line of brightly-decorated carriages containing brightly-decorated women slid and rolled through the city. Some of the students from Smolny were permitted to join in and 20 of the carriages, each drawn by six horses, were in the procession.

When it closed in 1917, the Institute was taken over by the **Petrograd Soviet of Workers' and Soldiers' Deputies and the Central Executive Committee.** Progress during the uprising against the Provisional Government following the fall of the Tsar was monitored here and Lenin made many of his early pronouncements from here. The Soviet Government moved to Moscow after four months but the Institute has remained the seat of the **St Petersburg Regional and City Committee of the Communist Party of the Soviet Union,** although there is a **museum** dedicated to that period when Lenin was in residence here.

The picturesque beauty of St Petersburg is exemplified in Rastrelli's unfinished masterpiece, the Smolny Cathedral (photo: Jim Helme).

Along Voina Street

It is a shame that the square named after Rastrelli (in front of the Cathedral) should be in an otherwise rather uninspiring area. The wide U1. Voinova (formerly Shpalernaya or Tapestry Street) runs westwards away from the square and the modern building on the left corner is the **House of Political Education of the St Petersburg Regional and City Committees of the CPSU.** The street was originally known as the First Row and on its right side, until the embankments were created, it was washed by the Neva. Owing to its location several factories were set up here, not least the **Tapestry Workshop** for the needs of the Court. An old palace on the right, looking out of place amid the uniform dullness, is Kikin.

Kikin Palace

This is one of the oldest buildings in the city, built in 1714. It belonged to the Boyar Kikin who, together with Peter's son Alexei, hatched a plot against Peter the Great. Kikin was executed and his palace used to house Peter's collection of rarities and curiosities, later rehoused in the Kunstkamer. The palace then became a regimental hospital and over the years altered beyond recognition. Damage during the WW II revealed much of the original decoration, making it easy to restore. Today it houses a **music school and art gallery.**

In the garden not far from the palace there is a **statue of Dzerzhinsky,** who was head of the forerunner of the KGB, the CHEKA.

Soon you will come to a red brick tower (right) behind barbed wire. Built in 1863, it is the tower of the main waterworks. Before its construction the citizens of St Petersburg had to rely on buckets, coloured according to the canal where it came from. The tower is still used to extract water from the Neva but now it is purified. (Even so it has a bad reputation, at least among foreigners.)

Taurida Palace

Across the street, at 47, is one of St Petersburg's magnificent palaces, the **Taurida Palace (Tavrichesky Dvorets).** It was built in 1783-9 by Catherine the Great for her lover and favourite Count Potemkin. Following Potemkin's success in annexing the Crimea to Russia from Turkey, he was made the Prince of Taurida, the old name for the Crimea.

The architect was Ivan Starov, a priest's son who had studied in Italy as well as in Moscow and St Petersburg and whose design of the exterior is strictly classical, much in favour in Catherine's court as a reaction to the baroque exuberance of her predecessors. The interior, on the other hand, is rather luxurious. Within there is a magnificent hall, leading to the imposing **Dome Room** and its murals. The **Catherine Room** is the most famous and splendid of all, decorated with 36 columns of artificial marble and bronze chandeliers. Starov's use of columns had a big effect on Russians and for the next half century no country house or palace was complete without them.

Potemkin was a powerful man but also known for his generosity and expansive gestures. The street outside was frequently crowded with carriages and the courtyards with people of all walks of life come to ask favours. In 1791 he gave a reception in honour of Catherine that eclipsed anything ever seen in Russia before. There were 3,000 guests and the host received the Empress wearing a tailcoat in red silk and studded with buttons of pure gold, each set with a diamond. His hat was so weighed down with diamonds that he couldn't wear it. There were several orchestras, Greek choirs, recitations by poets, a French comedy and a ballet composed by Potemkin himself.

Following his death, Catherine bought the palace back from his estate and spent several weeks there each spring and autumn until her death. Her son Paul I, no friend of Potemkin, turned the palace into stables for the Horse Guards, although it was restored later and inhabited briefly by Alexander I. During most of the later part of the nineteenth century it remained unoccupied, although it was used as a guest house from time to time. In 1905 however, Diaghilev, the man behind the success of the Russian Ballet, organised a fabulous art exhibition there, based on Russian portraiture from 1705 to 1905. He spent many months touring the country searching out what he wanted and in the end he acquired 3,000 paintings, sculptures and *objets d'art*. Bakst designed a sculptured court with green trellises, to be known as the **Winter Garden,** while Benois and Diaghilev hung the paintings. The Imperial family attended the grand opening and at a banquet given in honour of Diaghilev he uttered the following enigmatic words which, in view of subsequent events, may be seen as rather poignant: 'We are the witness of the greatest moment of summing up in history, in the name of a new and unknown culture, which will be created by us and which also will sweep us away.'

In the following year it was rebuilt for the state *Duma* (Parliament), the Winter Garden becoming a conference theatre. In

1917 it was used for many meetings both by the Provisional Government and by the Bolsheviks. Currently the palace houses the **Higher Party School.** Behind is the 30 hectare (74 acre) **Taurida Garden,** now a children's park.

Further up on the left, is a low modern building attached to another of older vintage. This is a huge **greenhouse** open to the general public from 11.00 to 20.00.

On the corner of the next street, Potyomkinskaya, number 41 is the pillared mass of the former barracks of the Cavalry Guards Regiment, built by Rusca between 1803 and 1806. Note the **statues of Mars and Bellona** (Roman gods of war) in the wings of the portico. The Cavalry Guards were originally 'the Tsar's own' but in 1800 they became an integral part of the Imperial Army. It is still used as a barracks.

Further down there are beautiful buildings at 35a and 27. Number 35a is a former church, built by Rusca in 1817-18 and today houses the **St Petersburg branch of the Voluntary All-Russia Society for the Preservation of Monuments of History and Culture.**

Number 34 is the **St Petersburg State Archives of Literature and Art.**

Number 6 Ul. Voinova, across Liteini Prospect was the home of the composers Rimsky-Korsakov, Mussorgsky and Kui.

The street ends at the junction with U1. Furmanova. From here you can turn right to the embankment, then left, to the Fontanka Canal, the Summer Garden and the Winter Palace; turning right at the embankment will bring you to the **Foundry Bridge (Liteini Most)** built in 1879. The intricate railings are original, but the bridge itself underwent considerable changes in the mid 1960s inorder to cope with larger ships. On the other side, along the embankment to the left, is the Leningrad Hotel.

For those interested in history of the Revolution, the **Finland Station** is nearby. Turn right on the other side of the Neva and then first left.

Buses 2, 14, 26 and 100 go directly back to Nevsky Prospect, not far from the metro station of the same name.

Museums

Many of the most important museums are mentioned in some detail in the course of the walks. They are mentioned again here as well as others that may be of interest. Opening times are given where known but they do change so you are advised to check.

The Hermitage (Winter Palace) (see p. 240).

The Russian Museum (Mikhailovsky Palace) (see p. 232).

Peter and Paul Fortress (containing Museum of History of St Petersburg) (see p. 254).

Peter's Cottage (see p. 257).

Summer Palace of Peter the Great (see p. 235).

Academy of Arts Museum
17 Naberezhnaya Universitetskaya. Open every day except Mondays and Tuesdays. Metro: Nevsky Prospect plus bus 7 or 44.

Pushkin Museum Flat
12, Naberezhnaya Moiki. Open every day except Tuesdays and the last Friday of each month 11.00-18.00. Metro: Nevsky Prospect.

Aurora
Naberezhenaya Petrogradskaya. Open every day 10.30-17.00; closed Fridays. Metro: Gorkovskaya.

Kazan Cathedral
(Also the museum of History of Religion and Atheism) on Nevsky. Open every day except Wednesdays and last Monday of each month 11.00-13.00, Tuesday 11.00-16.00; and Thursdays 13.00-20.00.

St Isaac's Cathedral
Open every day except Wednesdays and the second and last Monday of each month, 11.00-17.00 (gallery 11.00-16.00). Metro: Nevsky Prospect plus trolley bus 5 or 14.

Museum of History of Leningrad
44, Naberezhenaya Krasnovo-Flota. Open every day except Wednesdays and last Monday of each month, 11.00-17.00; Tuesdays 11.00-16.00, Fridays 13.00-20.00.

Victory Square (Ploshad Pobedy)
Monument and Museum to heroes of defence of Leningrad in WWII. Metro: Moskovskaya.

Piskaryovskoye Cemetery
74 Prospect Nepokoryonnykh. The cemetery for the Leningrad citizens who died during the WW II. Metro: Ploshad Moozhestva plus bus 75.

Literary Museum of the Institute of Russian Literature (Pushkin House)
4, Naberezhnaya Makarova. Open every day except Mondays and Tuesdays. Metro: Vasileostrovskaya.

Dostoyevsky Museum Flat
5, Kuznechny Pereulok. Open every day except Mondays and the last Wednesday of each month, 10.30-18.30. Metro: Vladimirskaya.

Museum of Ethnography of Soviet Peoples
Ul. Inzhenernaya (near the Russian Museum). Open every day except Mondays 1100-1800. Metro: Nevsky Prospect or Gostinny Dvor.

Anthropological and Ethnographic Museum of Peter the Great
Naberezhnaya Universitetskaya. Metro: Nevski Prospect plus bus 7 or 44 or Vasileostrovskaya.

Museum of Zoology of the Academy of Sciences
Universitetskaya. Metro: Nevski Prospect plus bus 7 or 44 or Vasileostrovskaya.

Menshikov Palace
15, Naberezhnaya Universitetskaya. Metro: Nevski Prospect plus bus 7 or 44 or Vasilieostrovskaya.

Yusupov Palace
On the Moika to the west of St Isaac's. Metro: Nevski Prospect plus bus 22 or Ploshad Mira.

There are also local museums in some quarters of the city. One, for example, is housed in a rather charming traditional wooden house, its charm heightened by the uninspiring blocks of flats that surround it. This is found not far from Ploshad Muzhestva metro station and then 5-10 minutes' walk along Prospect Schvernika. The museum is down an unmarked road on the right which is opposite block 41 on Prospect Schvernika.

Other places of interest within the city

Botanical Gardens
Ul. Professora Popova. Metro: Petrogradskaya.

Canals
Boats do tours of the canals during the summer months.

Churches
Chesma Church and Palace Built in the 1770s by the architect Felten, the name commemorates a naval victory over the Turks in 1770. The Palace was built for Catherine the Great (in the south of the city off Moskovski Prospect) so that she might have a place to rest on her way from St Petersburg to the Imperial country residences. The nearby church (at 12 Ul. Gastello) is in a rather unusual pseudo-gothic style and quite a contrast to most other churches in the city. Both are situated close to Moskovskaya metro station.

Cathedral of St Nicholas (Nikolski Sobor sometimes known as the Sailor's Church).
   On Plo. Kommunarov in the west of the city, it was built at the end of the eighteenth century by Chevakinski, a pupil of Rastrelli, in a style not dissimilar to Smolny Cathedral. Unlike Smolny it has a free-standing bell tower. It remains a functioning church.
   (There is no metro station close by but the nearest is Ploshad Mira, from which you can walk or take a bus 43 or 50, which go to Ploshad Kommunarov.)

Markets
When there is no food in the shops and for interest: Kuznyechny Rynok, near Vladimirskaya metro station; and Sytny Rynok not far from Gorkovskaya.

Parks and gardens
There are many parks dotted over the city. The islands to the north of and connected to Petrovsky Island all have parkland and make a pleasant walk in themselves. Metro: Petrogradskaya or Chornaya Riechka.

Otherwise there are the **Summer Garden,** the **Field of Mars,** and the **Mikhailovsky Garden** behind the Russian Museum. Also the **Moscow Victory Park (Moskovsky Park Pobedy)** for which you require the 'Park Pobedy' metro.

The Planetarium
Park V.I. Lenina. Metro: Gorkovskaya.

The zoo
Park V.I. Lenina. Metro: Gorkovskaya.

Peterhof. Destroyed by the Nazis, it has been entirely rebuilt.

Outside St Petersburg

There are several places to visit in the near vicinity of the city. One or two of these Imperial palaces are usually included in the Intourist itinerary. If not you can, obtain tickets for an organised visit to the palaces through Intourist for foreign currency; or you could take a taxi there and buy a ticket on the spot. You will, however, be compelled to take a guided tour in Russian if you want to see the apartments. Alternatively, you may merely wish to see the palaces only from the outside and wander the gardens. That they stand at all is a miracle — they were severely battered by the Nazi's in WW II and have required an astonishing amount of restoration. You will often be asked to wear special felt slippers (they fit over your footwear) which protect the beautiful wooden floors.

Petrodvorets (Peterhof)

This is the most famous of the palaces, with a spectacular location on the Gulf of Finland. It lies about 29 km (18 miles) west of the city. There is a regular train service from Baltic Station to Novi Peterhof which costs very little and which takes about forty minutes. Buy your ticket in advance from a machine at the station. Once at Novi Peterhof you can walk or take a bus (350, 351, 352). In the summer there is a regular hydrofoil service from beside the Winter Palace but you are likely to have to queue.

The palace is open 11.00-18.00 and closed on Fridays and the first Tuesday of each month. It was built for Peter the Great in the early eighteenth century to rival the palace at Versailles. The apartments are very ornate, not to everyone's taste, but the most spectacular part is the garden with its network of fountains (which are switched off in the winter).

Pavlovsk

This town lies about 29 km (18 miles) the south of the city. The train leaves from Vitebsky Station and the palace is a short walk from the station. The style of the palace is completely different from the others, much more restrained. The architect was the Scotsman Charles Cameron and he designed it for Catherine the Great's son Paul. Cameron was an enigma — summoned to Russia by Catherine he became her favourite architect. He stayed for 30 years, never learnt Russian and immediately after arriving, with a brigade of masons and artisans, he moved into the cottage belonging to the English gardener and married his daughter.

In many ways Pavlovsk is the most human of all the palaces and if you want something in contrast to the likes of the Winter Palace, this is the one to choose. The gardens are lovely too. Hours are 11.00-17.30; closed on Fridays and the first Monday of each month.

Pushkin

This is the former Tsarskoe Selo (Tsar's village) and is situated about 26 km (16 miles) south of the city, very close to Pavlovsk (so that a full day can easily include both). The railway station is still called Detskoe Selo (the name given to it after the Revolution) but the name changed to Pushkin in honour of the poet who studied here. Trains leave from Vitebsky Vokzal and you can take either the 371 or 382 bus to the Catherine Palace. Hours are 10.00-18.00; closed on Tuesdays and the last Monday of each month.

The palace was built by Rastrelli in 1752-6 very much in the style of the Winter Palace. The interior was later redesigned by Cameron. The garden is adorned with a pretty lake.

Gatchina

Pushkin, Pavlovsk and Petrodvorets are the usual Intourist destinations. Gatchina, the palace of Paul I, tends to get overlooked but is recommended. Trains to Gatchina leave from Baltic Station. On arrival you can walk to the palace.

The countryside

If you are in St Petersburg for any length of time you may like to get out of the city and enjoy the coast or the countryside where there are no palaces. The following places are all reached from Finland Station and are particularly attractive in the summer. The coastline is extremely pretty and the beaches good for swimming:

Solnechuse has a good beach.
Repino is also on the coast and named after the eminent Russian painter who lived here. His house and studio is open to the public and is not far from the railway station.
Zelenogorsk, also on the coast.
Komarova, where there is a lake, but which is a considerable walk from the station.

The magic of a Russian winter. Snow scene at Peterhof, outside St Petersburg.

Practical information

Shopping

As in most Russian cities, shopping is not a rewarding experience. However the situation is slowly improving.

Berioska and foreign currency shops
The best Berioska, or at least the largest, is attached to the **Pribaltiskaya Hotel,** which also has a foreign currency shop where you can get hold of domestic items. The next best is at the **Sovietskaya Hotel** and there are two fairly close to each other in the area of the Admiralty end of **Nevsky Prospect,** one in the same building as the Aeroflot office and another smaller one at U1, Guertsena 26. The **Leningrad Hotel** also has a duty-free shop. The Berioska in the **Moskva Hotel** will reopen soon.

Other shops
Theoretically the main shopping centre is along the Nevsky Prospect but the shops are disappointing on the whole. Still, from time to time something interesting turns up, so there is no point in ignoring them completely.

Art and craft
The choice is widening very slowly. Apart from the Berioska shops you should try the following for jewellery, paintings, laquerware and so on.

Ostrovsky Square. Artists sell outside by the railings.

Heritage. This shop is on Nevsky just by Ploshad Vostanya metro station and sells some interesting items for roubles.

The Artists Salon, 8 Nevsky Prospect.

Second-hand bookshops often deal in prints — see Books.

Beauty shops
There are some in the main hotels and a new one on Nevsky Prospect opposite Ostrovsky Square. It has a Wella sign outside it, seems to be called Salon Debut and works in foreign currency.

Books (Knigi)
The most well-known bookshop is **Dom Knigi** at 28 Nevsky
Prospect. It is the biggest and good if you read Russian. There is
not a great choice of books in foreign languages but interesting for
maps and posters.

Berioska shops are generally the best for foreign language books
although you might find something in the foreign language
bookshop **Planeta** which is on Liteini Prospect about two bus stops
down on the right going from Mevsky.

Second-hand and antiquarian bookshops are good hunting
grounds for foreign language publications. On Liteini Prospect
again on the left, close to Nevsky Prospect, there are several
specialist and second-hand bookshops. There is another second-
hand bookshop on Nevsky not far from Ploshad Vostanya on the
left as you head towards the Alexander Nevsky Monastery end; or
try **Staraya Knigi** at 18 Nevsky Prospect. Prints are also often sold
in second-hand bookshops.

Department stores
Pretty dispiriting on the whole but you never know:
Gostinny Dvor, 35 Nevsky Prospect.
Passazh, 48 Nevsky Prospect.
Dom Leningradskoi Torvogli, 21 Ulitsa Zelyabova.

Foods
Not a great selection. Items such as wine, vodka, good chocolate
and so on are on the whole restricted to the Berioska and Foreign
Currency shops.

Fresh food (fruit, vegetables, honey etc.) is more readily available
from the markets, although there is a co-operative greengrocers
along Nevsky Prospect between Ploshad Vostanya and Fontanka on
the left as you go towards the Admiralty.

There is a well-known bakery next to the Metropol Hotel in Ul.
Sadova and the shop at 104 Nevsky Prospect specialises in Central
Asian confections.

A shop called **Minutka** on Nevsky on the right (as you head for
the Admiralty) between Ul. Zhelyabova and the Moika sells meat
pancakes and broth.

Ice cream and other dairy products can be bought in special
parlours called *morozhenoe* — try the one at 24 Nevsky Prospect,
known as **Ligushatnik (The Little Frog)** because of its green interior.
Ice cream is sold from stalls and kiosks on the streets at all times

Western influence was beginning to make inroads into pre-revolutionary Russian life. Another view of the Singer sewing machine building on Nevsky Prospect, now the 'House of Books' (photo: Jim Helme).

of year. Similarly you can sometimes buy savoury snacks called *Pirozhki* in the same way.

Glass and porcelain
You might find the occasional bargain in the Forfar shops. There is one at 64 Nevsky Prospect and another at 147.

Jewellery
Apart from Berioskas and the shops mentioned under Art and Craft try *Beroza* which is on Nevsky Prospect on the left going towards the Admiralty not far from Pl. Vostanya. There is another in the old **Faberge** shop on Ul. Gertsena.

Posters
Dom Knigi at 28 Nevsky Prospect; and a specialist shop opposite the Sovietskaya Hotel.

Records
32 Nevsky Prospect or 28 Nevsky prospect **(Dom Knigi)**.

Shoes
Buying shoes is a real problem for Russians but a new joint venture called **Lenwest** has opened at 36 Sovorovski Prospect. It seems to deal only in women's shoes and there is always a queue but in an emergency it may be useful.

Ballet shoes are available in a bookshop at 9 Ul. Gertsena.

Entertainment

If you like opera and classical music, or if you speak Russian there is plenty to do in the evenings but far less for anyone else. You might consider going to the cinema if all else fails — it is surprisingly easy to enjoy what in effect becomes a silent film.

You can find out what is on from the service bureau in your hotel. Tickets for the opera and similar events can be bought from the same bureau for foreign currency or possibly from the various **Kassa** scattered around the city (e.g. the one in Rusca's pavilion by Gostinny Dvor). However, you will often find that in any case tickets for something like the **Kirov** are apparently unavailable — your best bet is to stand outside the theatre in question and wait for a black marketeer to show up. You may have to pay over the odds but it will be worth it.

Bars, cafés, clubs

There are not a lot of places for more casual entertainment. Most bars in the sense usually understood are in hotels and usually sell alcohol for foreign currency. The best are in the **St Petersburg, Pribaltiskaya** and **Moskva Hotels,** although when the **Astoria** and **Evropeiskaya** are completed the bars are likely to be good. Otherwise there is the **Pravda Jazz Club** on Zagorodni Prospect and a couple of restaurants with music (see Restaurants) and the **Rock Club** at 13 Ulitsa Rubinsteina which has live rock music. The Russian beer halls *(pivnoy bar),* traditionally low-life hang-outs, have dwindled to almost nothing and the most famous, on the Pervaya Linea on Vasilyevsky Island, has apparently been closed. A more respectable one is **Kolos** on the left embankment of the Griboyedev Canal as you face the Kazan Cathedral. Another is called **Byelaya Loshad** at 16 Ul. Chkalovski.

There are rather more cafés of varying quality. If it is real coffee that you wish for then atmosphere and presentation tell you nothing. Sniff the air for the aroma. The **café** around the corner from the Kavkazski restaurant at 25 Nevsky Prospect is good in most respects as is the **Kafe Metropol** on Ul. Sadovaya, not far from Gostinny Dvor. The **Saigon Café** (not its real name but everyone knows it by that name) is on Nevsky close to Liteiny Prospect — ask for Saigon and people will direct you. Otherwise there is the **Balkane** on Nevsky close to the Griboyedev Canal on the left as you walk to the Admiralty. The **Flora Café** on the Petrovski Island, on Ul. Bratyev Vasilyevik is not bad, and opposite it there is another new one called **Troitsky Most.** Hotel cafés are at least reliable from the point of view of good coffee.

Cinema
There are several along Nevsky showing contemporary films (including more these days from the West). Old films are shown at the Kinematograf in the Palace of Culture at 83 Bolshoi Prospect on Vasilyevsky Island.

Performing arts
The **Circus,** a Russian speciality, is at 3 Fontanka Embankment. Metro: Gostinny Dvor plus bus 25.

   Drama is perhaps of interest only to enthusiasts and Russian speakers. However, the Russian theatre has a wonderful tradition and the experience may be worthwhile for anyone — indeed the **Maly Theatre** (not the same as the Maly on Ploshad Iskusstv) recently won an award in Britain.
Maly Theatre, 18 Ul. Riubinstein (Vladimirskaya).
Pushkin, 2 Ploshad Ostrovskovo (Gostinny Dvor).
Comedy Theatre, 56 Nevsky Prospect (Gostinny Dvor).

Music. The **Big Hall** of the Philarmonia Dmitri Shostakovich at 2 Ul. Brodskovo and the **Small Glinka Hall** of the Philarmonia at 30 Nevsky Prospect (Nevsky Prospect or Gostinny Dvor). The **Capella** (which also has a good cafe) at 20 Moika Embankment close to the Winter Palace (Nevsky Prospect).

Opera and ballet. Kirov Opera Theatre, I Ploshad Teatralnaya (Nevsky Prospect plus bus 3 or 27 or Ploshad Mira plus 43 or 50). **Maly Theatre,** 1 Ploshad Iskusstv (Nevsky Prospect or Gostinny Dvor).

Puppets (another Russian tradition). **Bolshoi Puppet Theatre,** 10 Ul. Nekrasova (Mayakovskaya plus bus 6 or 43).
Puppet Theatre, 52 Nevsky Prospect (Gostinny Dvor). **Theatre of Fairy Tale Puppets.,** 121 Moskovski Prospect (Moskovski Vorota).

Sport
Tickets for supporting events such as soccer and ice hockey are available from any *Kassa* (Intourist service bureaux do not usually deal in sporting events) or from the Ubileini Dvorets Sporta near the Lenin Stadium on Petrovsky Island.

   If you want to do the same exercise yourself then there are a few choices. You can hire a rowing boat in the Central Park of Culture on Krestovsky Island in summertime and cross-country skis in the winter. Cross-country skiing is also popular in the towns mentioned under Countryside and skis can be hired on the spot. A good place for downhill skiing is Kavgolovo, about forty minutes by train from Finland Station. However, you will probably have to provide your own equipment.

Horse-riding is possible too, in the town of Pushkin and in the town of Olgina, reached by train from Finland Station. Once there ask for the motel, where you can ride and fish.

Services

Airlines
Aeroflot, 1 Nevsky Prospect. **Air France,** Pulkovo Airport. Tel: 122 6485. **Balkan Airlines (Bulgarian),** 36 Ulitsa Gertsena. Tel: 315 5030. **British Airways** (see Pan American). **CSA (Czechoslovak Airlines),** 36 Ul. Gertsena. Tel: 315 5229. **Finnair,** 19 Ul. Gogolya. Tel: 315 9736. Telex: 121533. **Interflug (East German Airlines),** 7 Prospect Mayorova. Tel: 215 1786. **KLM,** Pulkovo Airport, Tel: 122 1981. **Lufthansa,** Pulkova Airport. Tel: 122 5196. **Malev (Hungarian Airlines),** 7 Prospect Mayorova. Tel: 315 5455. **Pan-American,** 36 Ul. Gertsena. Tel: 311 5819. **LOT (Polish Airlines),** Pulkovo Airport. Tel: 296 7545.

Church services
The following are functioning places of worship. It seems likely that there will be more in the not too distant future.
Russian Orthodox: St Nicholas Cathedral, Pl. Kommunarov (Ploshad Mira then bus 43 or 50). Cathdral of the transfiguration, Pl. Radisheva (Chornishevskaya). Trinity Cathedral in Alexander Nevsky Monastery (Ploshad Alexander Nevskovo).
Roman Catholic: Church at Kovensky Pereulok. (Pl. Vostanya).
Synagogue: 2 Lermontovsky Prospect (Baltiskaya).
Mosque: 7 Prospect Maxim Gorkovskovo (Gorkovskaya).

Consulates
Bulgaria, 27 Ul. Yyleyeva. Tel: 273 7347.
China, 12 Third Liniya. Tel: 218 1721.
Cuba, 37 Ul. Ryleyeva. Tel: 279 0492.
Czechoslovakia, 5 Ul. Tverskaya. Tel: 271 0459.
Finland, 71 Ul. Chiakovskovo. Tel: 273 7321. Telex: 121536.
France, 15 Moikla Embankment. Tel: 314 1443.
Germany, 39 Ul. Petra Lavrova. Tel: 273 5598.
Hungary, 15 Ul. Marata. Tel: 312 6458.
Italy, 10 Pl. Teatralnaya. Tel: 312 2896.
Japan, 29 Moika Embankment. Tel: 312 1133.
Mongolia, 11 Saperny Pereulok. Tel: 243 4522.
Poland, 12 Ul. 5-Sovietskaya. Tel: 274 4331.
Sweden, 11 Tenth Line. 218 3526.
USA, 15 Ul. Petra Lavrova. Tel: 274 8235.
Great Britain has no prepresentation here — in the event of an emergency go to the American Embassy.

Emergencies
Ambulance Tel: 03; Fire 01; First Aid 278 0025; Police 02.

Lost Property
Tel: 97-0092 for items left on metro, 15-1862 for items on buses, 10-9873 for items on trams. Also 213 0039, 278 3690.

Pharmacy
The one at 63 Nevsky Prospect is open 24 hours.

Photographic developing
There is a shop on Ul. Sofia Perovsky (the first right after Dom Knigi as you head for the Admiralty) which will develop Western film.

INDEX

(M) Moscow; (P) St Petersburg

Academy of Arts (P) 250
accommodation 99, 120-1, 211-12
Admiralty (P) 229-30
air services and airports 23,
    (M) 113-14, 203, (P) 207, 281
Alexander Blok Library (P) 228
Alexander Column (P) 242
Alexander Gardens (M) 162
Alexander I, *Tsar* 61-3
Alexander II, *Tsar* 64-5
Alexander III, *Tsar* 65
Alexander Nevsky Monastery (P)
    218
Alexis the Gentle, *Tsar* 48-9
Alexis Tolstoy Street (M) 167
Anichkov Bridge (P) 221
Anichkov Palace (P) 222
Annunciation Square (P) 249
antiques 98
Apothecary's Island 260
Aragvi restaurant (M) 175
Arbat Street (M) 169-72
Architect Carlo Rossi Street (P)
    223
Armoury (M) 141-2
art and craft shops (M) 198
    (P) 274
Arts Square (P) 231
Aurora (P) 258, 267

ballet 110-12
banks (M) 203
bars and clubs (M) 201, (P) 278
Belfry of Ivan the Great (M) 140
Belorussia Square (M) 178
Belorussia Station (M) 178
Berioska shops 98, (M) 198,
    (P) 274
Blue Bridge (P) 245
Bolsheviks 69-70
Bolshoi Kamenni Bridge (M) 187
Bolshoi Theatre (M) 159
bookshops (M) 168, 170, 172,
    176, 180, 181, 199,
    (P) 219, 227, 275
Borovitskaya Square (M) 163
Bottle House 195

British Embassy (M) 183
Buddhist Temple (P) 260
buses, trolleybuses and trams 97,
    (P) 211

canal tours 269
Cannon Foundry (M) 179
car hire and spare parts 95,
    (M) 204
Cathedral of
    St Michael the Archangel (M)
        136
    St Nicholas (P) 269
    the Annunciation (M) 136-7
    the Assumption/Dormition (M)
        138-9
    the Dormition (Zagorsk) 197
    the Saviour (M) 192
    the Trinity (P) 218
    the Twelve Apostles (M) 139
Cathedral Square (M) 136-40
Catherine the Great, *Empress*
    56-61, 223
cemeteries (M) 193, 218
Central Exhibition Hall (M) 162,
    (P) 243
Central State History Archives
    (P) 243
Central Telegraph Office (M) 174
Chambers of the Boyars
    Troyekurov (M) 174
chemists (M) 204, (P) 282
Chesma Church and Palace
    (P) 269
Chess Club (M) 201
Church, The 82
church services 204, 281
Church of
    All Saints (M) 156
    John the Baptist under the
        Wood (M) 184
    John the Divine (M) 157
    Peter the Metropolitan (M) 181
    Ss Cosmas and Damian (M) 157
    St Barbara (M) 153
    St Elizabeth (P) 226
    St George (M) 153
    St Gregory Neokessarisky (M) 187
    St Maximus the Blessed (M) 153

Church of
St Michael and St Theodor
  Chernikovsky (M) 184
St Nicholas (M) 188
St Nicholas in Blinniki (M) 157
St Nicholas in Pyzhy (M) 186
St Theodore the Studious (M) 167
the Apostle Philip (M) 170
the Archangel Michael (M) 192
the Conception of St Anne
  (M) 154
the Deposition of the Virgin's
  Robe (M) 138
the Greater Ascension (M) 167
the Icon of the Mother of God
  (M) 184
the Lesser Ascension (M) 166
the Nativity of the Virgin in
  Putinki (M) 177
the Resurrection (P) 233
the Resurrection in Kadashi
  (M) 184
the Sign (P) 219
the Stylite (M) 165
the Tikhvin Icon of the Mother
  of God (M) 192
City Duma (P) 226
climate 21-2
clothes 27-8
costs 17
customs and immigration 89-90

Decembrists' Square (P) 243
Delovy Dvor 154
doctors 204
Dom Knigi (M) 168, (P) 227
Donskoi Monastery (M) 192
drinking water 20
drinks 108-10
driving 26, 90, 95-6
duty free 34
Dyetsky Mir (M) 158
Dzerzhinsky Square (M) 158-9

electricity 91
embassies and consulates
  London 19, (M) 205, (P) 281
emergency services 205, 282
entertainment 201-3, 277-80

Eternal Flame (M) 162
etiquette and custom 92-3
Evropeiskaya, hotel (P) 225
Exhibition of Economic
  Achievements (M) 193
Exhibition Hall...Nature
  Protection (M) 165

Facets Palace (M) 137
Field of Mars (P) 234
Finland Station (P) 266
folklore 85-7
Fontanka Canal (P) 221
food 33, 100-8, (M) 199, 200,
  (P) 275
Foundry Bridge (P) 266

Gatchina 272
Gayline (M) 205
Gnesins Musical and Educational
  Institute (M) 166
Gogol Street (P) 229
Gorbachev, Mikhail 80
Gorky, Maxim 164, 166, 167,
  179, 258
Gorky Park (M) 194
Gorky Street (M) 173-8
Gostinny Dvor, store (P) 224
Government Building (M)   133-4
Grabar Russian Art
  Restoration Centre (M) 186
Great Kremlin Palace (M)   140-1
GUM, store (M) 147

health precautions 19-20
Hermitage (P) 237, 240-2
Hermitage Park (M) 182
Hermitage Theatre (P) 237
Herzen Street (M) 166
Historical Archives Society (M)
  149
history 37-80, 127-9
Holy Trinity Cathedral
  (Zagorsk) 197
hotels 99, (M) 120-1, (P) 211-12
House of Columns (P) 228
House of Composers (M) 174-5
House of Friendship with
  Foreign Countries (M) 164

House of Simon Ushakov (M) 153
House of Soviets of the RSFSR
    (M) 168
House of St Petersburg
    Commerce 228
House of Towers (P) 259
House of Trade Unions (M) 160-1

Imperial Ballet School (P) 223
Imperial Stables (P) 247
Institute of Ethnography (P) 252
Institute of Folk Art (M) 166
Institute of Russian Literature
    (P) 253
Institute of the Arctic and
    Antarctic (P) 221
Intourist 15, 91, 161, 205
Intourist Hotel (M) 173
Ivan the Great, *Tsar* 42-3
Ivan the Terrible, *Tsar* 43-5
Ivanovsky Convent (M) 156
Izmailovo Park (M) 192

Kalinin Avenue (M) 163-5, 167
Karl Marx Avenue (M) 159
Kazan Cathedral (P) 226-7, 267
Khalturina Street (P) 236
Khrushchev, Nikita 79-80
Kikin Palace (P) 264
Kirov Opera Theatre (P) 279
Kirovski Street (P) 258
Kitai Gorod (M) 143, 148-54
Kolmenskoye Estate (M) 194
Komarova 273
Komsomol HQ (M) 157
Kremlin (M) 129-43
Krestovsky Island 260
Kuibyshev Street (M) 151-2
Kunstkammer (P) 252
Kuskovo Estate (M) 189
Kuznetski Most (M) 179

Lazarevskoye Cemetery (P) 218
Lenin 69-71
Lenin Hills 194
Lenin Library (M) 162-3, 205
Lenin's Mausoleum (M) 148
lost property (M) 205, (P) 282
luggage 26-7

Lutheran Church (P) 227

McDonalds (M) 177
Maly Opera House (P) 232
Maly Theatre (M) 159
Manege (M) 162
maps 35
Marble House (P) 236
Mariinsky Palace (P) 245
markets 200, 270
Matryoshka dolls 86
Mayakowski, statue (M) 178
medical services and supplies
    201, 204
Menishkov Palace (P) 268
metro 96-7, (M) 194, (P) 210
Metropole Hotel (M) 159
Mikhailovsky Palace (P) 232, 236
Ministry of Foreign Affairs (M)
    169
Mint (P) 255
Moika Canal (P) 245, 246-50
money 28-9, 92
Moscow Arts Theatre (M) 175
Moscow Operetta Theatre (M) 174
Moscow Satire Theatre (M) 178
Moscow State Conservatoire (M)
    166
Moscow University 161
mosque (P) 258
museums and galleries 189-90,
    267-9
  Abramtsevo Estate Museum 195
  Arkhangelskoye Estate Museum
    195
  Moscow
  Alexander Ostrovsky 185
  All Russia Society for
    Environment Protection 152
  Andrei Rublyov Museum of
    Old Russian Art 191
  Anthropological Museum 161
  Armoury 141-2
  Central Museum of the
    Revolution 177
  Chekhov House Museum 189
  Diamond Collection 143
  Exhibition of Economic
    Achievements 193

museums and galleries contd.

Gallery Art Moderne 186
Herzen Museum 170
Kalinin Museum 163
Konenkov Museum 176
Kuskovo Museum of Ceramics
189
Lenin Museum 160
Maxim Gorky Literary Museum
166, 167
Mayakovski Museum 158
Museum of Folk Art 167
Museum of Oriental Art 190
Museum of the History and
Reconstruction of Moscow 157
Polytechnical Museum 157
Pushkin Flat Museum 170
Pushkin Museum of Fine Arts
190
Scriabin Flat Museum 172
Shchussev Museum of Soviet
Architecture 164
Stanislavsky Flat Museum 190
State History Museum 147,
190
Tolstoy Museums 190
Tretyakov Gallery 185-6
Tropinin Museum 186
Zoological Museum 161
St Petersburg
Academy of Arts Museum 267
Anthropological... Museum of
Peter the Great 268
Artillery, Engineering and
Signals Museum 254
Aurora 267, 288
Botany Museum 260
Central Lenin Museum 237
Central Naval Museum 253
Central Soil Science Museum 253
Dostoyevsky Flat Museum 268
Ethnography Museum 233
Hermitage 237, 240-2
Institute of Ethnography 252
Kazan Cathedral 226-7, 267
Kunstkammer 252
Literary Museum of...Russian
Literature 253, 268

museums and galleries contd.

Menishkov Palace 268
Mikhail Lomonosov Museum 252
Mikhailovsky Palace 232-3
Mining Institute and Mining
Museum 250
Museum of...Architecture of
St Petersburg..255
Museum of Ethnography of
Soviet Peoples 268
Museum of Musical
Instruments 246
Museum of the Arctic and the
Antarctic 220
Museum of the History of
Leningrad 268
Museum of the History of
St Petersburg and Petrograd
257
Museum of the History of
Religion and Atheism 227
Museum of Urban Sculpture
218
Museum of Zoology of the
Academy of Sciences 268
Peter the Great Museum 252
Peter the Great's Log Cabin
257
Popov Communications
Museum 246
Pushkin Memorial Museum 247
Pushkin Flat Museum 267
Russian Museum 232-3
St Isaac's Cathedral 267
St Petersburg State Theatre
Museum 223
State History Museum 249
State Museum of...October
Socialist Revolution 257
Summer Palace of Peter the
Great 235
Victory Square 268
Yusupov Palace 269
Zoology Museum 252
*see also names of cathedrals,
churches and palaces*

National Hotel (M) 161

Neva Gate (P) 257
Neva River 216
Nevsky Prospect (P) 217-30
newspapers 98
Nicholas I, *Tsar* 63-4, 246
Nicholas II, *Tsar* 65-6, 69, 70
Nikitskiye Gates Square (M) 167
Nogin Square (M) 154
Novodevichy Convent (M) 191

October 25th Street 149-50
Old English Tavern (M) 153
Old State Court (M) 153
Ostankino Palace (M) 191
Ostrovsky Square (P) 223

Palace of Alexander
    Menshikov P) 250-1
Palace of Congresses (M) 133
Palace of the Secretary of the
    Duma (M) 157
Palace Square (P) 238-43
parks and gardens (M) 192,
    194, (P) 269, 270
passports 17
Patriarchs' Palace (M) 139
Paul I, *Tsar* 61
Pavlovsk 272
performing arts 201-2, 278
Peter and Paul Fortress (P) 254-7
Peter the Great, *Tsar* 50-4,
    243
Peter the Great's Log Cabin
    (P) 257
Petrodvorets (Peterhof) 271
photography 31-3, 172, 282
Piskaryovskoye Cemetery (P) 268
Pit, The (M) 147
Place of the Skull (M) 146
planetarium (P) 270
postal services 94, 205
Potieshny Palace (M) 143
Presidium (M) 134
public holidays 94
puppet theatres (P) 279
Pushkin 272
Pushkin Academic Drama
    Theatre (P) 223
Pushkin House (P) 253, 268

Pushkin Square (M) 176

Radio Moscow HQ 185
rail services 23-5, 95, 97
    stations (M) 114-15, (P) 210
Razhdest Venka Convent (M)
    182
Razin Street (M) 152-3
Red Square (M) 143-8
religion 82
Repin Square (M) 188
Repino 273
restaurants 99-100, (M) 122-5,
    (P) 212-14
revolution 67-9
Revolution Square (M) 160,
    (P) 257
Riding School (M) 162

Saltykov-Shchedrin Public
    Library (P) 224
Sandunovskiye Baths (M) 181
Savoy Hotel (M) 182
sea travel 25, 210
Second World War 75-6, 83
Shchussev Street (M) 167
shopping 97-8, (M) 198-200,
    (P) 274
Slavyansky Bazaar (M) 150
Smolny (P) 261-6
Smolny Cathedral (P) 261
Smolny Convent (P) 261, 262
Smolny Institute (P) 261, 262
Sokolniki Park (M) 192
Solnechuse 273
Soviet Square (M) 175
sports 201, 202-3, 279-80
Sretensky Monastery 179
St Basil's Cathedral (M) 145-6
St Catherine's Church (M) 186
St Clement's Church (M) 185
St Isaac's Cathedral (P) 244-5
St Isaac's Square (P) 245
St Peter and St Paul Cathedral
    (P) 255
St Petersburg Academic
    Comedy Theatre 222
St Petersburg Philharmonia
    building 231

St Petersburg State Archives 266
St Petersburg University 251
St Vladimir's Church (P) 220
Stalin 71-3, 75, 76, 77, 83
Stanislavsky Centre for Works in
    the Arts (P) 220
Stanislavsky Drama Theatre (M)
    178
State Bank of the USSR (M) 180
State Puppet Theatre (P) 222
Stock Exchange, former (M) 152
Stroganov Palace (P) 248
Sverdlov Square (M) 159-60
Summer Garden (P) 235
Summer Palace (P) 235

Tartar-Mongols 39-40
Taurida Palace (P) 264-6
taxis 97, 205
Tchaikovsky Concert Hall (M) 178
Terem Palace (M) 137-8
Tikhvinskoye Cemetery (P) 218
Tolstoy Estate 196
Tomb of the Unknown Soldier
    (M) 162
tour operators 14, 15-16
Tretyakov Passage (M) 150
Trinity Church in Nikitniki (M)
    154
Trinity Church in Vishnyati (M)
    185
Triumphal Arch (M) 169
Trubnaya Square (M) 182
Tsar's Cannon and Bell (M) 135
Tsentralnaya Hotel (M) 176
TSUM, store (M) 159, 181

Ukraine Hotel (M) 168
Union of Journalists (P) 221
University Embankment (P) 250-3
Ushinsky Scientific and
    Pedagogical Library (M) 185

vaccinations 19-20
Vaganova School of Choreography
    (P) 223
Vakhtangov Theatre (M) 172
Variety Theatre (M) 187
Vasilyevsky Island 250

Vasilyevsky Split (P) 252-3
Victory Square (P) 268
visas 17-18, 205
Voina Street (P) 264
Vorovsky Street (M) 165-6
Vysoko-Petrovsky Monastery (M)
    181

Winter Palace (P) 238-40
Workers Island 260

Yasnaya Polyana 196
Yelagin Island 260
Yermolova Theatre (M) 174
Yusupov Palace (P) 248, 269

Zagorsk 197
Zamoskvorechye (M) 183-9
Zelengorsk 273
zoos 193, 270